FRENCH
Step-By-Step

FRENCH

Step-By-Step

by

Charles

Berlitz

Charles Berlitz, world-famous linguist and author of more than 100 language-teaching books, is the grandson of the founder of the Berlitz Schools. Since 1967, Mr. Berlitz has not been connected with the Berlitz Schools in any way.

EVEREST HOUSE

Publishers   *New York*

Library of Congress Cataloging in Publication Data

Berlitz, Charles
French step-by-step

1. French language—Conversation and phrase books.
2. French language—Grammar—1950-   I. Title.
PC2121.B57.   448'.3'421   78-73614
ISBN 0-89696-026-9

Copyright © 1979 by Charles Berlitz
All Rights Reserved
Library of Congress Catalog Card Number: 78-73614
ISBN: 0-89696-026-9
Published simultaneously in Canada by
Beaverbooks, Pickering, Ontario
Manufactured in the United States of America by
American Book–Stratford Press, Inc.,
Saddle Brook, New Jersey
Designed by Sam Gantt and David Rogers
First Edition

PREFACE

French Step-By-Step is the first book of its kind and vastly different from other books designed to teach or review French.

This book will guide you to a knowledge of French step by easy step from first contact with the language to advanced conversation, including explanations that anyone can understand and conversational material that you can immediately use.

It will teach you to speak correct, colloquial French as it is spoken today and will teach you easily, without lengthy and involved explanations. From the first page you will learn instant communication in French.

This is because of the logical and unusual way that French is presented in the *Step-By-Step* approach. Every phrase of French construction, every use of French verbs, every turn of modern French idiom, and all sorts of situations that apply to everyday living and emotions are presented in short, easy-to-follow conversational patterns. These dialogues will not only hold your interest, but they will also stay in your memory, once you have used them, since it is relatively easy to remember words and phrases that you can readily use in conversations with French-speaking people.

If you are a beginner, you will be surprised at the ease with which you can learn to speak French and pronounce it so that French people can understand you. If you already know some French, you will find that this book will increase your understanding, your fluency, your ability to use the French vocabulary you already know, and, above all, your confidence in speaking French.

There are 26 steps to French in this book which, with a vocabulary selected on the basis of frequency in conversation, will take you from simple ordering in a café to an ability to understand what is said to you by French-speaking people you may meet and, better still, to reply; and finally, to be able to discuss books, politics, art, science, business, history, and any general topic of conversation. In addition, these conversational teaching selections constitute an excursion into the culture patterns of the French-speaking world—so that you will know not only what to say, but also when to say it.

You will learn how to start conversations with people—how to tell a story—how people speak when they are excited—and you will even acquire the language of romance.

Along the way you will absorb a vocabulary of several thousand words—actually more than most people use in speaking any language. You will be taught the verb forms and idiomatic constructions through the situational dialogues mentioned above; in other words, you will develop an *instinct* for correct use according to the situation—the same way you did when you learned your own language.

Explanations of these special constructions are given at the very spot where they are needed. These easy-to-understand explanations on the right side of each page refer directly to each new point of French idiom or construction.

At the end of each step, there is a section of instant conversation in the form of a short dialogue, the reading of which serves not only as a re-impression of the previous step, but shows French people talking naturally in situations that use the new material you have just learned in a normal, correct way. And, as you approach French in this natural *Step-By-Step* way, you will find yourself speaking it fluently and understanding it easily and, most important, you will enjoy the experience of learning it.

CONTENTS

Contents

Contents

Contents

When to use it — how it is formed — similarity
of endings with the conditional — the imperfect
as compared with the past tense (passé composé) — how to express "used to" and "would"
describing a habitual past action

The past *before* the past and the future *after* the
future. The past perfect forms with the imperfect
of *avoir* or *être* followed by the past participle —
used for action *finished* before another action
took place — used for an action that *will have finished* in the future.

Simple conditions — unreal or supposed conditions — suppositions about something that never
happened — place-names made into nouns — use
of infinitive with past participle

The subjunctive: a mood, not a tense — forma-
tion — using "that" ("que") as a signal for the
subjunctive — why the subjunctive is important

HOW TO PRONOUNCE FRENCH

Every sentence in the lessons and dialogues of this book is written three times — first in French, then in easy-to-read syllables that show how to pronounce it, and finally in English, so you can understand the meaning.

To pronounce the French correctly, say the second line out loud; read the separate syllables as if they were English and *voilà!* — they come out French.

Here is an example:

Savez-vous où est l'opéra?
Sa-vay voo oo ay lo-pay-ra?
Do you know where the opera is?

As you progress you should try to pronounce the French without looking at the second line, but it will still be there if you need it.

We have used two letter symbols in the phonetics to approximate important French sounds and to remind you how to pronounce them. The *u* with a circle over it (ů) to approximate the French *u* and the crossed *n* (n̦) to indicate the nasal sound so prevalent in French. When you see the ů in the phonetic line pronounce it like *ee* while holding your lips in a tight circle as though you were about to whistle. Practice this with the word for "street" — *rue* (rů). In the case of the n̦, pronounce it through your nose somewhat like the ng in sing. Practice this with the word for "pardon" — *pardon* (par-dohn̦).

The syllables in French are pronounced with equal value, without special stress. An English-speaking person, therefore, should emphasize the last syllable in a word, to counteract the tendency to accentuate the next-to-last syllable of English words.

You will notice in the phonetic lines that, quite often, a word will start with the sound of the last letter of the preceding word. This indicates the French liaison: when a word that ends with a consonant is followed by a word beginning with a vowel, the two words run together. Liaison is one of the factors that give French such a smooth and euphonious sound.

There are many instances in French when letters are silent. When you use the expression *coup d'état,* for example, the *p* and the final *t* are silent. The phonetics will indicate all cases in which letters are not sounded.

Other important pronunciation points to remember are:

1. The vowels a, e, i, o, u, are usually pronounced ah, ay, ee, oh, and ŭ (the last as described above). In the phonetics, oh is used only within a syllable or after t or d, to avoid confusion with English sounds.

2. The r should be slightly rolled and pronounced in the throat.

3. The *-ille, -eille* and *-aille* sounds are expressed in the phonetics as -ee', -ay', and -eye'.

famille	bouteille	Versailles
fa-mee'	**boo-tay'**	**Vair-sye'**
family	bottle	Versailles

But the sounds should be a bit more prolonged than they are in English, almost as though you were adding a very short and soft "yuh" after the phonetic sound: *fa-mee-(yuh); boo-tay-(yuh).*

4. As final letters of words are frequently silent, an apostrophe is used in the phonetics after a final r or bl to remind you to pronounce them with a slight emphasis or prolongation of the final sound:

quatre	possible
katr'	**po-seebl'**
four	possible

5. The French *j* is pronounced like the s in "treasure," and is indicated in the phonetics by zh.

6. You will notice various marks or accents over certain vowels (´, `, ˆ) and occasionally a mark under the c (ç). These are important in French spelling and pronunciation and they will be explained in the text as they occur.

After reading each lesson for the first time it is most important that you read the text and the instant conversation aloud. Read slowly at first and then gradually increase your speed to a normal conversational rate, reading the French line instead of the pronunciation line. This is an excellent and proven technique not only to help your pronunciation but also to imprint the key expressions in your mind. Whether you are studying alone or with someone else, try reading the different roles within the lessons, and especially in the "Instant Conversations," with expression and even gestures, and with increasing speed. By accustoming yourself to speaking naturally and easily you will attain a flow and rhythm which is the essence of speaking French the way the French do.

FRENCH
Step-By-Step

INSTANT CONVERSATION: AT A CAFÉ

The following phrases can be of immediate use in any French café. A dash before a sentence is the French way of showing a change of speakers, instead of quotation marks.

— Bonjour, monsieur.
Bohn-zhoor, muss-yuh.
Good morning, sir.

The important second line
The second line, which gives the French pronunciation, is meant to be read as if you were reading English syllables, and the result will come out as understandable French. The only phonetic letters to watch out for are the ů, which indicates that you should pronounce the letter as ee with your lips pursed, and the n to be pronounced like a nasal "ng" as in "sing." For complete value of each French letter see Preface.

Voilà une table libre.
Vwa-la ůne tabl' leebr'.
Here is an empty table.

Every object is masculine or feminine
All nouns are masculine or feminine. For "a" or "one" a masculine noun is translated by un, and when the noun is feminine it becomes une.

— Oh! Pardon, madame!
Oh! par-dohn, ma-dahm!
Oh! Pardon me, madam!

— Ce n'est rien, monsieur.
Suh nay r'yen, muss-yuh.
It's nothing, sir.

"Pardon"
The speaker has just said "pardon" to a lady
as he has pushed past a table to get to his. He
could also say "excusez-moi" or "pardonnez-
moi" or "je m'excuse."

— Un café, s'il vous plaît.
Un ka-fay, seel voo play.
A coffee, please.

— Oui. Tout de suite, monsieur.
Wee. Tood sweet, muss-yuh.
Yes. Right away, sir.

— Ah! Henri. Comment allez-vous?
Ah! Ahn-ree. Ko-mahn ta-lay-voo?
Ah! Henry. How are you?

Très bien, merci. Et vous?
Tray b'yen, mair-see. Ay voo?
Very well, thank you. And you?

— Pas mal. Asseyez-vous un moment. Je vous en prie.
Pa mahl. Ah-say-yay-voo zun mo-mahn. Zhuh voo zahn pree.
Not bad. Sit down for a moment. Please.

Politeness (La Politesse)
S'il vous plaît is the regular expression for
"please," while *je vous en prie,* which also
means "please," is even more polite. It can
also double for "You are welcome" or "Go
right ahead."

— Volontiers. Avec plaisir.
Vo-lohnt-yay. Ah-vek play-zeer.
Gladly. With pleasure.

— Garçon! Un autre café, s'il vous plaît.
Gar-sohn! Un no-truh ka-fay, seel voo play.
Waiter! Another coffee, please.

Garçon!
Garçon means "boy" and also means "waiter."
Note that the mark under the ç gives it the
sound of "s."

— Voilà, monsieur.
Vwa-la, muss-yuh.
Here it is, sir.

— Quel bon café!
Kel bohn̲ ka-fay!
What good coffee!

— N'est-ce pas?
Ness pa?
Isn't it?

Don't you think so?
N'est-ce pas? — "Isn't it?" — is a constantly used expression with many meanings, ranging from "Don't you think so?," "Am I right?" to "Isn't that so?"

— Garçon, l'addition!
Gar-sohn̲, la-dees-yohn̲!
Waiter, the check!

— Voilà, monsieur.
Vwa-la, muss-yuh.
Here you are, sir.

Voilà!
Voilà means "there it is," "there you are" or "here it is," "here you are," as well as "here is," "here are," depending on the context. A useful word, *n'est-ce pas?*

— Merci pour le café.
Mair-see poor luh ka-fay.
Thank you for the coffee.

— De rien. Au revoir!
Duh r'yen̲. Ohr-vwar!
Don't mention it. Good-bye!

— Au revoir et à bientôt.
Ohr-vwar ay ahb-yen̲-toh.
Good-bye and until soon.

5

TEST YOUR FRENCH

Match these phrases. Score 10 points for each correct answer. See answers below.

1. Good morning, sir.	Avec plaisir. ✓
2. Pardon me, madam.	Asseyez-vous un moment ✓
3. Don't mention it, sir.	Comment allez-vous? ✓
4. A coffee, please.	Au revoir et à bientôt.
5. Right away, sir.	Très bien, merci. ✓
6. How are you?	Pardon, madame. ✓
7. Very well, thank you.	Tout de suite, monsieur. ✓
8. Sit down for a moment.	De rien, monsieur. ✓
9. With pleasure.	Bonjour, monsieur. ✓
10. Good-bye and 'til soon.	Un café, s'il vous plaît ✓

Answers: 9 8 6 10 7 2 5 3 1 4

SCORE _⬚_ %

6

step 1 PLACES AND THINGS

Voici un hôtel, un restaurant,
Vwa-see uṇ no-tel, uṇ res-toh-rahṇ,
Here is a hotel, a restaurant,

> **Voici**
> *Voici* is used like *voilà* but for things close at
> hand. It means "here is," "here it is," "here
> you are," etc. However, *voilà* is often used in-
> stead of *voici* even for close things.

un théâtre, une banque.
uṇ tay-ahtr', ůne bahṇk.
a theater, a bank.

Est-ce un restaurant?
Ess uṇ res-toh-rahṇ?
Is this a restaurant?

Oui. C'est un restaurant.
Wee. Say tuṇ res-toh-rahṇ.
Yes. This is a restaurant.

Est-ce un hôtel?
Ess uṇ no-tel?
Is this a hotel?

Ce n'est pas un hôtel.
Suh nay pa zuṇ no-tel.
This is not a hotel.

> **"It is" and "it isn't"**
> *C'est* is the translation for "this is" or "it is"
> when you are introducing something. To form
> the negative, you bracket the verb *est* (*is*) with
> the construction *ne . . . pas*. However, as *est*

begins with a vowel, you drop the *e* of the *ne* and you get *ce n'est pas* — "this isn't." To say "is this" you reverse the order — *est-ce. . . ?*

Qu'est-ce que c'est?
Kess kuh say?
What is this?

C'est un théâtre.
Say tun tay-ahtr'.
This is a theatre.

Un taxi, un autobus.
Un tahk-see, un no-toh-bǔs.
A taxi, a bus.

Est-ce un taxi ou un autobus?
Ess un tahk-see oo un no-toh-bǔs?
Is this a taxi or a bus?

Est-ce l'autobus pour Versailles?
Ess l'oh-toh-bǔs poor Vair-sye'?
Is this the bus for Versailles?

C'est un taxi.
Say tun tahk-see.
This is a taxi.

Voici un cinéma, un magasin, un musée.
Vwa-see un see-nay-ma, un ma-ga-zen, un mǔ-zay.
Here are a movie theater, a shop, a museum.

Est-ce un magasin? — Oui, c'est un magasin.
Ess un ma-ga-zen? — Wee, say tun ma-ga-zen.
Is this a shop? — Yes, this is a shop.

Est-ce un musée? — Non, ce n'est pas un musée.
Ess un mǔ-zay? — Nohn suh nay pa zun mǔ-zay.
Is this a museum? — No, this is not a museum.

Qu'est-ce que c'est?
Kess kuh say?
What is this?

C'est un cinéma.
Say tun see-nay-ma.
It is a movie theater.

Une rue, une place, une statue.
Ůne rů, ůne plahss, ůn sta-tů.
A street, a square, a statue.

Quelle est cette rue?
Kell ay set rů?
What is this street?

C'est la rue de la Paix.
Say la rů duh la pay.
This is the rue de la Paix (Street of Peace).

Quelle est cette place?
Kell ay set plahss?
What is this square?

C'est la Place de l'Opéra.
Say la plahss duh lo-pay-ra.
This is the Place de l'Opéra (Square of the Opera).

Le, la and l'
The masculine word for "the" is *le* and the feminine is *la*. When a word begins with a vowel the *le* and the *la* drop the vowel and replace it with an apostrophe, as in the case of *L'Opéra* — "the opera." This also happens to "the hotel" — *l'hôtel* because, as the *h* is never pronounced in French, it is the same as if the word started with an *o*.

Quel est cet hôtel?
Kel ay set oh-tel?
What hotel is this?

Quel and quelle
Quel is masculine for "which?" or "what?" and *quelle* is the feminine form. Note the word order — in French you are saying "What is this hotel?" instead of "What hotel is this?"

9

The masculine word for "this" and also "that" is *ce* and the feminine is *cette*. *Ce* becomes *cet* when the word it refers to begins with a vowel or a silent *h* as in *hôtel*.

C'est l'Hôtel de Paris.
Say lo-tel duh Pa-ree.
This is the Hotel de Paris.

Quel est ce restaurant?
Kel ay suh res-toh-rahn?
What restaurant is this?

C'est le Café de la Paix.
Say luh ka-fay duh la pay.
This is the Café de la Paix.

Le café
The word for "the coffee" — *le café* is the same as the word café — a small restaurant.

Quelle est cette statue?
Kell ay set sta-tů?
What statue is this?

C'est une statue de Napoléon.
Say tůne sta-tů duh Na-po-lay-ohn.
It is a statue of Napoleon.

INSTANT CONVERSATION: A RIDE IN A TAXI

— Taxi, êtes-vous libre?
Tahk-see, ett-voo leebr'?
Taxi, are you free?

The hyphen for questions
The hyphen is written between the verb and the pronoun for questions when the word order is changed, as here.

— Oui, monsieur. Où allez-vous?
Wee, muss-yuh. OO ah-lay-voo?
Yes, sir. Where are you going?

— A l'Hôtel de Paris. Est-ce loin?
Ah lo-tel duh Pa-ree. Ess lwen?
To the Hotel de Paris. Is it far?

— Non, monsieur. Ce n'est pas loin.
Nohn, muss-yuh. Suh nay pa lwen.
No, sir. It is not far.

— Pardon. Où est l'Hôtel Ritz?
Par-dohn. Oo ay lo-tel ritz?
Pardon me. Where is the Ritz Hotel?

— Là-bas, à gauche.
La-ba, ah gohsh.
Over there, on the left.

— Est-ce un bon hôtel?
Ess un bohn no-tel?
Is it a good hotel?

— Oui, monsieur. Très bon . . . et très cher.
Wee, muss-yuh. Tray bohn . . . ay tray shair.
Yes, sir. Very good . . . and very expensive.

11

— Où est le Musée du Louvre?
Oo ay luh mŭ-zay dŭ Loovr'?
Where is the Louvre Museum?

— Au bout de cette rue, à droite.
Oh boo duh set rŭ ah drwaht.
At the end of this street, on the right.

> **de + le = du**
> **à + le = au**
> *De* is "of" and *à* is "to" or "at." When they combine with the masculine word for "the" the combination of *de* and *le* becomes *du* and *à* and *le* become *au*. *De la* and *à la* do not combine.

Ce grand bâtiment là-bas.
Suh grahn ba-tee-mahn la-ba.
That big building over there.

Nous voilà à l'Hôtel de Paris.
Noo vwa-la ah Lo-tel duh Pa-ree.
Here we are at the Hotel de Paris.

> **Word order**
> *Nous* is the word for "we" but it precedes *voilà*. French word order is often quite different from English as you will see.

— Très bien. Merci. C'est combien?
Tray b'yen. Mair-see. Say kohn-b'yen?
Very well. Thank you. How much is it?

> **How much?**
> "How much is it?" is *Combien est-ce?*, but you will more frequently hear *C'est combien?* — "It's how much?" used as a question.

— Quatre francs.
Katr' frahn.
Four francs.

— Voyons, un, deux, trois, quatre . . . et cinq.
Vo-yohn, un duh, trwa, katr' . . . ay sank.
Let's see, one, two, three, four . . . and five.

— Merci, monsieur.
Mair-see, muss-yuh.
Thank you, sir.

The importance of gender
People who study French for the first time often
ask why nouns are masculine and feminine.
There is no answer. You must simply learn their
gender as you meet them, and after using them
a while you will remember which are masculine
and which are feminine. Gender is especially
important because the word for ''a,'' ''the'' and
any adjective that refers to the noun or pronoun
must be either masculine or feminine to go
with it.

TEST YOUR FRENCH

Write *un* or *une*, according to gender, in front of each noun. Score 10 points for each correct answer. See answers below.

1. Voici _un_ hôtel.

2. C'est _un_ restaurant.

3. Voici _un_ théâtre.

4. C'est _un_ cinéma.

5. Ce n'est pas _un_ musée.

6. C'est _une_ statue de Napoléon.

7. Voici _une_ banque.

8. C'est _un_ taxi.

9. Voici _un_ magasin.

10. Ce n'est pas _un_ autobus.

SCORE _____%

	SINGULAR		PLURAL
	MAS.	FEM.	MAS. AND FEM.
my	*mon*	*ma*	*mes*
his, her, its	*son*	*sa*	*ses*
our	*notre*	*notre*	*nos*
your	*votre*	*votre*	*vos*
their	*leur*	*leur*	*leurs*

Où sont-ils?
Oo sohn-teel?
Where are they?

Je ne sais pas.
Zhuh nuh say pa.
I don't know.

I don't know
This expression is offered here simply as an extremely useful expression. The verb "to know" (*savoir*) will come in a later lesson.

Et voilà le verbe *parler:*
Ay vwa-la luh vairb *pahr-lay:*
And here is the verb *to speak:*

Parler
When you look up a verb in the dictionary you will find it given in its infinitive form, such as *parler* ("to speak"). Most French infinitives end in *-er* and are conjugated like *parler*. Here is the present tense of *parler:*

I speak (or) I am speaking	*je parle*
he (she) speaks (or) is speaking	*il (elle) parle*
we speak (or) are speaking	*nous parlons*
you speak (or) are speaking	*vous parlez*
they speak (or) are speaking	*ils (elles) parlent*

17

Notice that there is no difference between "I speak" and "I am speaking," as French has no progressive mood. In future tables we will give just the indicative equivalent.

Je parle français.
Zhuh pahrl' frahn̦-say.
I speak French.

Parlez-vous anglais?
Pahr-lay-voo zahn̦-glay?
Do you speak English?

Ma femme ne parle pas bien français.
Ma fahm nuh pahrl' pa b'yen frahn̦-say.
My wife does not speak French well.

No special word for "do."
There is no equivalent word for "do" in asking questions or for "do not" or "does not" in making negative constructions. For questions invert the order:
    "Do you speak?" — *Parlez-vous?*

For negatives put *ne* in front of the verb and *pas* after it:
    "I don't speak." — *Je ne parle pas.*

Nous parlons français avec nos amis français.
Noo pahr-lohn̦ frahn̦-say ah-vek no za-mee frahn̦-say.
We speak French with our French friends.

Ils ne parlent pas anglais.
Eel nuh pahrl' pa zahn̦-glay.
They do not speak English.

Le verbe *venir:*
Luh vairb *vuh-neer:*
The verb *to come:*

Venir
While most infinitives end in *-er* like *parler*, others end in *ir, -re* and *-oir*. We will take up the present tense of many verbs in Step 5, but we

introduce *venir* here because it occurs so often in basic conversation. Here is the present tense of *venir*:

> *Je viens, il (elle) vient, nous venons, vous venez, ils (elles) viennent*

Je viens de Montréal.
Zhuh v'yen duh Mohn-ray-ahl.
I come from Montreal.

D'où venez-vous?
Doo vuh-nay-voo?
Where do you come from?

Est-ce que Bertrand vient avec nous?
Ess-kuh Bair-trahn v'yen ta-vek noo?
Is Bertrand coming with us?

Simple questions
Est-ce que . . . is a convenient way of forming a question. You leave the word order the way it is (instead of inverting it) and preface the question with *est-ce que* — literally "is it that."

> *Vous êtes italien.* — "You are Italian."
> *Est-ce que vos êtes italien?* — "Are you Italian?"
> *Êtes-vous italien?* — "Are you Italian?"

Non, il ne vient pas avec nous.
Nohn, eel nuh v'yen pa za-vek noo.
No, he is not coming with us.

Nous venons de Californie.
Noo vuh-nohn duh Ka-lee-fohr-nee.
We come from California.

De quel pays viennent-ils?
Duh kel pay-ee v'yenn-teel?
What country do they come from?

Présentations:
Pray-zahn-tahs-yohn:
Introductions:

—Monsieur Dumas, un ami américain,
Muss-yuh Dǔ-ma, uɲ na-mee ah-may-ree-keɲ,
Mr. Dumas, an American friend,

Madame Latour.
Ma-dahm La-toor.
Mrs. Latour.

—Bonjour, monsieur.
Bohɲ-zhoor, muss-yuh.
Good morning, sir.

—Enchanté, madame.
Ahɲ-shah-tay, ma-dahm.
Delighted, madam.

La Politesse
Enchanté is a polite way to acknowledge an introduction. When a man is introduced to a lady an even more polite phrase is *Mes hommages, madame.* — "My respects, madam."

—Vous êtes américain, monsieur,
Voo zet za-may-ree-keɲ, muss-yuh,
You are American, sir,

In general *monsieur, madame* and *mademoiselle* are used more in French than "Sir," "Madam" and "Miss" are used in English. Also *madame* is used rather than *mademoiselle* to any woman past adolescence when you don't know if the lady is married or not.

mais votre nom est français.
may vo-truh nohɲ ay frahɲ-say.
but your name is French.

—Oui, mes parents sont français.
Wee, may pa-rahɲ sohɲ frahɲ-say.
Yes, my parents are French.

—Ah! C'est intéressant!
Ah! Say teɲ-tay-ray-sahɲ!
Ah! That is interesting!

Et de quelle région viennent-ils?
Ay duh kel ray-zhohɲ v'yenn-teel?
And from what region do they come?

— Ils sont de Marseille.
Eel sohɲ duh Mahr-say'.
They are from Marseilles.

Et vous, madame, êtes-vous parisienne?
Ay voo, ma-dahm, et-voo pa-reez-yenn?
And you, madam, are you Parisian?

— Oui, monsieur, je suis parisienne.
Wee, muss-yuh, zhuh swee pa-reez-yenn.
Yes, sir, I am a Parisian.

— Parlez-vous anglais?
Pahr-lay-voo zahɲ-glay?
Do you speak English?

— Un peu seulement. L'anglais est très difficile.
Uɲ puh suhl-mahɲ. Lahɲ-glay ay tray dee-fee-seel.
A little only. English is very difficult.

Mais vous, monsieur. Vous parlez très bien français.
May voo, muss-yuh. Voo pahr-lay tray b'yeɲ frahɲ-say.
But you, sir. You speak French very well.

Votre accent est très bon.
Vohtr ak-sahɲ tay tray bohɲ.
Your accent is very good.

— Merci, madame. Vous êtes bien aimable.
Mair-see, ma-dahm. Voo zet b'yeɲ nay-mahbl'.
Thank you, madam. You are very kind.

INSTANT CONVERSATION:
IN AN OFFICE

M. Rollin vient de New York.
Muss-yuh Ro-len v'yen duh New York.
Mr. Rollin comes from New York.

Il est américain, mais il parle aussi français.
Eel ay ta-may-ree-ken, may zeel parl' oh-see frahn-say.
He is American, but he also speaks French.

Il est dans un bureau à Paris, Legrand & Compagnie.
Eel ay dahn zun bŭ-ro ah Pa-ree, Luh-grahn ay Kohn-pahn-yee.
He is in an office in Paris, Legrand & Company.

Albert Rollin parle avec la secrétaire de Philippe Legrand.
Al-bair Roh-len parl ah-vek la suh-kray-tair de Fee-leep Luh-grahn.
Albert Rollin speaks with Philippe Legrand's secretary.

> **Belonging to**
> The genitive is formed by *de*, which means "of"
> as well as "from."
> *La voiture de Paul* — "Paul's car."

M. ROLLIN:
Bonjour. Est-ce bien le bureau de M. Legrand?
Bohn-zhoor. Ess b-yen luh bŭ-ro duh Muss-yuh Luh-grahn?
Good morning. Is this Mr. Legrand's office?

LA SECRÉTAIRE:
Oui, monsieur. Je suis sa secrétaire.
Wee, muss-yuh. Zhuh swee sa suh-kray-tair.
Yes, sir. I am his secretary.

M. ROLLIN:
Je suis un ami de M. Legrand.
Zhuh swee zun na-mee duh Muss-yuh Luh-grahn.
I am a friend of Mr. Legrand.

22

Voici ma carte. Je viens de New York.
Vwa-see ma kart. Zhuh v'yen duh New York.
Here is my card. I come from New York.

Et je suis ici de passage.
Ay zhuh swee zee-see duh pa-sahzh.
And I am here (just) passing through.

Est-ce que M. Legrand est très occupé?
Ess kuh Muss-yuh Luh-grahn ay tray zo-kǔ-pay?
Is Mr. Legrand very busy?

LA SECRÉTAIRE:

Excusez-moi, monsieur . . .
Ex-kǔ-zay-mwa, muss-yuh . . .
Excuse me, sir . . .

(Elle parle au téléphone)
(El parl' oh tay-lay-fohn)
(She speaks on the telephone)

Allô! monsieur . . . Êtes-vous libre un instant?
Ah-lo! muss-yuh . . . Et-voo leebr' un nens-tahn?
Hello! sir . . . Are you free for a moment?

M. Rollin est ici . . . un ami de New York.
Muss-yoh Roh-len ay tee-see . . . un na-mee duh New York.
Mr. Rollin is here . . . a friend from New York.

Très bien . . . Tout de suite.
Tray b-yen . . . Tood sweet.
Very well . . . Right away.

M. Legrand est dans son bureau, monsieur.
Muss-yuh Luh-grahn ay dahn sohn bǔ-ro, muss-yuh.
Mr. Legrand is in his office, sir.

Par ici, s'il vous plaît.
Par ee-see, seel voo play.
This way please.

M. ROLLIN:

Merci, mademoiselle, vous êtes bien aimable.

Mair-see, mad-mwa-zel, voo zet b'yen nay-mahbl'.

Thank you, miss, you are very kind.

LA SECRÉTAIRE:

Mais c'est un plaisir, monsieur.

May say tun play-zeer, muss-yuh.

But it is a pleasure, sir.

TEST YOUR FRENCH

Write number of English sentence which corresponds with French sentence in right hand column. Score 10 points for each correct answer. See answers below.

1. Do you speak English?
2. I speak French.
3. Where do you come from?
4. They are on a trip.
5. We are here visiting.
6. That is very interesting.
7. This way, please.
8. What country do they come from?
9. You are very kind.
10. You speak French very well.

Nous sommes ici en visite. ✓
C'est très intéressant. ✓
Par ici, s'il vous plaît. ✓
De quel pays viennent-ils? ✓
Vous êtes bien aimable. ✓
Je parle français. ✓
Parlez-vous anglais? ✓
Ils sont en voyage. ✓
Vous parlez très bien français. ✓
D'où venez-vous? ✓

Answers: 5 6 7 8 9 2 1 4 10 3

SCORE _100_ %

25

step 3 NUMBERS AND HOW TO USE THEM

Les nombres de 1 à 10:
Lay nohnᵣbr' duh unᵣ ah dees:
The numbers from 1 to 10:

Plural of le, la, l' = les
The plural of "the" (*le*, *la* or *l'*) is *les* for both genders:

le garçon — the boy
　　les garçons — the boys
la femme — the woman
　　les femmes — the women
l'homme — the man
　　les hommes — the men

The plural of nouns is usually formed by adding an *s*.

1	2	3	4	5
un	deux	trois	quatre	cinq
unᵣ	**duh**	**trwa**	**katr'**	**sank**

6	7	8	9	10
six	sept	huit	neuf	dix
sees	**set**	**weet**	**nuhf**	**deess**

de dix à seize:
duh deess ah sez:
from 10 to 16:

11	12	13
onze	douze	treize
ohnᵣz	**dooz**	**trez**

14	15	16
quatorze	quinze	seize
ka-torz	**kenᵣz**	**sez**

et ensuite
ay ahn-sweet
and then

17	18	19	20
dix-sept	dix-huit	dix-neuf	vingt
dees-set	**deez-weet**	**deez-nuhf**	**ven**

Et après vingt:
Ay ah-pray ven:
And after 20:

21	22	23	24
vingt et un	vingt-deux	vingt-trois	vingt-quatre
vent-ay-un	**vent-duh**	**vent-trwa**	**vent-katr'**

25 et cetera, jusqu'à 30:
vent-sank et say-tay-ra zhůs-ka trahnt:
25 et cetera, up to 30:

40	50
quarante	cinquante
ka-rahnt	**sen-kahnt**

60	70
soixante	soixante-dix
swa-sahnt	**swa-sahnt-deess**

"Sixty-ten" and "four-twenty"
Seventy is literally "sixty-ten" (*soixante-dix*)
and seventy-one is "sixteen and eleven" (*soixante et onze*, then "sixty-twelve" (*soixante-
douze*), etc.

Eighty is "four-twenty" (*quatre-vingt*) and 81,
82, etc. are *quatre-vingt-un, quatre-vingt-deux*,
etc. When we come to ninety it is literally "four-
twenty-ten," and 91, 92, etc. are "four-twenty-
eleven" (*quatre-vingt-onze*), "four-twenty-
twelve" (*quatre-vingt-douze*), etc. Rather like an
adding machine (*une machine à calculer*), *n'est-
ce pas?*

71	72	73
soixante et onze	soixante-douze	soixante-treize
swa-sahn̜t-ay-ohnz	**swa-sahn̜t-dooz**	**swa-sahn̜t-trays**

80	90
quatre-vingts	quatre-vingt-dix
katr'-ven̜	**katr'-ven̜-dees**

91	92	93
quatre-vingt-onze	quatre-vingt-douze	quatre-vingt-treize etc.
katr'-ven̜-ohnz	**katr'-ven̜-dooz**	**katr'-ven̜-trays et say-tay-ra.**

100	101	102 etc.	200	300
cent	cent un	cent deux etc.	deux cents	trois cents
sahn̜	**sahn̜ un̜**	**sahn̜ duh et say-tay-ra.**	**duh sahn̜**	**trwa sahn̜**

1,000	100,000	1,000,000
mille	cent mille	un million
meel	**sahn̜ meel**	**un̜ meel-yohn̜**

Big figures
In French numbers commas are used instead of decimal points — and vice versa.

ENGLISH	FRENCH
$1,000,000.00	$1.000.000,00

Les nombres sont très importants —
Lay nohn̜br' sohn̜ tray zen̜-pohr-tahn̜ —
Numbers are very important —

Adjectives in the plural
Importants has an *s* here because adjectives agree in number as well as gender with the noun they modify.

Dans un magasin . . .
Dahn zun̜ ma-ga-zen̜ . . .
In a shop . . .

   Un client: C'est combien?
   Un̜ clee-yahn̜: Say kohn̜-b'yen̜?
   A customer: How much is it?

La vendeuse: Dix-sept francs vingt-cinq centimes.
La vahn-duhz: Dees-set frahn vent-sank sen-teem.
Saleslady: Seventeen francs twenty-five centimes.

Au téléphone ...
Oh tay-lay-fohn ...
On the telephone ...

Une voix: Allo! C'est le 281-71-91?
**Une vwa: Ah-lo! Say luh duh sahn ka-truh-va-e-swa-sahnt-ay-
ohn zun, ka-tr'uh-van-ohnz?**
A voice: Hello! Is this 281-71-91?

Une voix qui répond: Non. Ici, c'est 282-72-92.
**Une vwa kee ray-pohn: Nohn. E-see, say luh duh sahn ka
truh-ve-duh, swa-sahn-dooz, ka-truh-van-dooz.**
A voice that answers: No. Here, it is 282-72-92.

La voix: Pardon. Excusez-moi!
La vwa: Par-dohn. Ex-kŭ-zay-mwa!
Voice: Pardon. Excuse me!

Pour les adresses ...
Poor lay za-dress ...
For addresses ...

— Quelle est votre adresse?
Kel ay vohtr' ah-dress?
What is your address?

— 116 rue du Quatre Septembre.
sahn-sez rŭ dŭ katr' sep-tahnbr.
116 rue du 4 Septembre. (September the fourth)

Pour savoir quelle heure il est ...
Poor sa-vwar kel err eel ay ...
To know what time it is ...

I don't know
Savoir means "to know." Pour ("for") is used
with savoir in the infinitive form in the sense of
"in order to know" or "for knowing." Literally it
is "for to know."

29

Time and the hour
Expressions relating to time or "o'clock" are expressed by *heure* ("hour").

> What time is it? — *Quelle heure est-il?*
> It's one o'clock. — *Il est une heure.*

Quelle heure est-il?
Kel err ay-teel?
What time is it?

Il est sept heures.
Eel ay set err.
It is seven o'clock.

Il est sept heures cinq . . . sept heures dix.
Eel ay set err sank . . . set err deess.
It is five past seven . . . ten past seven.

Il est sept heures et quart.
Eel ay set err ay kar.
It is a quarter past seven.

Sept heures vingt . . . sept heures vingt-cinq . . .
set err veṇ . . . set err veṇ-sank . . .
seven twenty . . . seven twenty-five . . .

Il est sept heures et demie.
Eel ay set err ay duh-mee.
It is half past seven.

Huit heures moins vingt-cinq . . . moins vingt . . .
Weet err mweṇ veṇt-senk . . . mweṇ veṇ . . .
Twenty-five to eight . . . twenty to eight . . .

Il est huit heures moins le quart.
Eel ay weet err mweṇ luh kar.
It is a quarter to eight.

Less a quarter
In French one says "8 hours less 25 minutes, 8 hours less a quarter." While *heures* means "hours" it is the equivalent of the English "o'clock."

Moins dix . . . moins cinq . . .
Mwen dees . . . mwen senk . . .
Ten to . . . five to . . .

Maintenant il est huit heures.
Ment-nahn eel ay weet err.
Now it is eight o'clock.

Pour les rendez-vous:
Poor lay rahn-day-voo:
For appointments:

— C'est bien pour demain à six heures, n'est-ce pas?
Say b'yen poor duh-men ah sees err, ness pa?
It is alright for tomorrow at six o'clock, isn't it?

— Non, non, c'est à cinq heures et demie.
Nohn, nohn, say-ta sank err ay duh-mee.
No, no, it is at half past five.

— Mais où?
May zoo?
But where?

— Place de la Liberté, sous l'horloge.
Plahss duh la Lee-bair-tay, soo lohr-lohzh.
Liberty Square, under the clock.

French words you already know
You may not realize it, but you have a head
start in many advanced French words. In the
case of those ending in *té* many are the same
as English words ending in *ty* and are feminine:

liberté	fraternité	unité
éternité	beauté	facilité
université	faculté	générosité
sincerité	possibilité	

— D'accord. Mais si je ne suis pas là
Dahk-kor. May see zhuh nuh swee pa la
Agreed. But if I am not there

à cinq heures et demie précises,
ah senk err ay duh-mee pray-seez,
at half past five on the dot,

> **Feminine and plural**
> *Précis* means "exact" or "precise." *Précises* is
> its feminine plural form because *heures* (to
> which it refers) is feminine and plural.

attendez-moi!
ah-tahn-day-mwa!
wait for me!

INSTANT CONVERSATION: AT A UNIVERSITY

Devant le Bureau de l'Administration de l'Université
Duh-vahn luh bŭ-ro duh lad-mee-nees-tras-yohn duh lŭ-nee-vair-see-tay
In front of the Administrative Office of the University

un jeune homme parle avec une jeune fille:
un zhuhn ohm parl ah-vek ŭn zhuhn fee':
a young man is talking with a girl:

> **Jeune fille = jeune personne**
> *Fille* means both "girl" and "daughter." But when it means "girl" remember to preface it with the adjective *jeune* ("young"). You can also say *jeune personne* for "girl."

PAUL:
Pohl:
PAUL:

Bonjour, mademoiselle.
Bohn-zhoor, mad-mwa-zell.
Good morning, mademoiselle.

Vous êtes une nouvelle étudiante n'est-ce pas?
Voo zet zŭne noo-vell eh-tŭ-d'yant, ness pa?
You are a new student, are you not?

> **Changes in adjectives**
> Most adjectives add an *e* for the feminine form but some make more basic changes. The masculine and feminine forms of "new," for example, are *nouveau* and *nouvelle*. Another word for "new" is *neuf* (neuve), used after the noun.
> *Le Pont Neuf* — "The New Bridge"

HENRIETTE:
Ahṇ-ree-yet:

HENRIETTE:

Oui, monsieur. Je suis en première année.
Wee, muss-yuh. Zhuh swee zahṇ pruhm-yair ah-nay.
Yes, Sir. I am in the first year.

PAUL:

Je suis le secrétaire de l'Administration de l'Université.
Zhuh swee luh suh-kray-tair duh lad-mee-nees-tras-yohṇ duh
lǔ-nee-vair-see-tay.
I am the secretary of the University administration.

Je m'appelle Paul Balard.
Zhuh ma-pell Pohl Ba-lar.
My name is Paul Balard.

Et vous, mademoiselle, . . .
Ay voo, mad-mwa-zell, . . .
And you, mademoiselle,

comment vous appelez-vous?
ko-mahṇ voo zap-lay-voo?
what is your name?

> **How do you call yourself?**
> "What is your name?" can be translated by
> *Quel est votre nom?*, but it is much more natu-
> ral and polite to use the expression *Comment*
> *vous appelez-vous?* literally "How do you call
> yourself." The answer to this is *Je m'ap-*
> *pelle. . . .* ("I call myself. . . ."). This reflexive
> verb construction will be explained in Step 12.
> For the time being simply memorize the two ex-
> amples as they are given.

HENRIETTE:

Moi, je m'appelle Henriette Leclerc.
Mwa, zhuh ma-pell ahṇ-ree-yett luh-klair.
Me, my name is Henriette Leclerc.

PAUL:

Quelle est votre adresse?
Kel ay votr' ah-dress?
What is your address?

HENRIETTE:

76, rue de la République.
Swa-sahɳt-sez rů duh la Ray-pů-bleek.
76, rue de la République.

PAUL:

Quel est votre numéro de téléphone?
Kel ay votr' nů-may-ro duh tay-lay-fohn?
What is your telephone number?

HENRIETTE:

C'est le 313-31-04.
Say luh trwa sahɳ trez, trahɳt-ay-uɳ zay-ro-katr'.
It is 313-31-04.

PAUL:

Merci, mademoiselle.
Mair-see, mad-mwa-zell.
Thank you, mademoiselle.

Au revoir, et . . . à bientôt.
Ohr-vwar, ay . . . ah b'yeɳ-toh.
Good bye, and . . . 'til soon.

JACQUES:

Bonjour, Henriette.
Bohɳ-zhoor, Ahɳ-ree-yett.
Good morning, Henriette.

Tiens! Ce type-là, c'est un de vos amis?
T'yen! Suh teep-lah, say tuɳ duh vo za-mee?
Well! That character, is he one of your friends?

This or that
As *ce* (or *cet* before a vowel) (mas.) and *cette* (fem.) can mean either "this" or "that" sometimes a *-ci* or *-là* is attached to the noun to specify "this" or "that" more clearly.

35

> *cet homme-ci* — "this man"
> *cet homme-là* — "that man"

A character
Type means "type" as in English, and it has an idiomatic connotation of "character." Another slightly derogatory word for "person" is *individu* — "individual."

HENRIETTE:

Pourquoi pas?
Poor-kwa pa?
Why not?

C'est le secrétaire de l'Administration de l'Université.
Say luh suh-kray-tair duh lad-mee-nees-tras-yohn̈ duh lũ-nee-vair-see-tay.
He is the secretary of the University Administration.

JACQUES:

Quelle blague!
Kel blahg!
What a joke!

C'est un étudiant comme nous. . . . Attention!
Say tun̈ nay-tũd-yahn̈ kohm noo. . . . Ah-tahn̈s-yohn̈!
He is a student like us. . . . Watch out!

TEST YOUR FRENCH

Translate these phrases into English. Score 10 points for each correct translation. See answers below.

1. C'est combien? _How much is it?_

2. Dix-sept francs vingt-cinq. _17 france twenty five_

3. Quelle est votre adresse? _what is your address_

4. Quelle heure est-il? _what time is it_

5. Il est sept heures et quart. _It is a quarter after 7._

6. Comment vous appelez-vous? _what is your name._

7. Quel est votre numéro de téléphone? _what is your tele #?_

8. C'est un de vos amis? _Is he one of your friends._

9. Si je ne suis pas là, attendez-moi. _If I am not there, wait for me.._

10. Quelle blague! _What a joke._

SCORE ____%

step 4   LOCATING THINGS AND PLACES

"Il y a . . ." est une expression très utile.
"Eel ee ya . . ." ay tŭne ex-press-yohn̠ tray zŭ-teel.
"There is (there are)" is a very useful expression.

Y a-t-il quelqu'un dans ce bureau?
Ee ya-teel kel-kun̠ dahn̠ suh bŭ-ro?
Is there anyone in this office?

Oui, il y a quelqu'un, il y a un directeur.
Wee, eel ee ya kel-kun̠, eel ee ya un̠ dee-rek-tuhr.
Yes, there is someone, there is an executive.

Combien de personnes y a-t-il dans cette pièce?
Kohn̠b-yen̠ duh pair-sohn' ee ya teel dahn̠ set p'yess?
How many people are there in this room?

> ### Combien + de
> *Combien* — "how many" or "how much" is followed by *de* without the article.
>
> How much? — *Combien?*
> How much money? — *Combien d'argent?*
> How many books? — *Combien de livres?*
> How many people? — *Combien de personnes?*

Il y a trois personnes dans cette pièce.
Eel ee ya trwa pair-sohn' dahn̠ set p'yess.
There are three people in this room.

Combien de bureaux y a-t-il ici?
Kohn̠b-yen̠ duh bŭ-ro ee ya-teel ee-see?
How many desks are there here?

Il y a deux bureaux ici.
Eel ee ya duh bŭ-ro ee-see.
There are two desks here.

Sur chaque bureau, il y a
Sûr shak bû-ro, eel ee ya
On each desk, there is

un téléphone et une machine à écrire.
un tay-lay-fohn ay ûne ma-sheen ah ay-kreer.
a telephone and a typewriter.

Combien de chaises y a-t-il dans cette pièce?
Kohnb-yen duh shez ee ya-teel dahn set p'yess?
How many chairs are there in this room?

> ### An extra "t" for sound
> For asking "is there" or "are there" the expression *il y a* is inverted or *est-ce que* is put in front of it without changing the word order.
>
> Is there. . . . ? — *Y a-t-il* . . . ?
> Is there. . . . ? — *Est-ce qu'il y a* . . . ?
>
> In the first example a *t* is inserted between *a* and *il* for reasons of pronunciation.
>
> In the second example *que* and *il* are contracted as *qu'il* for the same reason.

Il y a quatre chaises dans cette pièce;
Eel ee ya kahtr' shez dahn set p'yess;
There are four chairs in this room;

Deux près de chaque bureau.
Duh pray duh shak bû-ro.
Two near each desk.

Est-ce qu'il y a quelque chose sur le mur?
Ess keel ee ya kel-kuh shoz sûr luh mûr?
Is there anything on the wall?

Oui, il y a quelque chose.
Wee, eel ee ya kel-kuh shohz.
Yes, there is something.

Qu'est-ce qu'il y a sur le mur?
Kess keel ee ya sûr luh mûr?
What is on the wall?

Qu'est-ce qu'il y a?
The interrogative "what?," *qu'est'ce que?*, becomes *Qu'est-ce qu'il y a?* — "What is there?" as the *que* contracts with *il*. "What is this?" as in asking the name of something or a definition, is *Qu'est-ce que c'est?*

Il y a une pendule et deux tableaux.
Eel ee ya ûne pahn-dûl ay duh ta-blo.
There is a clock and two pictures.

Quelle heure est-il? Il est sept heures trente.
Kel err ay teel? Eel ay set err trahnt.
What time is it? It is seven thirty.

Est-ce qu'il y a quelqu'un dans les bureaux?
Ess keel ee ya kel-kun dahn lay bû-ro?
Is there anybody in the offices?

Non, il n'y a personne.
Nohn, eel nee-ya pair-sohn'.
No, there is nobody.

Nobody — somebody
Personne means "person" but used with the negative it means "nobody," "no one" or "not anybody." "Nobody is there." — *Personne n'est là.*

Quelqu'un is the word for "somebody," "someone" or "anybody."

Les bureaux sont fermés.
Lay bû-ro sohn fair-may.
The offices are closed.

Est-ce qu'il y a quelque chose sur cette table?
Ess keel ee ya kel-kuh shohz sûr set tahbl'?
Is there anything on this table?

Oui, il y a quelque chose.
Wee, eel ee ya kel-kuh shohz.
Yes, there is something.

Qu'est-ce qu'il y a?
Kess keel ee ya?
What is there?

Il y a des fleurs, des fruits, du pain, du fromage.
Eel ee ya day flerr, day frwee, du peɲ, dů fro-mahzh.
There are flowers, fruits, bread, cheese.

et une bouteille de vin.
ay ůne boo-tay duh veɲ.
and a bottle of wine.

(Et la plume de ma tante).
(Ay la plůme duh ma tahnt).
(And the pen of my aunt).

> **Some — du, de la, de l', des**
> Nouns must be used with definite ("the") or in-
> definite articles ("some"). In this case "flow-
> ers" and "fruits" must be accompanied by
> *des* — a contraction of *de* plus the definite arti-
> cle *les* — for "some."
> Observe:
>
> > some coffee — *du café*
> > some meat — *de la viande*
> > some money — *de l'argent*
> > some vegetables — *des légumes*

Est-ce qu'il y a quelque chose sur la chaise?
Ess keel ee ya kel-kuh shohz sůr la shayz?
Is there anything on the chair?

Non, il n'y a rien — absolument rien.
Nohɲ, eel nee ya r'yeɲ — ab-so-lu-mahɲ r'-yeɲ.
No, there is nothing — absolutely nothing.

> **Something — anything**
> "Anything" or "something" is *quelque chose*,
> "nothing" or "not anything" is *rien*. When *rien*
> is part of a sentence it must be used with *ne*.
>
> Is there something? — *Y a-t-il quelque chose?*
> *There is nothing.* — *Il n'y a rien.*

41

Il y a est très utile pour poser des questions,
Eel ee ya ay tray zů-teel poor po-zay day kest-yohn,
"There is (there are)" is very useful for asking questions,

en voyage, par exemple:
ahn vwa-yazh par ek-zahnpl':
on a trip for instance:

Pardon, monsieur, savez-vous . . .
Par-dohn, muss-yuh, sa-vay-voo . . .
Pardon me, Sir, do you know . . .

. . . où il y a un bon restaurant?
. . . oo eel ee ya un bohn res-toh-rahn?
. . . where there is a good restaurant?

. . . où il y a une pharmacie?
. . . oo eel ee ya ůne far-ma-see?
. . . where there is a drug store?

. . . où il y a une cabine téléphonique?
. . . oo eel ee ya ůne ka-been tay-lay-fo-neek?
. . . where there is a telephone booth?

. . . où il y a une boîte aux lettres?
. . . oo eel ee ya ůne bwat oh lettr'?
. . . where there is a mail box?

Dans un hôtel: Y a-t-il une chambre libre?
Dahn zun no-tel: Ee-ya-teel ůne shahnbr' leebr'?
In a hotel: Is there a room free?

Dans un restaurant: Y a-t-il une table libre?
Dahn zun res-toh-rahn: Ee ya teel ůne tabl' leebr?'
In a restaurant: Is there a table free?

Dans les affaires:
Dahn lay za-fair:
In business:

Le directeur — Est-ce qu'il y a quelque chose d'important dans le
courrier?
**Luh dee-rek-terr — Ess keel ee ya kel-kuh shohz den-por-tahn
dahn luh koor-yay?**
The director — Is there anything important in the mail?

La secrétaire — Non. Il n'y a rien d'important.
La suh-kray-tair — Nohn̞. Eel nee ya r'yen̞ den̞-por-tahn̞.
The secretary — No. There is nothing important.

> ### Quelque chose d'important
> Here are some other useful conversational phrases using *quelque chose* and *de*:
> *quelque chose d'intéressant* — something interesting
> *quelque chose d'amusant* — something amusing
> *quelque chose de différent* — something different

À la maison:
Ah la may-zohn̞:
At home:

Le fils — Qu'est-ce qu'il y a à manger?
Luh feess — Kess keel ee ya ah mahn̞-zhay?
The son — What is there to eat?

La mère — Il y a du pain, du beurre et du jambon dans la cuisine
La mair — Eel ee ya du pen̞, du berr et du zhahn̞-bohn̞ dahn̞ la kwee-zeen
The mother — There is bread, butter and ham in the kitchen.

Le mari: Est-ce qu'il y a quelque chose à boire?
Luh ma-ree: Ess keel ee ya kel-kuh shohz ah bwahr?
Husband: Is there anything to drink?

La femme: Oui, de la bière et du vin.
La fahm: Wee, duh la b'yair ay dů ven̞.
Wife: Yes, beer and wine.

Entre amis:
Ahn̞tr' ah-mee:
Between friends:

— Qu'est-ce qu'il y a de nouveau?
Kess keel ee ya duh noo-vo?
What's new?

— Oh, il n'y a rien de particulier.
Oh, eel nee ya r'yen duh par-tee-kůl-yay.
Oh, there is nothing special.

INSTANT CONVERSATION: GETTING MAIL AND MESSAGES

À la réception de l'hôtel
Ah lah ray-seps-yohn̲ duh lo-tel:
At the hotel desk:

UN CLIENT:
Un̲ klee-ahn̲:
A GUEST:

Ma clé, s'il vous plaît.
Ma klay, seel voo play.
My key, please.

Est-ce qu'il y a quelque chose pour moi?
Ess keel ee ya kel-kuh shohz poor mwa?
Is there anything for me?

L'EMPLOYÉ:
Lahn̲-plwa-yay:
THE CLERK:

Oui, monsieur. Il y a deux lettres,
Wee, muss-yuh. Eel ee ya duh lettr',
Yes, sir. There are two letters,

une carte postale et un assez gros paquet.
ûne kart pos-tahl ay un̲ na-say gro pa-kay
a postcard and a rather large package.

Une des lettres vient d'Italie et l'autre d'Espagne.
Un day lettr' v'yen̲ dee-ta-lee ay lohtr' des-pine'.
One of the letters comes from Italy and the other from Spain.

Les timbres sont très beaux.
Lay ten̲br' sohn̲ tray bo.
The stamps are very beautiful.

LE CLIENT:

Oui, c'est vrai. Pardon. Je suis un peu pressé. Il n'y a rien d'autre?

Wee, say vray. Pahr-dohn. Zhuh swee zun puh pres-say.

Yes, that's true. Pardon me. I am a bit in a hurry. Is there anything else?

L'EMPLOYÉ:

Si. Il y a aussi une lettre recommandée.

See. Eel ee ya oh-see ûne lettr' ruh'ko-mahn-day.

Yes. There is also a registered letter.

> *Si* is used as a special affirmative more forceful than *oui,* especially when an emphatic contradiction is involved.

Votre signature . . . ici, s'il vous plaît.

Vohtr' seen-ya-tûr . . . ee-see, seel voo play.

Your signature . . . here, please.

Beaucoup de courrier aujourd'hui, n'est-ce pas?

Bo-koo duh koor-yay oh-zhoor-dwee, ness pa?

Lots of mail today, isn't there?

> When an adverb of quantity such as *beaucoup* ("much" or "many," "a lot of," or "lots of") or *peu* ("few" or "little") comes before a noun the *de* is used without the article:
>
> *beaucoup d'argent* — much money
> *peu de courrier* — little mail
> *pas de messages* — no messages

LE CLIENT:

Oui, assez. Merci.

Wee, ah-say. Mair-see.

Yes, enough. Thank you.

L'EMPLOYE:

Oh, pardon, monsieur. Il y a aussi

Oh, par-dohn, muss-yuh. Eel ee ya oh-see

Oh, excuse me, sir. There are also

deux messages téléphoniques. Les voici.

duh may-sazh tay-lay-foh-neek. Lay vwa-see.

two telephone messages. Here they are.

LE CLIENT:

Merci bien. Et maintenant c'est tout?

Mair-see b'yen. Ay ment-nahn say too?

Thank you very much. And now is that all?

L'EMPLOYE:

Oui, c'est tout. Il n'y a rien d'autre.

Wee, say too. Eel nee ya r'yen dohtr'.

Yes, that's all. There is nothing else.

TEST YOUR FRENCH

Translate these phrases into English. Score 10 points for each correct answer. See answers below.

1. Qu'est-ce qu'il y a à manger?

2. Il y a du pain, du beurre et du jambon.

3. Est-ce qu'il y a quelque chose à boire?

4. Oui, de la bière et du vin.

5. Qu'est-ce qu'il y a de nouveau?

6. Oh, il n'y a rien de particulier.

7. Ma clé, s'il vous plaît.

8. Est-ce qu'il y a quelque chose pour moi?

9. Personne n'est là.

10. Il n'y a rien.

Answers: 1. What is there to eat? 2. There is bread, butter and ham. 3. Is there anything to drink? 4. Yes, beer and wine. 5. What is new? 6. Oh, there is nothing special. 7. My key, please. 8. Is there anything for me? 9. Nobody is there. 10. There is nothing.

SCORE _____%

step 5 HOW TO USE THE RIGHT VERB FORM

Les terminaisons des verbes changent avec le sujet.
Lay tair-mee-nay-zohṇ day vairb shahṇzh ah-vek luh sǔ-zhay.
The endings of verbs change with the subject.

Par exemple, avec *je* la terminaison du verbe est souvent – *e*
Par ex-ahṇpl', ah-vek *je* la tair-mee-nay-zohṇ dǔ vairb ay soo-vahṇ – e
For instance, with je the verb ending is often – *e*

Learn French through French
You will notice that in the first part of each step we frequently use French to explain verbs or other constructions. While this information is repeated more fully in the English notes, seeing it first in French is a more natural and direct approach and as you review, you will be learning French through the use of French.

Je parle un peu français.
Zhuh parl' uṇ puh frahṇ-say.
I speak a little French.

Je visite la France.
Zhuh vee-zeet la Frahṇs.
I am visiting France.

I speak or I am speaking
There is no difference in French between saying "I visit" or "I am visiting," "he speaks" or "he is speaking," etc. Both are expressed by the present tense of the verb.

J'habite à l'Hôtel Napoléon.
Zha-beet ah lo-tel Na-po-lay-ohṇ.
I live at the Hotel Napoléon.

Je m'appelle Rose Vidal.
Zhuh ma-pell Rose Vee-dahl.
My name is Rose Vidal.

Quelquefois, avec *je* la terminaison est *s:*
Kel-kuh-fwa, ah-yek *je* la tair-mee-nay-zohn ay *s:*
Sometimes, with *je* the ending is s:

Je suis dans une cabine téléphonique.
Zhuh swee dahn zǔn ka-been tay-lay-fo-neek.
I am in a telephone booth.

Je viens des Etats-Unis.
Zhuh v-yen day zay-ta-zǔ-nee.
I come from the United States.

Je vais au marché.
Zhuh vay zo mar-shay.
I am going to the market.

Je reviens tout de suite.
Zhuh ruh-vyen tood sweet.
I'm coming back right away.

Il y a une exception, *j'ai:*
Eel ee ya ǔn ex-seps-yohn, *zhay:*
There is an exception, "I have":

J'ai rendez-vous.
Zhay rahn-day-voo.
I have an appointment.

Avec *vous* la terminaison est *-ez:*
Ah-vek *voo* la tair-mee-nay-zohn ay *-ez:*
With "you" the ending is -ez:

Parlez-vous anglais?
Par-lay-voo zahn-glay?
Do you speak English?

Est-ce que vous me comprenez?
Ess kuh voo muh kohn-pruh-nay?
Do you understand me?

Attendez un moment.
Ah-tahn-day zun mo-mahn.
Wait a moment.

Commands

The ending of the present tense for *vous* is almost always *-ez*. The imperative of the verb, that is the form used for giving orders, is the same form as that used with *vous*, except that, when giving an order, *vous* is omitted:

You wait. — *Vous attendez.*
Wait! — *Attendez!*

But when using commands, don't forget *s'il vous plaît*.

Mettez ça là.
May-tay sa la.
Put this here.

À quelle heure finissez-vous?
Ah kel err fee-nee-say-voo?
At what time do you finish?

Venez avec moi!
Vuh-nay-za-vek mwa!
Come with me!

Où allez-vous?
Oo ah-lay-voo?
Where are you going?

Comment allez-vous?
Ko-mahn-ta-lay-voo?
How do you do?

How goes it?

"How are you?" is *Comment allez-vous?* — literally "How do you go?" Another, more idiomatic usage is *Comment ça va?* — "How goes it?"

Où habitez-vous?
Oo ah-bee-tay-voo?
Where do you live?

Avez-vous l'heure? — Avez-vous le temps?
Ah-vay-voo lerr? — Ah-vay-voo luh tahn?
Have you the time? — Do you have time?

> **Time and the hour**
> *Temps* means "time" only when it refers to a period of time. For telling time, "time" is translated by *heure*.
>
> > Do you know the time? — *Savez-vous l'heure?*
> > I haven't time. — *Je n'ai pas le temps.*

Avez-vous une cigarette? — Avez-vous une allumette?
Ah-vay-voo zŭne see-ga-ret? — Ah-vay-voo zŭne ah-lŭ-met?
Have you a cigarette? — Have you a match?

Il y a quelques exceptions: *vous êtes, vous faites, vous dites.*
Eel ee ya kel-kuh zek-seps-yohn: *voo zet, voo fet, voo deet.*
There are some exceptions: "You are," "you do," "you say."

Où êtes-vous?
Oo et-voo?
Where are you?

Qu'est-ce que vous faites?
Kess-kuh voo fet?
What are you doing?

Dites-moi, s'il vous plaît, ...
Deet-mwa, seel voo play, ...
Tell me, please ...

Avec *nous* la terminaison est *-ons:*
Ah-vek *noo* la tair-mee-nay-zohn ay *-ons:*
With "we" the ending is *-ons:*

Que faisons-nous aujourd'hui?
Kuh fuh-zohn-noo oh-zhoor-dwee?
What are we doing to-day?

> **Que and qu'est-ce que**
> When "what" is used as an object its form is *que* or *qu'est-ce que*.

What are you doing? —*Qu'est-ce que vous faites?*
(or) *Que faites-vous?*

Note that in the second example the word order of the verb is inverted.

Nous allons à la campagne.
Noo zah-lohn za la kahn-pine'.
We are going to the country.

Nous avons une nouvelle voiture.
Noo za-vohn zůn noo-vel vwa-tůr.
We have a new car.

Prenons la route de Versailles.
Pruh-nohn la root duh Vair-sye'.
Let us take the road to Versailles.

Où déjeunons-nous?
Oo day-zhuh-nohn-noo?
Where are we having lunch?

Nous revenons à six heures.
Noo ruhv-nohn za see zerr.
We are coming back at six o'clock.

Nous dînons en ville.
Noo de-nohn zahn veel.
We are dining in town.

Il a une exception: *Où sommes-nous?*
Eel ee ya ůne ek-seps-yohn: *Oo sohm-noo?*
There is one exception: "Where are we?"

Avec *il, elle* ou *on* la terminaison est *-e* et quelquefois *t* ou *d:*
Ah-vek *eel, el* oo *ohn* la tair-mee-nay-zohn ay *-e* ay kell-kuh-fwa *-t* oo *-d:*
With "he," "she" or "one" the ending is e and sometimes t or d:

À quelle heure commence le concert?
Ah kel err koh-mahns luh kohn-sair?
At what time does the concert start?

À quelle heure finit-il?
Ah kel err fee-nee-teel?
At what time does it end?

La banque ouvre à neuf heures.
La bahnk oovr' ah nuh verr.
The bank opens at nine o'clock.

Elle ferme à quatre heures.
El fairm ah katr' err.
It closes at four o'clock.

Est-ce qu'on passe à droite ou à gauche?
Ess-kohn pass ah drwat oo ah gohsh?
Does one pass on the right or on the left?

Il part pour Londres.
Eel par poor Lohndr'.
He is leaving for London.

Elle est en voyage.
El ay tahn vwa-yazh.
She is travelling.

Elle ne prend pas le train.
El nuh prahn pa luh tren.
She is not taking the train.

Quand part-on?
Kahn par-tohn?
When are we leaving? (lit: When is one leaving?)

Qui sait?
Kee say?
Who knows?

Des exceptions: *il (elle) va, il (elle) a*
Day zek-seps-yohn: *il (elle) va, il (elle) a*
Some exceptions: "he (she) goes," "he (she) has"

Elle va au marché; elle ne va pas au restaurant.
El va oh mar-shay; el nuh va pa zo res-toh-rahn.
She goes to the market (marketing); she does not go to the restaurant.

Il a une affaire intéressante et il n'a pas de difficultés.
Eel ah ǔn ah-fair eɲ-tay-ray-sahɲ ay eel na pa duh dee-fee-kǔl-tay.
He has an interesting business and he has no problems.

Où va-t-on?
Oo va-tohɲ?
Where is one (are we, you) going?

Au pluriel, avec *ils* ou *elles,* la terminaison est *-ent:*
Oh plǔr-yel, ah-vek *ils* oo *elles,* la tair-mee-nay-zohɲ ay-*ent:*
In the plural with "they" the ending is *-ent:*

Les Robin visitent Paris.
Lay Ro-beɲ vee-zeet Pa-ree.
The Robins are visiting Paris.

Liaison

The present tense the verb forms for *ils* and *elles* almost always end in *-ent.* However, the *-ent* ending, as you will see in the phonetics, is generally silent, although the *t* is frequently sounded in *liaison,* that is, when the next word starts with a vowel.

Ils ne comprennent pas bien le français.
Eel nuh kohɲ-prenn pa b'yeɲ luh frahɲ-say.
They do not understand French well.

Mais ils prennent des leçons,
May zeel prenn day luh-sohɲ,
But they are taking lessons,

et ils commencent à comprendre.
ay eel ko-mahɲss a kohɲ-prahɲdr'.
and they are beginning to understand.

Renée et Marcelle habitent chez leurs parents.
Ruh-nay ay Mar-sel ah-beet shay lerr pa-rahɲ.
Renée and Marcelle live with their parents.

Elles travaillent dans une librairie,
El tra-vye' dahɲ zǔne lee-bray-ree,
They work in a bookshop,

et elles sortent beaucoup.
ay el sohrt bo-koo.
and they go out a lot.

> **Verbs ending in -er**
> Since the majority of regular verbs end in -er
> you can get the present tense form of most of
> them by consulting the conjugation of *parler* in
> Step 2. Other verbs, with infinitives ending in
> -ir, -re, and -oir will be dealt with more fully in
> Step 8.

Il y a quelques exceptions comme *vont, sont, ont, font.*
Eel ee ya kel-kuh zek-seps-yohn kohm vohn, sohn, ohn, fohn.
There are some exceptions such as (they) "go," "are," "have," "make."

Où vont ces gens-là?
Oo vohn say zhahn-la?
Where are those people going?

Ce sont des touristes.
Suh sohn day too-reest.
They are tourists.

Ils ont des appareils photographiques.
Eel zohn day za-pa-ray fo-to-gra-feek.
They have cameras.

Ils font des photos.
Eel fohn day fo-to.
They are taking pictures.

Ils vont au Musée du Louvre.
Eel vohn toh Mŭ-zay dŭ Loovr'.
They are going to the Louvre Museum.

INSTANT CONVERSATION: AN INVITA-
TION TO THE MOVIES

— Bonjour, mes jolies. Où allez-vous donc?
Bohn-zhoor, may zho-lee. Oo ah-lay-voo dohnk?
Hello, my pretty ones. Where are you going now?

Linking words
Certain words such as *donc, alors* and *ensuite*
are constantly used in conversation. They all
mean "then" as an intensifier or as a transition
to the next thing you are saying or telling. *Donc*
can be translated by a variety of words —
"then," "now," "really," "indeed"; and *alors,*
besides meaning "then" also means "well," or
"well then," as you hesitate before choosing
the next phrase.

— Nous allons au cinéma.
Noo za-lohn oh see-nay-ma.
We are going to the movies.

— A quel cinéma?
Ah kel see-nay-ma?
To which movie?

— On va au Richelieu.
Ohn va oh Ree-shuh-l'yuh.
We are going to the Richelieu.

"On dit" — "one says"
On va means "one goes" but also can be translated as "you," "we" or "they go" in an impersonal sense. *On* uses the same verb form as
il or *elle:*

on dit — one says (they say, it is said, etc.)
on part — one is leaving (we are leaving,
                they are leaving, etc.)

57

on joue — one plays (they are playing, it is being played, etc.)
on parle français — *one speaks French* (we speak French, French is spoken)

The use of *on* is so important in French that, if you wish to speak French in France immediately, as a short cut you could start using the *on* form of the verb while still learning the other forms. Your meaning can usually be understood by context, and also, you would sound very French, as this form permeates all conversation.

— Quel film joue-t-on?
Kel feelm zhoo-tohn?
What film are they playing?

— "Intrigue," un nouveau film de Danièle Darasse.
"En-treeg," un noo-vo film duh Dan-yel Da-rahss.
"Intrigue," a new Danièle Darasse film.

— On dit qu'il est très amusant.
Ohn dee keel ay tray za-mů-zahn.
They say that it is very amusing.

— Vous ne venez pas avec nous?
Voo nuh vuh-nay pa za-vek noo?
You are not coming with us?

— Je ne sais pas si j'ai le temps.
Zhuh nuh say pa see zhay luh tahn.
I don't know if I have time.

Quand commence le film?
Kahn ko-mahns luh feelm?
When does the film start?

— Il commence bientôt, à huit heures et demie.
Eel koh-mahns b'yen-toh, ah weet err ay duh-mee.
It starts soon, at half past eight.

— Et savez-vous à quelle heure il finit?
Ay sa-vay-voo ah kel err eel fee-nee?
And do you know at what time it ends?

— Je crois qu'il finit à dix heures et demie.
Zhuh krwa keel fee-nee ah dee zerr ay duh-mee.
I believe it ends at half past ten.

— Ça n'est pas trop tard. Alors j'ai le temps.
Sa nay pa tro tahr. Ah-lohr zhay luh tahn.
That is not too late. Then I have time.

Je vous accompagne . . . et j'achète les billets.
Zhuh voo za-kohn-pine' ay zha-shet lay bee-yay.
I'll accompany you and I'll buy the tickets.

Word order
In French word order the pronoun (*vous* in this case) comes before the verb, except after an affirmative command.

The present for the future
Note that, in conversation, the present tense often can be used for the future.

— Oh, ça c'est gentil!
Oh, sa say zhan-tee!
Oh, that is nice!

Mais ce n'est pas la peine.
May suh nay pa la pain.
But it is not necessary.

Chacun paie sa place.
Sha-ken pay sa plahss.
Each one pays for his seat.

Masculine dominates (!)
"Each one" is *chacun* for masculine and *chacune* for feminine. The girl here uses the masculine form because the boy is included in the group and one male turns a feminine group masculine — at least grammatically!

59

TEST YOUR FRENCH

Fill in the correct verb forms. Score 10 points for each correct answer. See answers below.

1. I am visiting France.
   Je _____ la France.

2. What are you doing?
   Qu'est ce que vous _____?

3. We have a new car.
   Nous _____ une nouvelle voiture.

4. The bank opens at nine o'clock.
   La banque _____ à neuf heures.

5. It closes at four o'clock.
   Elle _____ à quatre heures.

6. They are going to the Louvre Museum.
   Ils _____ au Musée du Louvre.

7. We are going to the movies.
   Nous _____ au cinéma.

8. Let us take the road to Versailles.
   _____ la route de Versailles.

9. Come with me.
   _____ avec moi.

10. Where do you live?
    Où _____ - vous?

Answers: 1. visite 2. faites 3. avons 4. ouvre 5. ferme 6. vont 7. allons 8. Prenons 9. Venez 10. habitez

SCORE _____%

step 6 FAMILY RELATIONSHIPS

Une famille
Ůne fa-mee'
A family

Le mari et la femme
Luh ma-ree ay la fahm
The husband and the wife

Les parents et les enfants
Lay pa-rahṇ ay lay zahn-fahṇ
The parents and the children

Le père et le fils
Luh pair ay luh feess
The father and the son

La mère et la fille
La mair ay la fee'
The mother and the daughter

Le frère et la soeur
Luh frair ay la serr
The brother and the sister

Le grand-père et sa petite-fille
Luh grahṇ-pair ay sa puh-teet-fee'
The grandfather and his
granddaughter

La grand-mère et son petit-fils
**La grahṇ-mair ay sohṇ
puh-tee-feess**
The grandmother and her grandson

M. André Lafont est un homme d'affaires.
Muss-yuh Ahṇ-dray La-fohṇ ay tuṇ nohm da-fair.
Mr. Andrew Lafont is a businessman.

Il a un bureau à Paris.
Eel ah uṇ bů-ro ah Pa-ree.
He has an office in Paris.

Les Lafont ont deux enfants,
Lay La-fohn ohn duh zahn-fahn,
The Lafonts have two children,

To have
The verb *avoir* ("to have") forms its present as follows:

> *j'ai, il (elle) a, nous avons
> vous avez, ils (elles) ont*

Leur fils, Guillaume, est étudiant.
Lerr feess, Ghee-yohm, ay tay-tůd-yahn.
Their son, William, is a student.

Il est à l'Ecole Centrale.
Eel ay ta Lay-kohl Sahn-trahl.
He is in the Central School.

Marie-Louise, sa soeur,
Ma-ree-Loo-eez, sa serr,
Marie-Louise, his sister,

fait ses études à la Sorbonne.
fay say zay-tůd ah la Sohr-bohn.
is studying at the Sorbonne.

To make — to do
Faire ("to make" or "to do") has many idiomatic meanings. Here is its present tense:

> *je fais, il (elle) fait, nous faisons
> vous faites, ils (elles) font*

Elle est fiancée. Son fiancé est avocat.
El ay fee-ahn-say. Sohn fee-ahn-say ay ta-vo-ka.
She is engaged. Her fiancé is a lawyer.

Le père de M. Lafont, M. George Lafont,
Luh pair duh Muss-yuh La-fohn, Muss-yuh Zhohrzh La-fohn,
Mr. Lafont's father, Mr. George Lafont,

grand-père de Guillaume et de Marie-Louise,
grahn-pair duh Ghee-yohm ay duh Ma-ree Loo-eez,
William's and Marie-Louise's grandfather,

est en retraite.
ay tahn ruh-tret.
is retired.

C'est un ancien officier de marine.
Say tun nahns-yen no feess-yay duh ma-reen.
He is a former Navy officer.

The descriptive "de"
De is often used as a descriptive:

> *un homme d'affaires* — a businessman
> *un officier de marine* — a Navy officer

Souvent dans une famille on a aussi
Soo-vahn dahn zůne fa-mee ohn na oh-see
Often in a family one also has

des oncles et des tantes,
day zohn-kl' zay day tahnt,
uncles and aunts,

des neveux et des nièces,
day nuh-vuh zay day n'yess,
nephews and nieces,

des cousins et des cousines.
day koo-zen zay day koo-zeen.
cousins (male) and cousins (female).

Don't forget "des"
Remember that nouns rarely are used alone —
in, as here, the case of uncles, aunts, cousins,
etc., unless you give them a number, you must
preface the words by *des* ("some").

Dans une famille on a généralement
Dahn ůne fa-mee ohn na zhay-nay-rahl-mahn
In a family we have (one has) generally

un beau-père et une belle-mère,
un bo-pair ay ůne bell-mair,
a father-in-law and a mother-in-law,

un gendre et une belle-fille,
uṇ zhahṇdr' ay ůne bell-fee',
a son-in-law and a daughter-in-law,

un beau-frère et une belle-soeur.
uṇ boh-frair ay ůne bell-serr.
a brother-in-law and a sister-in-law.

Toujours la politesse
The equivalent word for in-law is "beautiful" (*beau* or *belle*). This in itself is an outstanding example of French politeness — *la politesse française.*

INSTANT CONVERSATION: TALKING ABOUT ONE'S FAMILY

— Est-ce que vous êtes mariée?
Ess-kuh voo zett mar-yay?
Are you married?

— Oui, mon mari est là-bas.
Wee, mohn ma-ree ay la-ba.
Yes, my husband is over there.

— Celui qui a une barbe?
Suh-lwee kee ah ûne barb?
The one who has a beard?

> **The one who . . . this one — that one**
> *Celui* — there are (mas.); *ceux* (mas. pl.)
> *celle* — there are (fem.); *celles* (fem. pl.).
>
> The demonstratives *-ci* and *là* are frequently added to these pronouns for the more exact identification.
>
> *Pas celui-ci, celui-là* — "not this one — that one." *Ceci* and *cela* (often shortened to *ça*) are shorter forms which mean "this" and "that" without specifying the gender.

— Non, l'autre; celui qui a une moustache.
Nohn, lohtr'; suh-lwee kee ah ûne moos-tash.
No, the other; the one who has a mustache.

— Avez-vous des enfants?
Ah-vay-voo day zahn-fahn?
Do you have children?

— Oui, nous en avons quatre, trois fils et une fille.
Wee, noo zahn na-vohn kahtr' trwa feess ay ûne fee'.
Yes, we have four (of them), three sons and daughter.

65

En — a key word
En is a very important and useful word, meaning "of it," "of them," "any," or "some," if the word referred to has already been mentioned. This is one of the little words that are in constant conversational use in French and offer a source of bewilderment to the student. Actually, if you remember that it means any one of several things — and fit in its appropriate meaning, there's nothing to it.

Et vous, avez-vous des enfants?
Ay voo, ah-vay-voo day zahn̞-fahn̞?
And you, have you any children?

— Non, je n'en ai pas, je ne suis pas marié.
Nohn̞, zhuh nahn̞ nay pa, zhuh nuh swee pa mar-yay.
No, I don't have any (of them), I am not married.

Est-ce que vos enfants sont ici?
Ess-kuh voh zahn̞-fahn̞ sohn̞ tee-see?
Are your children here?

— Non, un de mes fils habite Londres.
Nohn̞, un̞ duh may feess ah-beet Lohn̞dr'.
No, one of my sons lives in London.

Sa femme est anglaise.
Sa fahm ay tahn̞-glez.
His wife is English.

Mes deux autres fils et ma fille Catherine,
May duh zo-tr' feess ay ma fee' Kaht-reen,
My two other sons and my daughter Catherine,

sont encore au lycée.
sohn̞ tahn̞-kohr oh lee-say.
are still in high school.

— Avez-vous une photo de vos enfants?
Ah-vay-voo zŭne fo-toh duh vo zahn̞-fahn̞?
Have you a photo of your children?

Oui, j'en ai une. Les voici tous ensemble.
Wee, zhan̞ ay ůne. Lay vwa-see toos ahn̞-sahn̞bl'.
Yes, I have one. Here they are all together.

> **"En" with numbers**
> "I have one" — *j'en ai une* — Note the use of
> *en* which is necessary to express the idea of
> "of them," when a quantity is mentioned in the
> answer. Another example:
>
> How many tickets have you? *Combien de billets
> avez-vous?*
> I have four. *J'en ai quatre.*

— Quels beaux enfants!
Kel bo zahn̞-fahn̞!
What beautiful children!

Quel âge a l'aîné?
Kel azh ah lay-nay?
How old is the eldest?

— André, celui de Londres, a vingt-trois ans.
Ahn̞-dray, suh-lwee duh Lohn̞dr', a ven̞t-trwa zahn̞.
Andrew, the one in London, is twenty-three.

Pierre a dix-sept ans,
P'yair ah dees-set ahn̞,
Peter is seventeen,

> **How old are you?**
> For determining ages, use *avoir:*
>
> *Quel âge avez-vous?* How old are you? *J'ai
> vingt et un ans.* I am twenty-one years old.

— Catherine est très jolie.
Kaht-reen ay tray zho-lee.
Catherine is very pretty.

A quel lycée vont-ils?
Ah kel lee-say vohn̞-teel?
To what high school are they going?

— Pierre est au lycée Henri IV à Paris.
P'yair ay toh lee-say Ahn-ree Kahtr' ah Pa-ree.
Peter is at the lycée Henry IV in Paris.

— Il habite chez sa grand-mère.
Eel ah-beet shay sa grahn-mair.
He lives at his grandmother's.

— Et les autres?
Ay lay zohtr'?
And the others?

— Les autres vont au Lycée Français.
Lay zohtr' vohn toh lee-say frahn-say.
The others go to the French Lycée.

— Alors, tous vos enfants parlent très bien français, n'est-ce pas?
Ah-lohr, too vo zahn-fahn parl tray b'yen frahn-say, ness pa?
Then all your children speak very good French, don't they?

— Oh oui, mieux que moi.
Oh wee, m'yuh kuh mwa.
Oh yes, better than I.

— Mais vous parlez très bien français,
May voo par-lay tray b'yen frahn-say,
But you speak very good French,

et vous avez un très bon accent.
ay voo za-vay un tray bohn ak-sahn.
and you have a very good accent.

— Vous êtes bien aimable.
Voo zett b'yen nay-mabl'
You are very kind.

Ah! Voilà mon mari.
Ah! Vwa-lah mohn ma-ree.
Ah! Here comes my husband.

Il est sans doute temps de partir.
Eel ay sahn doot tahn duh par-teer.
It's no doubt time to leave.

"De" with the infinitive

De is put in front of the infinitive in certain infinitive phrases and is not translated since in this case *partir* already means "to leave."

TEST YOUR FRENCH

Translate these phrases into English. Score 10 points for each correct translation. See answers below.

1. Est-ce que vous êtes mariée?

2. Oui, mon mari est là-bas.

3. Avez-vous des enfants?

4. Oui, nous en avons quatre.

5. Quels beaux enfants!

6. Il est homme d'affaires.

7. Il a un bureau à Paris.

8. Je ne suis pas marié.

9. Vous avez un très bon accent.

10. Vous êtes bien aimable.

Answers: 1. Are you married? 2. Yes, my husband is over there. 3. Do you have children? 4. Yes, we have four. 5. What beautiful children! 6. He is a businessman. 7. He has an office in Paris. 8. I am not married. 9. You have a very good accent. 10. You are very kind.

SCORE _____%

HOW TO READ, WRITE, SPELL, AND PRONOUNCE FRENCH

Comment pronounce-t-on les lettres de l'alphabet?
Ko-mahn pro-nohns-tohn lay lettr' duh lahl-fa-bay?
How does one pronounce the letters of the alphabet?

Comme ceci:
Kohm suh-see:
Like this:

A	B	C	D	E	F
ah	bay	say	day	uh	ef

G	H	I	J
zhay	ahsh	ee	zhee

K	L	M	N	O
ka	el	em	en	oh

P	Q	R	S	T
pay	ků	air	ess	tay

U	V	W
ů	vay	doo-bluh-vay

X	Y	Z
eeks	ee-grek	zed

W pronounced as V
The "w" is pronounced the same as the "v." It is not properly a French letter, but it is included in the alphabet because it is used in so many foreign words and place names.

— Pardon, comment vous appelez-vous?
Par-dohn ko-mahn voo za-puh-lay-voo?
Pardon, what is your name?

— Je m'appelle Paul Champeaux.
Zhuh ma-pelle Pohl Shaṇ-po.
My name is Paul Champeaux.

— Est-ce qu'on écrit cela, C H A M P O T ?
Ess kohṇ nay-kree suh-lay, say, ahsh, ah, em, pay, oh, tay?
Do you write that, C H A M P O T ?

— Non, pas comme ça, C H A M P E A U X .
Nohṇ, pa kohm sa, say, ahsh, ah, em, pay, uh, ah, ů, eeks.
No, not like that, C H A M P E A U X .

Il y a trois accents en français:
Eel ee ya trwa zak-sahṇ ahṇ frahṇ-say:
There are three accents in French:

L'accent aigu (´) et l'accent grave (`)
Lak-sahṇ tay-gů ay lak-sahṇ grahv
The acute accent and the grave accent

changent la prononciation de *e* en *é* ou *è,*
shahṇzh la pro-nohṇs-yahs-yohṇ duh *uh* eṇ *ay* oo *eh,*
change the pronunciation of e into é or è,

par exemple, l'Amérique, l'Algérie, l'élève.
par ekzahṇpl, la-may-reek, lal-zhay-ree, lay-lehv.
for example, America, Algeria, the pupil.

Written accents ´ ` and
The written accents affect the pronunciation only of the "e" making it like *ay* instead of "uh." The *accent aigu* (é) is sharper than the *accent grave* (è) which is more open. However, the best way to hear the difference between these sounds is to have a French person say the words we have given as examples.

The *accent grave* over *a* and *u* do not influence the sound but are used to differentiate between the meaning of short words that are spelled the same.

a — has
à — to
ou — or
où — where
la — the
là — there

On trouve des circonflexes sur les mots:
Ohn troov day seer-kohn-flex sûr lay mo:
One finds circumflexes on the words:

château, être, dîner, hôtel, dû,
sha-toh, etr', dee-nay, oh-tel, dû,
castle, to be, dinner, hotel, owed,

et sur beaucoup d'autres mots.
ay sûr bo-koo dohtr' mo.
and on many other words.

The circonflexe (^)
The *accent circonflexe* (^) appears over vowels
in certain words. When the ^ is used over an *e*
and *o* it gives the *e* a shorter sound, and the *o* a
longer one. The ^ also often shows that the letter "s" used to follow the vowel. This was in old
French so the (^) is really a sort of reminder of
the past.

Le petit signe sous le c dans les mots
Luh puh-tee seen soo luh say dohn lay mo
The little sign under c in the words

ça, garçon, reçu, etc.
sa, gar-sohn, ruh-sû, etc.
"that," "boy," "receipt," etc.

s'appelle la cédille.
sa-pel la say-dee'.
is called the cedilla.

The ç
The c before o, a, or u would normally be hard — like a k, so the *cedilla* is used to keep the c sounding like an s.

As you have seen, French written accents are used as part of the spelling of a word. Don't worry if you miss them sometimes. The French do too!

On écrit une lettre à la main ou à la machine.
Ohn nay-kree ůn lettr' ah la men oo ah la ma-sheen.
One writes a letter by hand or on the typewriter.

The many uses of "à"
À ("to") or "at" can also mean "on," "by," "by means of," "for," "in," or "with," depending on how it is used.

Quand la lettre est finie,
Kahn la lettr' ay fee-nee,
When the letter is finished,

on met le nom et l'adresse sur l'enveloppe.
ohn may luh nohn ay la-dress sůr lahnv-lohp.
one puts the name and the address on the envelope.

Ensuite, on met les timbres nécessaires,
Ahn-sweet, ohn may lay tenbr' nay-say-sair,
Then, one puts on the required stamps,

et on porte la lettre à la boîte aux lettres.
ay ohn pohrt la lettr' ah la bwaht oh lettr'.
and one takes the letter to the mailbox.

INSTANT CORRESPONDENCE:
A THANK-YOU NOTE AND A
POSTCARD

Voici une courte lettre à un ami:
Vwa-see ůn koort lettr' ah uṇ na-mee:
Here is a short letter to a friend:

le 10 mai
luh deess may
May 10th

> When writing in French, remember that capital
> letters are not used for days of the week,
> months, names of languages, or nationalities
> when used as adjectives:
>
> *il est canadien* — he is Canadian.
> C'est un Canadien — He's a Canadian.

Mon cher Guillaume,
Mohṇ shair Ghee-yohm,
My dear William,

Merci beaucoup pour les jolies fleurs.
Mair-see bo-koo poor lay zho-lee flerr.
Thank you very much for the pretty flowers.

Elles sont très belles!
El sohṇ tray bell!
They are very beautiful!

Les roses rouges sont mes fleurs favorites.
Lay rohz' roozh sohṇ may flerr fa-vo-reet.
Red roses are my favorite flowers.

A bientôt, j'espère.
Ah b'yeṇ-toh, zhes-pair.
Til soon, I hope.

Bien amicalement, Yvette.
B'yen na-mee-kal-mahn, Ee-vet.
Cordially, Yvette.

Voici une carte postale à une amie:
Vwa-see ûn kart pos-tahl ah ûn ah-mee:
Here is a postcard to a friend:

Ma chère Janine.
Ma shair Zha-neen.
My dear Janine.

Bons souvenirs de Cannes.
Bohn soov-neer duh Kahn.
Remembrances from Cannes.

Tout est très beau ici.
too tay tray bo ee-see.
Everything is very beautiful here.

Le temps est magnifique,
Luh tahn mahn-yee-feek,
The weather is magnificent,

et les gens sont très aimables.
ay lay zhan sohn tray zay-mabl'.
and the people are very nice.

Mais, malheureusement, vous n'êtes pas là.
May, ma-luh-ruhz-mahn, voo nett pa la.
But, unfortunately, you are not here.

> **Là**
> Là can mean "here" or "there" according to context.

Meilleures amitiés, Jacques.
May-yerr za-meet-yay, Zhahk.
Best regards, Jacques.

TEST YOUR FRENCH

Translate these phrases into French. Score 10 points for each correct translation. See answers below.

1. Thank you very much for the pretty flowers.
   _____

2. They are beautiful!
   _____

3. Red roses are my favorite flowers.
   _____

4. See you soon, I hope.
   _____

5. Remembrances from Cannes.
   _____

6. Everything is very beautiful here.
   _____

7. The weather is magnificent.
   _____

8. The people are very nice.
   _____

9. But, unfortunately, you are not here.
   _____

10. Best regards.
    _____

Answers: 1. Merci beaucoup pour les jolies fleurs. 2. Elles sont très belles! 3. Les roses rouges sont mes fleurs favorites. 4. A bientôt, j'espère. 5. Bons souvenirs de Cannes. 6. Tout est très beau ici. 7. Le temps est magnifique. 8. Les gens sont très aimables. 9. Mais, malheureusement, vous n'êtes pas là. 10. Meilleures amitiés.

SCORE _____%

step 8 BASIC VERBS RELATING TO SENSES

Voilà quelques verbes très importants:
Vwa-la kel-kuh vairb tray zeɲ-pohr-tahɲ:
Here are some very important verbs:

voir, regarder, lire, écrire, entendre, écouter,
vwar, ruh-gahr-day, leer, ay-kreer, ahɲ-tahɲdr', ay-koo-tay,
"to see," "to look," "to read," "to write," "to hear," "to listen,"

marcher, courir, danser, et plusieurs autres.
mar-shay, koo-reer', dahɲ-say ay pluz-yerr zohtr'.
"to walk," "to run," "to dance," and several others.

The three verb groups
You already know the present tense of several of these new verbs — the ones that end in er — *regarder, écouter, marcher, danser, chanter,* because they are conjugated like *parler* in Step 5 — by simply taking off the er and adding the appropriate ending — e for *je*, il, elle, ons for *nous*, ez for *vous*, and ent for *ils* or *elles*. These er verbs are called 1st conjugation verbs. Verbs in *ir* are 2nd conjugation verbs while those whose infinitives end in re or oir are classified as 3rd conjugation verbs and, as you will see, have a somewhat different conjugation pattern.

Nous voyons avec les yeux.
Noo vwa-yohɲ za-vek lay z'yuh.
We see with the eyes.

Je vous vois — Vous me voyez.
Zhuh voo vwa — Voo muh vwa-yay.
I see you — You see me.

Il ne nous voit pas, mais il la voit.
Eel nuh noo vwa pa, may zeel la vwa.
He does not see us, but he sees her.

Direct object pronouns
The direct object is placed before the verb. *Je vous vois* is literally "I you see." For the negative, the *ne* comes before the pronoun object.

Here are the direct object pronouns:

me	*me*
him or it	*le*
her or it	*la*
us	*nous*
you	*vous*
them	*les*

Nous voyons la mer de notre maison.
Noo vwa-yohn la mair duh notr' may-sohn.
We see the sea from our house.

Nous regardons la télévision.
Noo ruh-gar-dohn la tay-lay-veez-yohn.
We look at television.

Il la regarde — Elle le regarde.
Eel la ruh-gard — El luh ruh-gard.
He looks at her. — She looks at him.

Ils ne me regardent pas.
Eel nuh muh ruh-gard pa.
They do not look at me.

Ces personnes lisent.
Say pair-sohn leez.
These people are reading.

Cet homme lit le journal.
Set ohm lee luh zhoor-nahl.
This man reads the newspaper.

Cette femme ne lit pas le journal.
Set fahm nuh lee pa luh zhoor-nahl.
This woman does not read the newspaper.

Elle lit un magazine.
El lee tun ma-ga-zeen.
She reads a magazine.

Nous écrivons avec un crayon ou avec un stylo.
Noo zay-kree-vohn za-vek un kray-yohn oo ah-vek
un stee-lo.
We write with a pencil or with a fountain pen.

Irregular verbs
According to their endings, *dire, voir, lire,* and
écrire are all 3rd conjugation verbs and should
be conjugated the same way. However, some of
the commonest verbs are often irregular — that
is, they do not follow a pattern and therefore
must be considered separately: here is the present of these four verbs (from now on we will
give just the *il*-forms as the same form goes for
elle) —

dire (to say)	*voir* (to see)
je dis	*je vois*
il dit	*il voit*
nous disons	*nous voyons*
vous dites	*vous voyez*
ils disent	*ils voient*

lire (to read)	*ecrire* (to write)
je lis	*j'écris*
il lit	*il écrit*
nous lisons	*nous écrivons*
vous lisez	*vous écrivez*
ils lisent	*ils écrivent*

J'écris à la main — Elle écrit à la machine.
Zhay-kree ah la men — El ay-kree ah la ma-sheen.
I write by hand — She writes with the typewriter.

Il m'écrit — Elle vous écrit.
Eel may-kree — El voo zay-kree.
He writes to me — She writes to you.

On entend avec les oreilles.
Ohn̪ nahn̪-tahn̪ ah-vek lay zo-ray'.
One hears with the ears.

"Entendre" — to ~~listen~~ h ear
Entendre ("to listen") is a typical verb of the
3rd conjugation (with the *re* infinitive):
> *j'entends, il entend, nous entendons, vous
> entendez, ils entendent.*

You will meet other common verbs which follow
this pattern in future steps and we will call to
your attention verbs which have the same pattern as *entendre.*

Nous entendons parler les gens.
Noo zahn̪-tahn̪-dohn̪ par-lay lay zhan̪.
We hear the people talking (literally — "to talk").

Je vous parle — Vous m'écoutez.
Zhuh voo parl — Voo may-koo-tay.
I speak to you — You listen to me.

Indirect object pronouns
The indirect object pronouns are as follows:

> me, (or) to me — *me*
> him, her, (or) to him, to her, to it — *lui*
> us, (or) to us — *nous*
> you, (or) to you — *vous*
> them (or) to them — *leur*

Vous me parlez — Je vous écoute.
Voo muh par-lay — Zhuh voo zay-koot.
You speak to me — I listen to you.

Qu'est-ce que vous écoutez?
Kess kuh voo zay-koo-tay?
What are you listening to?

Nous sommes en train d'écouter la radio.
Noo sohm zahn̪ tren̪ day-koo-tay la rahd-yo.
We are listening to the radio.

En train de = in the process of
You will remember that French has no
progressive tense — for example "I speak" or
"I am speaking" are both expressed by *je
parle*. To give the idea of the English
progressive of something that is going on right
now, use the expression *être en train de*, followed by the verb.
  Je suis en train d'écrire une lettre.
  I am writing a letter. — (right now).
  Literally: I am in the process of writing a
  letter.

Paul écoute les nouvelles.
Pohl ay-koot lay noo-vel.
Paul is listening to the news.

Hélène écoute un disque.
Ay-layn ay-koot un deesk.
Helene is listening to a record.

Une dame chante. Les auditeurs l'écoutent.
Ůne dahm shant. Lay zo-dee-terr lay-koot.
A lady is singing. The audience is listening to her.

Elle finit de chanter.
El fee-nee duh shan-tay.
She finishes singing.

Finir — a pattern for the second conjugation
Finir gives the typical pattern for the 2nd conjugation. Its forms are: *je finis, il finit, nous finis-
sons, vous finissez, ils finissent.* The normal
pattern for 3rd conjugation verbs has already
been given by *entendre* (page 81). Incidentally,
as the 2nd and 3rd conjugations contain numerous exceptions, it is better to consider each important verb individually (and the most common
verbs are generally the irregular ones) and learn
these verbs and their irregularities through
using them.

Tout le monde dit:
Tool mohnd dee:
Everybody says:

Bravo! C'est magnifique! Formidable!
Bra-vo! Say mahn-yee-feek! Fohr-mee-dahbl'!
Bravo! It is magnificent! Terrific!

> **Everybody = Tout le monde**
> The word for "everybody" is *tout le monde*, literally "all the world" — a rather good synonym for "everyone," *n'est-ce pas?*

Avec la bouche, nous mangeons et nous buvons.
Ah-vek la boosh, noo mahn-zhohn zay noo bŭ-vohn.
With the mouth, we eat and we drink.

Nous mangeons du pain, de la viande, des légumes et des fruits.
Noo mahn-zhotn dŭ pen, duh lav-yahnd, day lay-gŭm zay day frwee.
We eat bread, meat, vegetables and fruit.

Nous buvons du café, du thé, du vin, de la bière, de l'eau.
Noo bŭ-vohn dŭ ka-fay, dŭ tay, dŭ ven, duh la b'yair, duh lo.
We drink coffee, tea, wine, beer, water.

> **The Partitive — 3 examples**
> Note how the three singular forms of the partitive are used in one line — *du, de la, de l'*.

Mon oncle Jules ne boit pas de lait.
Mo nohnkl' Zhŭl nuh bwa pa duh lay.
My uncle Julius doesn't drink milk.

> **Negative partitive = "de" without the article**
> For the negative of the partitive no article is used — just the *de:*
>
> > What! You don't eat cheese? — *Quoi! Vous ne mangez pas de fromage?*

Il boit du champagne.
Eel bwa du shahn-pine.
He drinks champagne.

Nous marchons et courons avec les jambes et les pieds.
Noo mahr-shohn zay koo-rohn za-vek lay zhahn br'ay lay p'yay.
We walk and run with the legs and feet.

Quand on danse, on remue tout le corps.
Kahn tohn dahns, ohn ruh-mü tool kor.
When one dances, one moves the whole body.

Avec le corps nous sentons
Ah-vek luh kor noo sahn-tohn
With the body we feel

> **"Sentir" means both "to feel" and "to smell"**
> Although it is a verb ending in -ir, sentir and a group of other verbs form their present tense in a somewhat different way than finir:
>
> *je sens, il sent, nous sentons, vous sentez, ils sentent.*
>
> Some other verbs that follow the pattern of sentir include sortir ("to go out"), dormir ("to sleep"), courir ("to run"), partir ("to depart").

si nous avons froid ou chaud,
see noo za-vohn frwa oo sho,
if we are cold or hot,

si nous avons faim ou soif,
see noo za-vohn fen oo swahf,
if we are hungry or thirsty,

> **"To have" instead of "to be"**
> In order to explain that you are hot or cold, hungry or thirsty, use avoir with the words given here:
>
> | | |
> |---|---|
> | I am hot | j'ai chaud |
> | I am cold | j'ai froid |
> | I am hungry | j'ai faim |
> | I am thirsty | j'ai soif |
>
> | | |
> |---|---|
> | Are you hot? | Avez-vous chaud? |
> | Are you cold? | Avez-vous froid? |
> | Are you hungry? | Avez-vous faim? |
> | Are you thirsty? | Avez-vous soif? |

Incidentally, be careful about pronouncing *faim*
("hunger") like *femme* ("woman") as it might
lead to an interesting misunderstanding.

et nous savons aussi si nous sommes malades
ay noo sa-vohn̗ zo-see see noo sohm ma-lahd
and we also know whether we are sick

ou en bonne santé.
oo ahn̗ bonn sahn̗-tay.
or in good health.

Voilà des exemples
Vwa-la day zex-ahn̗-pl'
Here are some examples

de l'emploi des pronoms compléments.
duh lahn̗-plwa day pro-nohn̗ kohn̗-play-mahn̗.
of the use of the pronoun objects.

Pierre aime la campagne.
P'yair aim la kahn̗-pine'.
Peter likes the country.

Il l'aime.
Eel laym.
He likes it.

Il regarde les oiseaux et les arbres.
Eel ruh-gard lay zwa-zo ay lay zarbr'.
He looks at the birds and the trees.

Il les regarde.
Eel lay ruh-gard.
He looks at them.

Un taureau mange l'herbe.
Un toh-ro mahn̗zh lairb.
A bull is eating the grass.

Il la mange.
Eel la mahn̗zh.
He eats it.

En — a reminder
If the bull eats "the" grass, the object pronoun
is *la*. To express "some grass" we would use
de l'herbe and "he is eating *some*" would be *il
en mange.*

Pierre ne voit pas le taureau.
P'yair nuh vwa pa luh toh-ro.
Peter does not see the bull.

Il ne le voit pas.
Eel nuh luh vwa pa.
He does not see it.

Le taureau regarde Pierre.
Luh toh-ro ruh-gard P'yair.
The bull looks at Peter.

Il le regarde.
Eel luh ruh-gard.
It looks at him.

Pierre entend le taureau.
P'yair ahn-tahn luh toh-ro.
Peter hears the bull.

Il l'entend et il le voit.
Eel lahn-tahn ay eel luh vwa.
He hears it and sees it.

Il court vers la barrière . . .
Eel koor vair la bar-yair' . . .
He runs toward the gate . . .

et vite, il saute par-dessus.
ay veet, eel soht pahr duh-sů.
and quickly, he jumps over (it).

INSTANT CONVERSATION: AT A DISCO

PIERRE:
P'yair:
PETER:

Vous voyez cette femme là-bas?
Voo vwa-yay set fahm la-ba?
Do you see that woman over there?

JEAN-PAUL:
Zohn Pohl:
JOHN-PAUL:

Comment? Je ne vous entends pas bien à cause de la musique.
Koh-mahn? Zuh nuh voo zahn-tahn pa b'yen ah kohz duh la mŭ-zeek.
What? I do not hear you well because of the music.

Il y a trop de bruit.
Eel ee ya tro duh brwee.
There is too much noise.

PIERRE:

Je vous dis: Voyez-vous cette femme là-bas?
Zhuh voo dee: Vwa-yay-voo set fahm la-ba?
I am saying to you: Do you see that woman over there?

JEAN-PAUL:

Laquelle? Il y en a beaucoup.
La-kel? Eel ee yahn na bo-koo.
Which one? There are many of them.

Which one?
Lequel — which one (mas.)
Laquelle — which one (fem.)
Lesquels — which ones (mas. pl.)
Lesquelles — which ones (fem. pl.)

PIERRE:

Celle qui est près du micro.
Sell kee ay pray dǔ mee-kro.
The one who is near the mike.

JEAN-PAUL:

La blonde qui est en train de chanter,
La blohn̪ kee ay tahn̪ tren̪ duh shan̪-tay,
The blond who is singing,

ou la brune qui danse toute seule là-bas.
oo la brǔne kee dahn̪ss toot suhl la-ba.
or the brunette who is dancing all alone over there.

PIERRE:

Mais non. La jolie aux cheveux noirs.
May nohn̪. La zho-lee oh shuh-vuh nwar.
But no. The pretty one with black hair.

JEAN-PAUL:

Celle qui danse avec le vieux monsieur?
Sell kee dahn̪ss ah-vek luh v'yuh muss-yuh?
The one who dances with the old gentleman?

PIERRE:

Oui, celle-là.
Wee, sell-la.
Yes, that one.

JEAN-PAUL:

Tiens! Elle est assez jolie. Et en plus elle danse bien.
T'yein̪! El ay ah-say zho-lee. Ay ahn̪ plǔs el dahn̪ss b'yen̪.
Well! She is pretty enough. And besides she dances well.

La connaissez-vous?
La ko-nay-say-voo?
Do you know her?

PIERRE:

Non, je ne la connais pas; et vous?
Nohn̪, zhuh nuh la ko-nay pa; ay voo?
No, I don't know her; and you?

JEAN-PAUL:

Moi non plus, bien sûr. Voilà pourquoi je vous le demande.

Mwa nohn̪ plŭ, b'yen̪ sûr. Vwa-la poor-kwa zhuh vool'duh-mahn̪d.

Neither do I, of course. That is why I'm asking you.

PIERRE:

Ça va. Je vois bien qu'elle vous intéresse.

Sa va. Zhuh vwa b'yen̪ kell voo zen̪-tay-ress.

O.K. I can see that she interests you.

Allons voir Louis. Il connaît tout le monde.

Ah-lohn̪ vwahr Lwee. Eel ko-nay tool mohn̪d.

Let's go see Louis. He knows everybody.

Il va sûrement vous présenter.

Eel va sûr-mahn̪ voo pray-zahn̪-tay.

He'll surely introduce you.

TEST YOUR FRENCH

Write number of English sentence which corresponds with French sentence in right hand column. Score 10 points for each correct answer. See answers below.

1. I see you.	Il connaît tout le monde.
2. You see me.	Elle danse bien.
3. He looks at them.	Cette dame chante.
4. He likes it.	Il y a trop de bruit.
5. He writes to me.	La connaissez-vous?
6. This lady is singing.	Vous me voyez.
7. Do you know her?	Il les regarde.
8. There is too much noise.	Il l'aime.
9. She dances well.	Il m'écrit.
10. He knows everybody.	Je vous vois.

Answers: 10 9 6 8 7 2 3 4 5 1

SCORE _____%

step 9 PROFESSIONS AND OCCUPATIONS

Pour connaître la situation ou la profession
Poor ko-netr' la see-tu-ass-yohn oo la pro-fess-yohn
To know the position or the profession

d'une personne, on demande:
dune pair-sonn, ohn duh-mahnd:
of a person, one asks:

"Quelle est votre profession?"
"Kell ay vo-truh pro-fess-yohn?"
"What is your profession?"

ou: "Quel métier faites-vous?"
oo: "Kel met-yay fet-voo?"
or: "What work do you do?"

Voici quelques métiers ou professions:
Vwa-see kel-kuh met'yay zoo pro-fess-yohn:
Here are some jobs or professions:

Un homme d'affaires travaille dans un bureau.
Un nohm da-fair' tra-vye' dahn zun bu-ro.
A businessman works in an office.

Les ouvriers travaillent dans des usines.
Lay zoovr-yay tra-vye' dahn day zu-zeen.
The workers work in factories.

Les médecins soignent les malades.
Lay med-sen swahn-yuh lay ma-lahd.
The doctors take care of the sick.

Les acteurs et les actrices
Lay zahk-tuhr ay lay zahk-treess
The actors and actresses

font du théâtre ou du cinéma.
fohn dŭ tay-ahtr' oo dŭ see-nay-ma.
work in the theatre or in the movies.

> **Faire=to make — to engage in**
> *Faire du théâtre* is an idiom equivalent to "engage in" or "work in." Another example is *faire de la politique* — "to engage in politics."

Un peintre fait des portraits ou des paysages.
Un pentr fay day por-tray oo day pay-ee-zahzh.
A painter makes portraits or landscapes.

Un auteur écrit des livres ou des articles.
Un no-tuhr ay-kree day leevr' oo day zahr-teekl'.
An author writes books or articles.

Un musicien joue du piano ou d'un autre instrument.
Un mŭ-zeess-yen zhoo dŭ p'yah-no oo dun nohtr' ens-trŭ-mahn.
A musician plays the piano or another instrument.

> **Jouer à, — jouer de**
> With *jouer* — "to play" — *de* must be used with the instrument played.
>
> > *Jouez-vous du violon?*
> > *Do you play the violin?*
>
> In playing sports, à is used with the definite article.
>
> > Do you play tennis? *Jouez-vous au tennis?*

Un mécanicien répare des autos.
Un may-ka-neess-yehn ray-pahr day zo-toh.
A mechanic repairs cars.

Le facteur apporte le courrier.
Luh fak-terr ah-port' luh koor-yay.
The mailman brings the mail

Un conducteur d'autobus conduit un autobus.
Un kohn-dŭk-terr doh-toh-bŭss kohn dwee un no-toh-bŭs.
A bus driver drives a bus.

Les chauffeurs de taxis conduisent des taxis.
Lay sho-ferr duh tak-see kohn-dweez day tahk-see.
Taxi drivers drive taxis.

Les pompiers éteignent les incendies.
Lay pohnp-yay ay-tain-yuh lay zen-sahn-dee.
The firemen put out fires.

Les agents de police maintiennent l'ordre dans la rue,
Lay za-zhahn duh po-leess men-yehn lordr' dahn la rů,
The policemen maintain order in the streets,

et arrêtent les criminels.
ay ah-ret lay kree-mee-nel.
and arrest the criminals.

Check with Step 5
Most of the verbs used above are regular first conjugation verbs — *demander, travailler, soigner, jouer, apporter* and *arrêter* and therefore all follow the form of *parler*. The infinitives of the other verbs are *faire, écrire, conduire, éteindre* and *maintenir*.

INSTANT CONVERSATION:
AT A *SOIRÉE* (EVENING PARTY)

— Quelle agréable réunion!
  Kel ah-gray-ahbl' ray-ûne-yohṇ!
  What a pleasant gathering!

— Oui, les invités sont très intéressants.
  Wee, lay zeṇ-vee-tay sohṇ tray zeṇ-tay-ray-sahṇ.
  Yes, the guests are very interesting.

  Madame de Laramont a beaucoup d'amis,
  Ma-dahm duh La-ra-mohṇ ah bo-koo da-mee,
  Mrs. de Laramont has many friends,

  dans des milieux très divers.
  dahṇ day meel-yuh tray dee-vair.
  in very different circles.

  Dans ce groupe là-bas près de la fenêtre,
  Dahṇ suh groop la-ba pray duh la fuh-netr',
  In that group over there by the window,

  il y a un avocat, un compositeur,
  eel ee ya uṇ na-vo-ka, uṇ kohṇ-po-zee-terr,
  there is a lawyer, a composer,

  un banquier, un architecte,
  uṇ bahṇk-yay, uṇ nar-shee-tekt',
  a banker, an architect,

  un dentiste et une vedette de cinéma.
  uṇ dahṇ-teest ay ûne vuh-dett duh see-nay-ma.
  a dentist and a movie star.

— Tiens! Je me demande de quoi ils parlent,
  T'yeṇ! Zhuh muh duh-mahṇd duh kwa eel pahrl',
  Well! I wonder what they are talking about,

architecture, finance, musique, droit . . . Qui sait?
ahr-shee-tek-tŭr, fee-nahⁿs, mŭ-zeek, drwa . . . Kee say?
architecture, finance, music, law . . . Who knows?

> *Demander* means "to ask," but *se de-mander* — "to ask oneself" — means "to wonder."

— Pensez-vous! Ils parlent sûrement de cinéma.
Pahⁿ-say-voo! Eel parl' sŭr-mahⁿ duh see-nay-ma.
You can imagine! They surely talk about the movies.

— Savez-vous qui est cette très jolie femme brune,
Sa-vay-voo kee ay set tray zho-lee fahm brŭn,
Do you know who that very pretty brunette is,

dans un élégant tailleur noir?
dahⁿ zuⁿ nay-lay-gahⁿ ta-yerr nwahr?
in an elegant black suit?

— C'est une danseuse étoile de l'Opéra.
Say tŭne dahⁿ-suhz' ay-twahl duh lo-pay-ra.
She is a star dancer from the Opera.

Elle s'appelle Yvonne Thomas.
Ell sa-pell E-vohn Toh-ma.
Her name is Yvonne Thomas.

— Et les deux hommes qui parlent avec elle?
Ay lay duh zohm kee parl ah-vek ell?
And the two men who are talking with her?

— Le vieux monsieur est chef d'orchestre
Luh v'yuh muss-yuh ay shef dor-kestr'
The old gentleman is a conductor

et le beau jeune homme est acteur, assez mauvais d'ailleurs.
ay luh bo zhuhn nohm ay tak-terr, ah-say mo-vay da-yerr.
and the handsome young man is an actor, rather a bad one really.

— Regardez! Vous voyez qui arrive maintenant?
Ruh-gahr-day! Voo vwa-yay kee ah-reev' meⁿt'-nahⁿ?
Look! Do you see who is arriving now?

C'est le Commandant Marcel Bardet,
Say luh Koh-mahn-dahn Mar-sell Bar-day,
It is Commander Marcel Bardet,

l'explorateur du fond de la mer.
lex-plo-ra-terr dü fohn duh la mair.
the explorer of the bottom of the sea.

> **N.B. the descriptive "de"**
> The French do not use nouns as adjectives. We
> can say either "sea bottom" or "bottom of the
> sea" but the French say it only the longer way.
> They don't say "gas station" or "fire engine"
> but "station of gas" (*poste d'essence*) and "en-
> gine for (a) fire" (*pompe à incendie*).

— Tiens! Savez-vous qu'il y a un article sur lui
T'yen! Sa-vay voo keel ee ya un nar-teekl' sür lwee
Well! Do you know that there is an article about him

dans le Figaro d'aujourd'hui?
dahn luh Fee-ga-ro doh-zhoor-dwee?
in today's Figaro?

Quelle vie aventureuse!
Kel vee ah-vahn-tü-rerrz!
What an adventurous life!

—... et dangereuse! Vous savez, je le connais bien.
... ay dahn-zhuh-rerrz! Voo sa-vay, zhuh luh ko-nay b'yen.
... and dangerous! You know, I know him well.

Il raconte toujours des choses très intéressantes.
Eel ra-kohnt too-zhoor day shohz' tray zen-tay-ray-sahn.
He always tells (about) very interesting things.

Allons bavarder un moment avec lui.
Ah-lohn ba-vahr-day un mo-mahn ah-vek lwee.
Let's go and talk to him for a while.

> **Let's see**
> *Allons* — "we go" or "we are going" — also
> can be used for "let's" when it is followed by
> the infinitive of the next verb.
> Allons voir — Let's see.

Je vais vous le présenter.
Zhuh vay voo luh pray-zahn-tay.
I'll introduce him to you.

Order priority for pronouns
When two pronoun objects are used together before the verb, they follow a sort of priority in their order. *Me, vous,* and *nous* come first, then *le, la* and *les,* and finally *lui* and *leur.*

TEST YOUR FRENCH

Match these people to the work they do. Score 10 points for each correct match. See answers below.

1. Un homme d'affaires	fait des paysages. (A)
2. Les médecins	éteignent les incendies. (B)
3. Un auteur	joue du piano. (C)
4. Les acteurs et les actrices	arrêtent les criminels. (D)
5. Un peintre	travaille dans un bureau. (E)
6. Un musicien	apporte le courrier. (F)
7. Le facteur	répare des autos. (G)
8. Les pompiers	soignent les malades. (H)
9. Un mécanicien	écrit des livres. (I)
10. Les agents de police	font du cinéma. (J)

Answers: 1. E 2. H 3. I 4. J 5. A 6. C 7. F 8. B 9. G 10. D.

SCORE _____%

step 10 HOW TO ASK AND GIVE DIRECTIONS — CAR TRAVEL

Voici quelques exemples de l'emploi
Vwa-see kel-kuh-zek-zahnpl' duh lahn-plwa
Here are a few examples of the use

de l'impératif et des pronoms compléments.
duh len-pay-ra-teef ay day pro-nohn kohn-play-mahn.
of the imperative and pronoun objects.

L'homme dans la voiture parle à un piéton.
Lohm dahn la vwa-tůr pahrl ah un pee-ay-tohn.
The man in the car is speaking to a pedestrian.

Il lui demande: "Est-ce que je suis bien sur la route d'Avignon?"
**Eel lwee duh-mahnd: "Ess kuh zhuh swee b'yen sůr, la root
da-veen-yohn?"**
He asks him: "Am I really on the road to Avignon?"

Le piéton lui répond: "Non, monsieur.
Luh pee-ay-tohn lwee ray-pohn: "Nohn, muss-yuh.
The pedestrian answers him: "No, sir.

Vous n'y êtes pas du tout.
Voo nee ett pa dů too.
You are not on it at all.

> ### The importance of "y"
> The one-letter word y means "there," "on it,"
> "in it," "at that place," "to there," "to it" — to
> give just a few of its meanings. This is another
> of the well-known "small words" which perme-
> ate French. Y and en are really very useful as
> they can substitute for a whole phrase.

Pour retrouver la route d'Avignon,
Poor ruh-troo-vay la root da-veen-yohn,
To get back on the road to Avignon,

Continuez tout droit jusqu'à la deuxième rue.
Kohn-tee-nway too drwa zhûs-ka la duhz-yem rû.
Continue straight ahead up to the second street.

Puis tournez à gauche.
Pwee toor-nay-za gohsh.
Then turn to the left.

Allez jusqu'au troisième feu rouge.
Ah-lay zhûs-ko trwaz-yem fuh roozh.
Go up to the third red light.

Là, vous tournez à droite.
Lah, voo toor-nay za drwat'.
There, you turn to the right.

Ensuite vous êtes sur la bonne route.
Ahn-sweet voo zet sûr la bunn root.
Then you are on the right road.

Mais, attention à la police.
May, ah'tahns-yohn ah la po-leess.
But, watch out for the police.

Il y a une limite de vitesse."
Eel ee ya ûne lee-meet duh vee-tess."
There is a speed limit."

L'automobiliste le remercie
Lo-toh-mo-bee-leest luh ruh mair-see
The motorist thanks him

et suit ses indications;
ay swee say zen-dee-kahs-yohn;
and follows his instructions;

Il tourne à gauche dans la deuxième rue,
Eel toorn a gohsh dahn la duhz-yem rû,
He turns to the left into the second street,

continue jusqu'au troisième feu rouge,
kohn-tee-nû zhûs-ko trwaz-yem fuh roozh,
continues up to the third red light,

Red & green lights
Feu is "fire." A red light for traffic is called a
feu rouge ("red fire"), while the green light is a
feu vert.

et tourne à droite.
ay toorn ah drwat.
and turns right.

Mais un agent de police en motocyclette le voit.
May zun̩ na-zhan̩ duh po-lees ahn̩ mo-toh-see-klet luh vwa.
But a policeman on a motorcycle sees him.

Il le suit, le dépasse et l'arrête.
Eel luh swee, luh day-pahss ay la-ret.
He follows him, passes him and stops him.

Il lui dit: "Et alors, le feu rouge?
Eel lwee dee: "Ay ah-lor, luh fuh roozh?
He says to him: "And what about the red light?

Alors
French colloquial conversation leans heavily on
alors — said in all sorts of tones and ways —
including sarcasm — as the policeman uses it
here.

Montrez-moi votre permis de conduire."
Mohn̩-tray-mwa vohtr' pair-mee duh kohn̩-dweer."
Show me your driving license."

The negative imperative
When pronoun objects are used after an im-
perative, "me" becomes *moi.*
Donnez-le-moi! — Give it to me!

This affirmative imperative changes the regular
priority order of pronoun objects and puts the
indirect objects last. But the negative imperative
goes back to the regular order.
Ne me le donnez pas! — Don't give it to me!

L'automobiliste le lui donne.
Lo-toh-mo-bee-leest luh lwee dunn.
The motorist gives it to him.

"Donnez-moi aussi la carte grise."
"Dohn-nay-mwa oh-see la kart greez."
"Give me also the registration (the gray card)."

Il la lui donne.
Eel la lwee donn.
He gives it to him.

L'agent écrit une contravention
La-zhan ay-kree ûn kohn-tra-vahns-yohn
The policeman writes a summons

et la donne à l'automobiliste.
ay la dunn ah lo-toh-mo-bee-leest.
and gives it to the motorist.

Il lui rend le permis et la carte grise.
Eel lwee rahn luh pair-mee ay la kart greez.
He gives him back the license and the registration.

"Tenez," lui dit-il, "et à l'avenir faites attention."
"Tuh-nay," lwee-dee-teel, "ay ah lahv'-neer fait za-tahns-yohn."
"Here, you are (have it)," he says to him, "and in the future pay attention
(be careful)."

INSTANT CONVERSATION:
GIVING ORDERS

LA DAME:
La dahm:
THE LADY:

> Marie, vous n'entendez pas, on sonne,
> **Ma-ree', voo nahn-tahn-day pa, ohn sunn,**
> Marie, don't you hear, someone is ringing,

> Il y a quelqu'un à la porte. Ouvrez, s'il vous plaît.
> **Eel ee ya kel-kun ah la pohrt. Oo-vray, seel voo play.**
> There is someone at the door. Open it, please.

> Qui est-ce?
> **Kee ess?**
> Who is it?

MARIE:
Ma-ree:
MARIE:

> C'est le garçon-boucher qui livre la viande.
> **Say luh gar-sohn-boo-shay kee leevr' la vee-ahn.**
> It's the boy from the butcher that delivers the meat.

LA DAME:

> Mettez-la dans le réfrigérateur.
> **Met-tay-la dahn luh ray-free-zhay-ra-terr.**
> Put it into the refrigerator.

> Avez-vous la note?
> **Ah-vay-voo la noht?**
> Have you the bill?

MARIE:

> C'est lui qui l'a, madame.
> **Say lwee kee la, ma-dahm.**
> He is the one who has it, madam.

C'est moi!

After forms of *être* — like *c'est* and also when pronouns stand entirely alone — another pronoun form is used:

It is I	*C'est moi*
It is he	*C'est lui*
It is she	*C'est elle*
It is we	*C'est nous*
It is you	*C'est vous*
It is they (mas.)	*C'est eux*
It is they (fem.)	*C'est elles*

French has an advantage over English in this case, as English-speaking people are usually undecided about whether to say "it is I" or "it's me." This form is also used with prepositions.

avec moi — with me
sans elle — without her

LA DAME:

Dites-lui de la laisser sur la table de la cuisine.
Deet-lwee duh la lay-say sûr la tahbl' duh la kwee-zeen.
Tell him to leave it on the kitchen table.

Je ne la paie pas tout de suite.
Zhuh nuh la pay pa tood' sweet.
I am not paying it right now.

Voilà la liste pour demain. Prenez-la et donnez-la-lui.
Vwa-la la leest' poor duh-men. Pruh-nay-la ay dun-nay-la-lwee.
Here is the list for to-morrow. Take it and give it to him.

MARIE:

Oui, madame. Tout de suite.
Wee, ma-dahm. Tood sweet.
Yes, madam. Right away.

LA DAME:

Et maintenant je sors.
Ay ment-nahn zhuh sohr.
And now I am going out.

Je vais d'abord chez le coiffeur,
Zhuh vay da-bohr shay luh kwa-ferr,
I am going first to the hair dresser's

Chez le coiffeur
The following vocabulary will be useful when speaking to the *coiffeur* — "Hairdresser" or "barber"

For ladies:
une mise en plis — a set
un shampoing — a shampoo
un rinçage — a rinse
plus clair — lighter
plus foncé — darker
comme ça — like this
une manucure — a manicure

and for men:
une coupe de cheveux — a hair cut
pas trop court — not too short
un massage — a massage
la barbe aussi — a shave too
(this last implies either "a shave," or "to trim the beard" according to whether you have a "beard" — *barbe*—or not)

et ensuite je vais faire des courses.
ay ahn-sweet zhuh vay fair day koors.
and then I am going shopping.

More expressions with "faire"
Some idiomatic expressions with *faire*:

faire des courses — to go shopping
faire une promenade — to take a walk (or ride)
faire du ski — to go skiing
faire du sport — to engage in sport
faire réparer — to have fixed
faire nettoyer — to have cleaned
faire repasser — to have pressed

Pendant ce temps, nettoyez la maison
Pahn-dahn suh tahn, nay-two-yay la may-zohn
Meanwhile, clean the house

et préparez le dîner.
ay pray-pa-ray luh dee-nay.
and prepare the dinner.

Voilà deux robes, une jupe et un complet.
Vwa-la duh rohb, ŭne jŭp ay un̦ kohn̦-play.
Here are two dresses, a skirt and a suit.

Portez-les chez le teinturier.
Pohr-tay-lay shay luh ten̦-tŭr-yay.
Take them to the cleaner's.

Allons bon . . . Encore le téléphone . . .
Ah-lohn̦ bohn̦ . . . Ahn̦-kohr luh tay-lay-fohn . . .
Well now . . . Again the telephone . . .

Répondez, s'il vous plaît. . . .
Ray-pohn̦-day, seel voo play. . . .
Answer (it), please. . . .

Qui est-ce?
Kee ess?
Who is it?

MARIE:
C'est mon ami Jules.
Say mohn̦ na-mee Zhŭl.
It's my friend Jules.

Il m'invite au bal ce soir.
Eel men̦-veet oh bahl suh swar.
He is inviting me to a dance tonight.

LA DAME:
Mais nous avons des invités.
Mai noo za-vohn̦ day zen̦-vee-tay.
But we have guests.

Bon . . . allez-y. Mais servez d'abord le dîner.
Bohn̦ . . . Ah-lay-zee. May sair-vay da-bohr luh dee-nay.
Well then . . . go there. But serve dinner first.

TEST YOUR FRENCH

Translate these imperatives into French. Where pronouns are used, gender is indicated. Score 5 points for each correct answer. See answers below.

1. Come here!	11. Give it to me! (mas.)
2. Go!	12. Open it! (fem.)
3. Continue straight ahead!	13. Close it! (mas.)
4. Turn right!	14. Take it! (fem.)
5. Turn left!	15. Carry them! (mas.)
6. Tell me!	16. Clean them! (mas.)
7. Show me!	17. Give it to him! (fem.)
8. Wait!	18. Put it here! (fem.)
9. Answer!	19. Do it! (mas.)
10. Pay attention!	20. Don't do it! (mas.)

Answers: 1. Venez ici! 2. Allez! 3. Continuez tout droit! 4. Tournez à droite! 5. Tournez à gauche! 6. Dites-moi! 7. Montrez-moi! 8. Attendez! 9. Répondez! 10. Faites attention! 11. Donnez-le-moi! 12. Ouvrez-la! 13. Fermez-le! 14. Prenez-la! 15. Portez-les! 16. Nettoyez-les! 17. Donnez-la-lui! 18. Mettez-la ici! 19. Faites-le! 20. Ne le faites pas!

SCORE _____%

107

step 11 HOW TO SAY "WANT," "CAN," "MAY," "MUST", AND "WOULD LIKE TO"

Un jeune homme veut voir le match de football,
Un zhuhn ohm vuh vwar luh match duh football,
A young man wants to see the soccer game,

mais il ne peut pas entrer.
may zeel nuh puh pa zahn-tray.
but he cannot get in.

Pourquoi ne peut-il pas entrer?
Poor-kwa nuh puh-teel pa zahn-tray?
Why can't he get in?

Parce qu'il n'a pas de billet.
Par-suh keel na pa duh bee-yay.
Because he doesn't have a ticket.

Pourquoi n'achète-t-il pas un billet?
Poor-kwa na-shet-teel pa zun bee-yay?
Why doesn't he buy a ticket?

Parce qu'il n'a pas assez d'argent.
Par-suh keel na pa za-say dar-zhahn.
Because he doesn't have enough money.

Sans argent il ne peut pas voir le match.
Sahn zar-zhahn eel nuh puh pa vwar luh match.
Without money he cannot see the game.

S'il veut le voir, il doit payer.
Seel vuh luh vwar, eel dwa pay-yay.
If he wants to see it, he must pay.

To want, can, and must
Vouloir "to want," *pouvoir* "can," or "to be able" and *devoir* "must," or "to owe" combine

108

directly with the infinitive of the next verb or can be used alone. Here is their present tense:

	vouloir	pouvoir	devoir
(je)	veux	peux	dois
(il)	veut	peut	doit
(nous)	voulons	pouvons	devons
(vous)	voulez	pouvez	devez
(ils)	veulent	peuvent	doivent

Mais voilà un de ses amis:
May vwa-la un duh say za-mee:
But here is a friend of his:

"Dites donc," lui dit-il, "voulez-vous me prêter 10 francs
"Deet dohnk," lwee dee-teel, "voo-lay-voo muh preh-tay dee fran
"Say there," he says to him, "will you lend me 10 francs

An invitation

Voulez-vous? is another easy way to offer an invitation or to give an implied command.

Voulez-vous une cigarette? — Do you wish (want) a cigarette?
Voulez-vous fermer la fenêtre? — Will you (do you want to) close the window?

pour aller voir le match?"
poor ah-lay vwar luh match?"
to go and see the match?"

"Peut-être," dit-il, "Quand pouvez-vous me les rendre?"
"Puh-tetr'," dee-teel, "Kahn poo-vay-voo muh lay rahndr'?"
"Perhaps," he says, "When can you give them back to me?"

"Oh! Demain, certainement, sans faute," répond son ami.
"Oh! Duh-men, sair-tane-mahn, sahn foht," ray-pohn so na-mee.
"Oh! Tomorrow, certainly, without fail," replies his friend.

Ma voiture ne peut pas démarrer.
Ma vwa-tůr' nuh puh pa day-ma-ray.
My car cannot start.

Pourquoi ne peut-elle pas démarrer?
Poor-kwa nuh puh-tel pa day-ma-ray?
Why can't it start?

Parce qu'il n'y a pas d'essence dans le réservoir.
Par-suh keel nee a pa day-sahns dahn luh ray-zair-vwar.
Because there is no gas in the tank.

Quand il n'y a pas d'essence dans le réservoir
Kahn teel nee a pa day-sahns dahn luh ray-zair-vwar
When there is no gas in the tank

le moteur ne peut pas marcher.
luh mo-terr nuh puh pa mar-shay.
the motor cannot go.

Il faut mettre de l'essence.
Eel fo mettr' duh lay-sahns.
One must put in gas.

> **"Il faut" — "must" or "need"**
> The impersonal expression *il faut* is used for "I
> (he, you, we or they) must" or "it is necessary
> to" and combines with the infinitive when the in-
> finitive follows.
>
> > *Il faut partir* — "We must go."
>
> *Il faut* with the indirect object pronoun means
> "one needs" or "must have" something.
> > *Il me faut de l'argent* — I need money.

Où peut-on acheter de l'essence?
Oo puh-tohn ash-tay duh lay-sahns?
Where can one buy gas?

On peut en acheter dans un poste d'essence.
Ohn puh tahn nash-tay dahn-zun pohst day-sahns.
One can buy some at a gas station.

> **Dans un poste d'essence**
> While on the subject of service stations, note
> the following key expressions:
>
> > Fill it! — *Faites le plein!*
> > Check the oil. — *Vérifiez l'huile.*

Check the tires. — *Vérifiez les pneus.*
Check the battery. — *Vérifiez la batterie.*
This isn't working well. — *Ceci ne marche pas bien.*
Can you fix it? — *Pouvez-vous le réparer?*
This tire must be changed. — *Il faut changer ce pneu.*
How long must we wait? — *Combien de temps faut-il attendre?*

Deux jeunes filles sont en difficulté.
Duh zhuhn fee' sohn tahn dee-fee-kŭl-tay.
Two girls are in trouble.

Un pneu de leur voiture est à plat.
Un p'nuh duh lerr vwa-tŭr ay ah pla.
A tire of their car is flat.

Elles ne peuvent pas changer la roue parce qu'elles n'ont pas de cric.
Ell nuh puhv pa shan-zhay la roo par skel nohn pa duh kreek.
They cannot change the wheel because they haven't a jack.

Mais voilà un jeune homme qui arrive dans une voiture de sport.
May vwa-la un zhuhn ohm kee ah-reev dahn zŭn vwa-tŭr duh spohr.
But here is a young man who arrives in a sports car.

Il leur demande: — "Puis-je vous aider?"
Eel lerr duh-mahnd: — "Pwee-zhuh voo zay-day?"
He asks them: — "May I help you?"

"Certainement! Pouvez-vous nous prêter un cric?"
"Sair-tane-mahn! Poo-vay voo noo preh-tay un kreek?"
"Certainly! Can you lend us a jack?"

"Mais je peux faire encore mieux," dit-il.
"May zhuh puh fair ahn-kor m'yuh," dee-teel.
"But I can do even more," he says.

"Je peux moi-même vous changer la roue."
"Zhuh puh mwa-mem voo shahn-zhay la roo."
"I can change the wheel (for) you myself."

Que faut-il faire si nous voulons aller au cinéma?
Kuh fo-teel fair see noo voo-lohn zah-laz oh see-nay-ma?
What must we do if we want to go to the movies?

Il faut acheter des billets.
Eel fo tahsh-tay day bee-yay.
We must buy tickets.

Si la télévision ne marche pas, que faut-il faire?
See la tay-lay-veez-yohn nuh marsh pa, kuh fo-teel fair?
If the television does not go (work), what must we do?

Il faut la faire réparer.
Eel fo la fair ray-pa-ray.
It is necessary to have it repaired.

To have something done.
To have something done is expressed by *faire* followed by the verb in the infinitive. For your travels, this is especially useful in hotels.

Voulez-vous faire repasser ceci? — Will you have this pressed?
Voulez-vous faire monter un petit déjeuner? — Will you have breakfast sent up?

Both cases use *faire* because you don't expect the person you are talking to do it personally — but to have it done.

INSTANT CONVERSATION:
A TV PROGRAM

ROGER:
Ro-zhay:
ROGER:

Vous savez, on va donner
Voo sa-vay, ohn va dun-nay
You know, they are going to give

un programme très intéressant
un pro-gram tray zen-tay-ray-sahn
a very interesting program

ce soir à la télévision.
suh swahr ah la tay-lay-veez-yohn.
this evening on television.

Malheureusement, je ne peux pas le voir.
Ma-luh-ruhz-mahn, zhuh nuh puh pa luh vwar.
Unfortunately, I cannot see it.

Parce que mon poste ne marche pas.
Par-suh kuh mohn post nuh marsh pa.
Because my set is not working.

ALBERT:
Ahl-bair:
ALBERT:

Voyons . . . téléphonez donc au service de réparations.
Voh-yohn . . . tay-lay-fo-nay dohnk oh sair-vees duh ray-pa-rahs-yohn.
Well then . . . telephone the repair service.

ROGER:

À quoi bon? Vous savez bien
Ah kwa bohn? Voo sa-vay b'yen
What's the use? You well know

113

qu'ils ne peuvent jamais venir tout de suite.
keel nuh puhv zha-may vuh-neer tood-sweet.
that they can never come right away.

ALBERT:

Alors, si vous tenez vraiment à voir
Ah-lohr, see voo tuh-nay vray-mahŋ ah vwar
Then, if you really want to see

ce programme, venez chez moi.
suh pro-grahm, vuh-nay shay mwa.
this program, come to my house.

ROGER:

C'est gentil, mais je ne veux pas vous déranger.
Say zhaŋ-tee, may zhuh nuh vuh pa voo day-rahŋ-zhay.
It's kind (of you), but I don't want to bother you.

ALBERT:

Mais je vous en prie, vous ne me dérangez pas du tout.
May zhuh voo zahŋ pree, voo nuh muh day-rahŋ-zhay pa dǔ too.
But I assure you, you won't bother me at all.

D'ailleurs, si c'est si intéressant,
Da-yerr, see say see en-tay-ray-sahŋ,
Besides, if it is so interesting,

Moi aussi, je voudrais le voir.
Mwa oh-see, zhuh voo-dray luh vwahr.
I too would like to see it.

> ### "I want" or "I would like"
> "I want" is *je veux,* and "I would like" is *je vou-drais.* While the latter is in the conditional mood, which we will take up in a later Step, *je voudrais* is so frequent in conversation that we introduce it here as a special and more polite form.

Nous pouvons le regarder ensemble.
Noo poo-vohŋ luh ruh-gar-day ahŋ-sahŋbl'.
We can look at it together.

Au fait, qu'est-ce que c'est que ce programme?
Oh fett, kess kuh say kuh suh pro-gram?
By the way, what is the program?

ROGER:

C'est le Festival de Cannes
Say luh Fes-tee-vahl duh Cahnn
It is the Cannes Festival

transmis directement avec toutes les vedettes.
trahns-mee dee-rek-tuh-mahn ah-vek toot lay vuh-det.
directly transmitted with all the stars.

ALBERT:

A quelle heure est-ce que ça commence?
Ah kel err ess kuh sa koh-mahns?
At what time does it start?

ROGER:

A neuf heures précises.
Ah nuhv err pray-seez.
At nine o'clock precisely.

ALBERT:

Alors, nous pouvons dîner d'abord.
Ah-lohr, noo poo-vohn dee-nay da-bor.
Then, we can have dinner first.

Voulez-vous dîner avec moi?
Voo-lay-voo dee-nay ah-vek mwa?
Will you have dinner with me?

ROGER:

Volontiers, mais je voudrais vous inviter.
Vo-lohnt-yay, may zhuh voo-dray a voo zen-vee-tay.
Gladly, but I would like to invite you.

ALBERT:

Mais non, je vous en prie.
May nohn, zhuh voo zahn pree.
But no, please.

ROGER:

Si, j'insiste.
See, zhen-seest.
Yes, I insist.

> **"Si" — an emphatic "yes"**
> *Si* is a forceful form of *oui*, when one insists on something to affirm, deny or contradict. Usually, because of the tradition of politeness, routines of polite refusals about invitations, who goes first, etc., are customary. Here again, the expression *je vous en prie,* said by either party, is quite useful.

ALBERT:

Alors, si vous insistez, je ne peux pas refuser.
Ah-lohr, see voo zen-sees-tay, zhuh nuh puh pa ruh-fů-zay.
Then, if you insist, I cannot refuse.

ROGER:

Très bien. Nous pouvons dîner
Tray b'yen. Noo poo-vohn dee-nay
Very well. We can have dinner

dans un petit restaurant du quartier tout près d'ici.
dahn zun puh-tee res-toh-rahn dů kart-yay too pray dee-see.
in a little restaurant in the area very close to here.

On n'y mange pas mal.
Ohn nee mahnzh pa mahl.
One does not eat badly there.

Allons-y tout de suite.
Ah-lohn-zee tood sweet.
Let's go right away.

ALBERT:

Oui. Il faut dîner vite
Wee. Eel fo dee-nay veet
Yes. We must eat fast

si nous ne voulons pas manquer le début du programme.
see noon voo-lohn pa mahn-kay luh day-bů dů pro-grahm.
if we don't want to miss the beginning of the program.

TEST YOUR FRENCH

Translate these phrases into English. Score 10 points for each correct answer. See answers below.

1. Il me faut de l'argent. _____

2. Il faut partir. _____

3. Allons-y tout de suite. _____

4. Voulez-vous dîner avec moi? _____

5. Pouvez-vous me prêter dix francs? _____

6. Je ne veux pas vous déranger. _____

7. Je voudrais le voir. _____

8. Venez chez moi. _____

9. Pourquoi n'achète-t-il pas un billet? _____

10. Parce qu'il n'a pas assez d'argent. _____

SCORE _____%

step **12**

HOW TO USE REFLEXIVE VERBS

Monsieur Leblanc se lève de bonne heure.
Muss-yuh Luh-blahn suh lev duh bonn err.
Mr. Leblanc gets up early.

Il se lave les dents, il se lave la figure, et il se rase.
Eel suh lahv lay dahn, eel suh lahv la fee-gŭr, ay eel suh rahz.
He cleans his teeth, he washes his face, and he shaves.

Reflexive verbs & pronouns
Se laver ("to wash oneself") is a reflexive verb,
like *s'appeler* in Step 7. Reflexive verbs are so
called because the subject of the verb acts on
itself, as in the case of to wash, to dress, etc.
Here are the reflexive pronouns as used with *se
laver* in the present tense:

> *je* **me** *lave, il* **se** *lave, nous* **nous** *lavons,
> vous* **vous** *lavez, ils* **se** *lavent.*

Ensuite, il s'habille.
Ahn-sweet, eel sa-bee'.
Then he gets dressed.

The silent "h"
The *se* drops an *e* in *s'habiller* because the
word sonically begins with *a* as the *h* is always
silent.

Un peu plus tard ses enfants se lèvent.
Un puh plŭ tahr say zahn-fahn suh lev.
A little later his children get up.

Il se lavent, se peignent et se brossent les cheveux
Eel suh lahv, suh pane ay suh brohss lay shuh-vuh
They wash, comb and brush their hair

et s'habillent en vitesse.
ay sa-bee' tahɲ vee-tess.
and get dressed quickly.

Et puis ils se mettent à table
Ay pwee eel suh met ah tahbl'
And then they sit down at the table

pour prendre leur petit déjeuner.
poor prahɲdr' lerr puh-tee day-zhuh-nay.
to take their breakfast.

> **Breakfast or lunch**
> Remember that petit déjeuner is "breakfast"
> and déjeuner "lunch."

Pour leur petit déjeuner,
Poor lerr puh-tee day-zhuh-nay,
For their breakfast,

ils prennent du jus d'orange,
eel prenn dů zhů doh-rahɲzh',
they take orange juice,

des petits pains avec du beurre et du café au lait.
day puh-tee peɲ ah-vek dů berr ay dů ka-fay oh lay.
rolls with butter and coffee with milk.

> **The descriptive "à"**
> A plus the definite article can mean "with"
> especially if, as is the case with café au lait, the
> thing it refers to is mixed in. You will often see it
> so used in restaurant items.

Après le déjeuner Monsieur Leblanc
Ah-pray luh day-zhuh-nay Muss-yuh Luh-blahɲ
After breakfast, Mr. Leblanc

met son manteau et son chapeau
may sohɲ mahɲ-toh ay sohɲ sha-po
puts on his coat and his hat

et va à son bureau.
ay va ah sohɲ bů-ro.
and goes to his office.

Les enfants mettent leurs manteaux et leurs bérets.
Lay zahɲ-fahɲ met lerr mahɲ-toh ay lerr bay-ray.
The children put on their coats and their berets.

The plural with x
Words ending in *eau* or *eu* form the plural by adding an *x*. Words ending in *al* do the same. Two common words of this sort are often confused by students:

un cheveu — a hair	*des cheveux* (hair, pl.)
un cheval — a horse	*des chevaux* (horses)

Ils prennent leurs serviettes et vont à l'école.
Eel prain lerr sairv-yet ay vohɲ ta lay-kohl
They take their bookbags and go to school.

Alors, Madame Leblanc se sent fatiguée,
Ah-lohr, Ma-dam Luh-blahɲ suh sahɲ fa-tee-gay,
Then, Mrs. Leblanc feels tired,

et elle se recouche pour se reposer.
ay el suh ruh-koosh poor suh ruh-po-zay.
and she goes to bed again to rest.

Bientôt elle s'endort.
B'yeɲ-toh el sahɲ-dohr.
Soon she falls sleep.

"Dormir" and "s'endormir"
dormir — to sleep   *s'endormir* — to fall asleep

Dormir is conjugated like *sentir* in Step 8: *je dors, il dort, nous dormons, vous dormez, ils dorment.*

En France, comme en Amérique,
Ahɲ Frahɲs', kom ahɲ Ah-may-reek,
In France, as in America,

on déjeune entre midi et deux heures,
ohɲ day-zhun ahɲtr' mee-dee ay duh-zerr,
one has lunch between noon and two o'clock,

mais pour beaucoup de Français
may poor bo-koo duh Frahn̨-say
but for many French people

le déjeuner est le repas le plus important.
luh day-zhuh-nay ay luh ruh-pa luh plu zen̨-pohr-tahn̨.
lunch is the most important meal.

Souvent ils rentrent chez eux
Soo-vahn̨ eel rahn̨tr' shay zuh
Often they return home

> **Chez**
> *chez* — at the house (home) of
> *chez moi* — at my house
> *chez nous* — at our house
> *chez eux* — at their house (masc.)
> *chez elles* — at their house (fem.)
> *chez soi* — at one's house
> *allons chez Henri* — let's go to Henry's

et retournent à leur bureau l'après-midi.
ay ruh-toorn' ah lerr bů-ro la-pray-mee-dee.
and return to their office in the afternoon.

Dans beaucoup de villes françaises,
Dahn̨ bo-koo duh veel frahn̨-sez,
In many French cities,

les magasins ferment de midi à deux heures.
lay ma-ga-zen̨ fairm duh mee-dee ah duh zerr.
the stores close from noon to two o'clock.

En France, on quitte son bureau
Ahn̨ Frahn̨s', ohn̨ keet sohn̨ bů-ro
In France, one leaves his office

à six heures ou même plus tard
ah see zerr oo mem plů tahr
at six o'clock or even later

et on rentre dîner chez soi, rarement avant huit heures.
ay ohn̨ rahn̨tr' dee-nay shay swa, rahr-mahn̨ ah-vahn̨ weet err.
and returns home to dinner, rarely before eight o'clock,

Adverbs ending in "-ment"
As most English adverbs end in "ly," French adverbs end in *ment*. See whether you can recognize these adverbs without translation:

généralement, sûrement, énormément, possiblement, probablement, certainement, terriblement, rapidement.

Were you able to guess them?

They were: "generally," "surely," "enormously," "possibly," "probably," "certainly," "terribly," and "rapidly."

INSTANT CONVERSATION:
GOING TO A BUSINESS MEETING

— Dépêchez-vous. Il faut s'en aller.
Day-pay-shay-voo. Eel fo sahn na-lay.
Hurry up. We must leave.

Nous allons arriver en retard à la réunion.
Noo za-lohn ah-ree-vay ahn ruh-tahr ah la ray-ŭn-yohn.
We are going to be late for the meeting.

— Ne vous inquiétez pas.
Nuh voo zenk-yay-tay pa.
Don't worry.

Reflexive verbs describing emotions
Many of the reflexive verbs denote an emotional
state of one's own personality.

> *s'inquiéter* — to worry
> *se fâcher* — to get angry
> *s'ennuyer* — to be annoyed (or) bored
> *s'énerver* — to get nervous
> *se calmer* — to calm oneself

Nous avons encore presque une demi-heure.
Noo za-vohn zahn-kohr presk ŭne duh-mee-err.
We still have almost half an hour.

Nous ne voulons pas arriver trop tôt.
Noo nuh voo-lohn pa za-ree-vay tro toh.
We do not want to arrive too early.

Tôt ou tard
There are two words for "early" — *de bonne
heure* and *tôt*. "In advance" is *en avance*;
"late" is *tard*, and late to an appointment is *en
retard*. "On time" is *à l'heure*. And, discussing
punctuality, here is an old French proverb:

123

L'exactitude est la politesse des rois —
Punctuality is the courtesy of kings.

— Mais la réunion se tient
May la ray-ûne-yohɲ suh t'yeɲ
But the meeting is taking place

de l'autre côté de la ville.
duh lohtr' kot-tay duh la veel.
on the other side of town.

Il faut vraiment se dépêcher.
Eel foh vray-mahɲ suh day-pay-shay.
We really must hurry.

— Voyons, vous vous chargez
Vwa-yohɲ, voo voo shar-zhay
Let's see, you are taking care

d'apporter les documents,
da-pohr-tay lay doh-kû-mahɲ,
of bringing the documents.

— Oui. Voilà la correspondance concernant le contrat.
Wee. Vwa-la la koh-ress-pohɲ-dahɲs kohn-sair-nahɲ luh kohɲ-tra.
Yes. Here's the correspondence concerning the contract.

The verbal ending -ant

The present participle of the verb ends in -ant
and is equivalent to the English "ing," but is
not used as the progressive mood. It is employed in adverbial phrases as an adjective:

En marchant — while walking
En passant — in passing, while passing
Que c'est étonnant! — How surprising!
C'est fatigant! — That's tiring!

— Mais le contrat lui-même —
May luh kohɲ-tra lwee-maim —
But the contract itself —

Mon Dieu! Où se trouve-t-il?
Mohɲ D'yuh! Oo suh troov-teel?
My God! Where is it?

Se trouver = to be located
Oy se trouve-t-il? Literally, "Where does it find itself?" "Where is it?" or "Where is it located?"

— C'est vous qui l'avez — dans votre serviette.
Say voo kee la-vay — dahɲ vohtr' sairv-yet.
You're the one that has it — in your brief case.

— Ah oui, je me souviens maintenant.
Ah wee, zhuh muh soov-yeɲ meɲt'-nahɲ.
Ah yes, I remember now.

Attendez-moi ici. Je vais chercher un taxi.
Ah-tahɲ-day-mwa ee-see. Zhuh vay shair-shay uɲ tahk-see.
Wait for me here. I'm going to get a taxi.

— Ne vous dérangez pas.
Nuh voo day-rahɲ-zhay pa.
Don't bother.

Il y a un taxi qui attend en bas devant la porte.
Eel ee ya uɲ tahk-see kee ah-tahɲ ahɲ ba duh-vahɲ la port'.
There is a taxi waiting downstairs in front of the door.

— Bon. Partons — et vite.
Bohɲ. Par-tohɲ — ay veet.
Good. Let's go — and quickly.

— Mais calmez-vous, mon vieux.
May kal-may-voo, mohɲ v'yuh.
But calm yourself, (my) old fellow.

Et surtout — ne vous énervez pas pendant la réunion.
Ay sûr-too — nuh voo zay-nair-vay pa pahɲ-dahɲ la ray-ûne-yohɲ.
And above all — don't get nervous during the meeting.

TEST YOUR FRENCH

Translate into French, using reflexive verbs. Score 10 points for each correct answer. See answers below.

1. They get up early.
   _____

2. He shaves (himself).
   _____

3. He washes his face.
   _____

4. She feels tired.
   _____

5. She falls asleep.
   _____

6. Don't worry.
   _____

7. Hurry up.
   _____

8. Don't get nervous.
   _____

9. Don't bother.
   _____

10. Calm yourself.
   _____

SCORE _____%

step 13 EXPRESSING PREFERENCES AND OPINIONS

Nous sommes au bord de la mer. C'est l'été.
Noo sohm zo bor duh la mair. Say lay-tay.
We are at the seashore. It is summer.

La mer est bleue.
La mair ay bluh.
The sea is blue.

Le ciel est bleu clair.
Luh see-el ay bluh klair.
The sky is light blue.

Les nuages sont blancs.
Lay nů-ahzh sohṇ blahṇ.
The clouds are white.

Trois jeunes filles se reposent sur la plage.
Trwa zhuhn fee' suh ruh-poz sůr la plazh'
Three girls are resting on the beach.

Elles ne veulent pas nager.
El nuh vuhl pa na-zhay.
They don't want to swim.

L'eau est trop froide.
Lo ay tro frwahd.
The water is too cold.

Mais le soleil est très chaud.
May luh so-lay' ay tray sho.
But the sun is very hot.

Elles préfèrent prendre un bain de soleil sur le sable.
El pray-fair prahṇdr' uṇ beṇ duh so-lay' sůr luh sahbl'.
They prefer to take a sun bath on the sand.

127

L'une d'elles a un costume de bain rouge.
Lûne dell a un kos-tûme duh ben roozh.
One of them has a red bathing suit.

The agreement of colors
Colors, being adjectives, agree in gender and number with the noun or pronoun. However, if they already end in -e, they do not change for the feminine singular. "The Red Sea" — *la Mer Rouge.*

La deuxième a un bikini vert.
La duhz-yem a un bee-kee-nee-vair.
The second has a green bikini.

La troisième porte un costume noir.
La trwahz-yaim pohrt un kohs-tûme nwar.
The third one wears a black suit.

Devant les jeunes filles
Duh-vahn lay zhuhn fee'
In front of the girls

quelques garçons sont en train
kel-kuh gar-sohn sohn tahn tren
some boys are

de jouer de la guitare et de chanter.
duh zhoo-ay duh la ghee-tar ay duh shahn-tay.
playing a guitar and singing.

Les jeunes filles aiment entendre la musique.
Lay zhuhn fee aim ahn-tahndr' la mû-zeek.
The girls like to hear the music.

Ça leur plaît beaucoup.
Sa lerr play bo-koo.
It pleases them very much.

I like — it pleases me
Plaire — *"to please"* — is used with the indirect object. Instead of saying "I like," in French we say "it pleases me."
I like that. — *Cela me plaît.*
He (or she) likes it. — *Cela lui plaît.*

When the objects you like are in the plural, they take the plural form of the verb.
I like those. — *Ceux-là me plaisent.*

The expression for "please" — *s'il vous plaît* literally means "if it pleases you."

La bonde dit à la brune:
La blohnd dee ta la brûne:
The blonde girl says to the dark-haired girl:

"Comme ils chantent bien, n'est-ce pas?"
"Kom eel shahnt' b'yen, ness-pa?"
"How well they sing, don't they?"

"C'est vrai," lui répond son amie.
"Say vray," lwee ray-pohn sohn na-mee.
"It's true," her friend replies to her.

"Ils chantent tous bien
"Eel shahnt toos b'yen
"They all sing well

mais c'est celui de droite qui chante le mieux."
may say suh-lwee duh drwaht kee shahnt luh m'yuh."
but it's the one on the right who sings the best."

Comparison of adverbs
Adverbs are compared like this: "slowly," "more slowly," "the most slowly" — *lentement, plus lentement, le plus lentement,* with the exceptions "well," "better," "best" — *bien, mieux, le mieux,* and "badly," "worse," "the worst" — *mal, pis, le pis.*

"Vous vous trompez," dit la blonde,
"Voo voo trohn-pay," dee la blohnd,
"You are mistaken," says the blonde,

"Celui qui est à gauche chante mieux que lui."
"Suh-lwee kee ay tah gohsh shahnt m'yuh kuh lwee."
"The one who is on the left sings better than he."

Quand les garçons s'arrêtent de chanter, l'un d'eux dit aux autres:
Kahn lay gahr-sohn sa-rett duh shahn-tay, lun duh dee toh zohtr':
When the boys stop singing, one of them says to the others:

> **A reminder — "de" + infinitive**
> *De* is used after various verbs before the infinitive. Stop doing that! — *Cessez de faire ça!*

"Elles sont jolies, hein, ces petites?
"El sohn zho-lee, en, say puh-teet?
"They are pretty, aren't they, those girls? (lit. "little ones")

> **What did you say?**
> *Hein?* is a word asking for assent like *n'est-ce pas?*, but considerably more colloquial.

"Moi, je trouve que la brune est la plus jolie."
"Mwa, zhuh troov kuh la brūne ay la plū zho-lee."
"I think that the brunette is the prettiest."

"Pas moi" dit un autre,
"Pa mwa," dee tun nohtr',
"Not me," says another,

"à mon avis, la blonde est plus jolie qu'elle."
"ah mohn na-vee, la blohnd ay plū zho-lee kell."
"in my opinion, the blond is prettier than she."

"Je ne suis pas d'accord," dit le troisième. "C'est la rousse
"Zhuh nuh swee pa da-kohr," dee luh trwa-s'yem. "Say la rooss
"I do not agree," says the third. "It is the red-haired one

> **D'accord!**
> *D'accord*, literally meaning "in accord," is another way of saying "all right, agreed."
>
> *Êtes-vous d'accord?* — Do you agree?
> *Oui, d'accord.* — Yes, agreed.

qui est la plus belle de toutes."
kee ay la plū bell duh toot."
who is the most beautiful of all."

Comparism of adjectives
Adjectives are compared by prefixing *plus* for
the comparative, and *le plus* or *la plus* (sing.) or
les plus (pl.) for the superlative.

> big, bigger, biggest — *grand, plus grand, le
> plus grand*
> small, smaller, smallest — *petit, plus petit, le
> plus petit*

and the irregulars

> good, better, best — *bon, meilleur, le
> meilleur*
> bad, worse, worst — *mauvais, pire, le pire*

INSTANT CONVERSATION: SHOPPING

UNE DAME:
Un dahm:
A LADY:

> Il faut acheter des cadeaux pour la famille et pour les amis.
> **Eel fo tash-tay day ka-doh poor la fa-mee' ay poor lay za-mee.**
> We must buy some presents for the family and friends.

> Voilà un petit magasin, entrons.
> **Vwa-la en puh-tee ma-ga-zen, ahn-trohn.**
> Here's a little shop, let us go in.

LA VENDEUSE:
La Vahn-derrz:
THE SALESGIRL:

> Vous désirez, madame?
> **Voo day-zee-ray, ma-dahm?**
> You wish (something), madam?

LA DAME:

> S'il vous plaît, montrez-nous quelques foulards.
> **Seel voo play, mohn-tray-noo kel-kuh foo-lahr.**
> Please, show us some scarves.

LA VENDEUSE:

> En voilà deux, madame,
> **Ahn vwa-la duh, ma-dahm,**
> Here are two, madam,

> en noir et blanc et en vert et bleu.
> **ahn nwahr ay blahn ay ahn vair ay bluh.**
> in black and white and in green and blue.

> Est-ce qu'ils vous plaisent?
> **Ess keel voo playz?**
> Do you like them?

132

LA DAME:
Celui-ci me plaît.
Suh-lwee-see muh play.
I like this one.

Les couleurs me plaisent
Lay koo luhr muh playz
I like the colors

et le dessin est plus joli. C'est combien?
ay luh day-sen ay plů zho-lee. Say kohnb-yen?
and the design is prettier. How much is it?

LA VENDEUSE:
Cent cinquante-cinq francs.
Sahn sen-kahnt-sen frahn.
A hundred and fifty-five francs.

LA DAME:
Tiens. C'est un peu cher.
T'yen. Say tun puh shair.
Well. That's a little expensive.

Avez-vous quelque chose de meilleur marché?
Ah-vay-voo kel-kuh shohz duh may-yuhr mar-shay?
Have you something cheaper?

> **Something cheaper, please.**
> *Meilleur marché*, a colloquial expression for
> "cheaper," literally means a "better market."
> "Cheap" is *bon marché*.

LA VENDEUSE:
Oui. Mais pas en soie naturelle.
Wee. May pa zen swa na-tů-rell.
Yes. But not in natural silk.

Nous en avons
Noo zahn na-vohn
We have some

en jaune, en rose, en orange, en marron, en violet . . .
ahn zhon, ahn rohz, ahn no-rahnzh, ahn ma-rohn, ahn vee-oh-lay . . .
in yellow, pink, orange, brown, purple . . .

133

C'est un peu moins cher — trente francs.
Say tun puh mwen shair — trahnt frahn.
It's a little less expensive — thirty francs.

LA DAME:

Ils ne sont pas aussi jolis que les autres.
Eel nuh sohn pa zo-see zhoh-lee kuh lay zotr'.
They are not as pretty as the others.

> **"as" and "not so"**
> The comparative with "as" and "not so . . . " is
> as follows:
>
>> as big as he — *aussi grand que lui*
>> not so intelligent as she — *pas aussi intelli-*
>> *gent qu'elle*

Quand même, achetons celui-ci, le violet
Kahn maim, ahsh-tohn suh-lwee-see, luh vee-oh-lay
Anyway, let's buy this one, the purple one

pour tante Isabelle.
poor tahnt Ee-za-bell.
for aunt Isabelle.

LE MARI:
Luh ma-ree:
THE HUSBAND:

D'accord. Et maintenant,
Da-kohr. Ay ment'-nahn,
O.K. And now,

Qu'est-ce que nous allons acheter pour maman?
Kess kuh noo za-lohn zash-tay poor ma-mahn?
what are we going to buy for mother?

LA VENDEUSE:

Regardez ce beau collier, monsieur.
Ruh-gar-day suh bo kohl-yay, muss-yuh.
Look at this beautiful necklace, sir.

Il ne coûte que cent trente francs.
Eel nuh koot kuh sahn trahnt frahn.
It costs only a hundred and thirty francs.

Only = ne . . . que
"Only" is *ne . . . que,* with the verb placed between the *ne* and the *que.*
It's only I — *Ce n'est que moi.*

Il est charmant, n'est-ce pas?
Eel ay shahr-mahn, ness-pa?
It's charming, isn't it?

LA DAME:
Oui, vraiment ravissant.
Wee, vray-mahn ra-vee-sahn.
Yes, really delightful.

Pour quoi ne pas l'acheter, mon chéri?
Poor-kwa nuh pa lahsh-tay, mohn shay-ree?
Why not buy it, dear?

LE MARI:
C'est vrai. Pourquoi pas? Je le prends.
Say vray. Poor-kwa pa? Zhuh luh prahn.
That's true. Why not? I'll take it.

Et maintenant je voudrais acheter
Ay men-tuh-nahn zhuh voo-dray zahsh-tay
And now I would like to buy

du parfum pour ma secrétaire.
dü par-fen poor ma suh-kray-tair.
some perfume for my secretary.

LA VENDEUSE:
Cette grande bouteille-là — "Beau Rêve"
Sett grahnd boo-tay'-la — "Bo Rev"
That large bottle there — "Beau Rêve" (Beautiful Dream)

LE MARI:
Oui, c'est cela. — Voulez-vous me la montrer?
Wee, say suh-la. — Voolay-voo muh la mohn-tray?
Yes, that's it. — Will you show it to me?

LA VENDEUSE:

Avec plaisir, monsieur.
Ah-vek play-zeer, muss-yuh.
With pleasure, sir.

LA DAME:

Vraiment, Alfred!
Vray-mahn, Al-frayd!
Really, Alfred!

Nous ne pouvons pas dépenser tant d'argent en cadeaux.
Noo nuh poo-vohn pa day-pahn-say tahn dahr-zhan ahn ka-doh.
We cannot spend so much money on presents.

Pourquoi ne pas acheter ce petit flacon?
Pour-kwa nuh pa zash-tay suh puh-tee flah-kohn?
Why not buy this little bottle?

On peut le mettre dans son sac à main.
Ohn puh luh mettr' dahn sohn sack ah men.
One can put it in one's handbag.

C'est très pratique.
Say tray pra-teek.
It's very practical.

LE MARI:

Bon. Alors — je prends le petit flacon.
Bohn. Ah-lohr — zhuh prahn luh puh-tee fla-kohn.
All right. Then — I'll take the little bottle.

LA VENDEUSE:

Voulez-vous essayer "Beau Rêve," Madame?
Voo-lay-voo zay-say-yay "Bo Rev," Ma-dahm?
Do you wish to try "Beau Rêve," Madam?

Ça sent bon, n'est-ce pas?
Sa sahn bohn, ness-pa?
It smells good, doesn't it?

LA DAME:

Oh oui, c'est exquis! Est-ce que c'est cher?
Oh wee, say tex-skee! Ess-kuh say shair?
Oh yes, it's exquisite! Is it expensive?

LA VENDUSE:

C'est notre meilleur parfum.
Say notr' may-yuhr par-fun.
It's our best perfume.

Il coûte cent quatre-vingt quinze francs.
Eel koot sahn katruh-ven kenz frahn.
It costs a hundred ninety-five francs.

LE MARI:

Ca ne fait rien. Je le prends pour ma femme.
Sa nuh fay r'yen. Zhur luh prohn poor ma fahm.
It doesn't matter. I'll take it for my wife.

LA DAME:

Ça, c'est chic! Merci, mon chou.
Sa, say sheek! Mair-see, mohn shoo.
How nice! Thank you, my dear (lit. "cabbage").

Endearments and insults
Words of endearment (or insult) can vary sur-
prisingly from language to language. *Mon
chou* — ("my cabbage") or *mon petit chou* is a
general term of endearment, as is *mon chéri*
and *ma chère* — ("my dear one"), to a man or
woman respectively, *mon amour* — ("my
love"), *mon trésor* — "my treasure," and *mon
âme* — "my soul." On the obverse side, some
words that are not especially insulting in English
constitute super insults in French — *vache* —
"cow," *chameau* — "camel," and *cochon* —
"pig."

137

TEST YOUR FRENCH

Fill in the verb forms. Score 10 points for each correct answer. See answers below.

1. I like that.
   Cela me ———————.

2. She likes those.
   Ceux-là lui ———————.

3. Let us go in.
   ———————.

4. Let's buy this one.
   ——————— celui-ci.

5. It costs eighty francs.
   Il ——————— quatre-vingts francs.

6. They sing very well.
   Ils ——————— très bien.

7. Show us some scarves.
   ——————— quelques foulards.

8. They are wearing sunglasses.
   Elles ——————— des lunettes de soleil.

9. She has a green bikini.
   Elle ——————— un bikini vert.

10. You are mistaken.
    Vous vous ———————.

Answers: 1. plaît 2. plaisent 3. Entrons 4. Achetons 5. coûte 6. chantent 7. Montrez-nous 8. portent 9. a 10. trompez.

SCORE _____%

step 14 MARKETING AND NAMES OF FOODS

Madame Delatour va au marché.
Ma-dahm Duh-la-toor va oh mar-shay.
Mrs. Delatour is going to the market.

Elle va acheter de la viande,
El va ash-tay duh la v'yahnd,
She is going to buy meat,

de la charcuterie, des légumes et des fruits,
duh la shar-ků-tree, day lay-gůme zay day frwee,
cold cuts, vegetables and fruit,

du poisson et du pain.
dů pwa-sohn ay dů pehn.
fish and bread.

> **The partitive for lists**
> Remember that, in naming lists of food or other
> things, you must always use the partitive, that is
> *de* with the article, whether "some" would be
> said in English or not.

Elle va d'abord chez le boucher.
El vah da-bohr shay luh boo-shay.
She goes first to the butcher.

Elle demande au boucher:
El duh-mahnd oh boo-shay:
She asks the butcher:

"Avez-vous du filet de boeuf bien tendre?"
"Ah-vay-voo dů fee-lay duh buhf b'yen tahndr'?"
"Have you some very tender beef fillet?"

Le boucher lui répond: "Oui madame.
Luh boo-sha lwee ray-pohn: "Wee ma-dahm.
The butcher replies: "Yes madam.

Je vous prépare un rôti de deux kilos environ."
Zhuh voo pray-pahr un ro-tee duh duh kee-lo ahn-vee-rohn."
I'll fix for you a roast of about two kilos."

Elle achète aussi des escalopes de veau et des biftecks.
El ah-shett oh-see day zais-ka-lohp duh vo ay day beef-tek.
She also buys veal cutlets and some steaks.

Chez le charcutier, elle achète du jambon,
Shay luh shar-kŭt-yay, el ah-shett dŭ zhahn-bohn,
At the pork butcher's she buys some ham,

des côtelettes de porc, et de la tête de veau.
day koht-lett duh pohr, ay duh la tet duh vo.
some pork chops, and some calf's head.

La cuisine française

Some French specialties, although a little strange to American tastes, are nevertheless delicious. *Tête de veau,* for example, is a selection of the brains, tongue and cheeks of the veal. Other particularly French specialties include: *des cuisses de grenouilles* — "frogs' legs (thighs)"; *des escargots* — "snails"; *des tripes* — "tripe"; and *des ris de veau* — "calves' sweetbreads."

Puis elle va chez le marchand de légumes
Pwee zel va shay luh mar-shahn duh lay-gŭme
Then she goes to the vegetable stand

pour acheter des pommes de terre, des haricots verts,
poor ash-tay day pohm duh tair, day ah-ree-ko vair,
to buy some potatoes, some green beans,

une laitue et un kilo de tomates.
ŭn lay-tŭ ay un kee-lo duh toh-maht.
a lettuce and one kilo of tomatoes.

"C'est combien le kilo de prunes aujourd'hui?"
"Say kohn-b'yen luh kee-lo duh prûne oh-zhoor-dwee?"
"How much for the kilo of plums today?"

demande-t-elle au marchand.
duh-mahn-duh-tel oh mar-shahn.
she asks the shopkeeper.

Elle achète aussi des poires, des bananes et des pêches.
El ah-shett oh-see day pwar, day ba-nahn ay day pesh.
She also buys pears, bananas and peaches.

Chez l'épicier, elle achète du riz,
Shay lay-peess-yay, el ah-shett dû ree,
At the grocer's she buys rice,

des nouilles, du café et du sucre.
day nwee', dû ka-fay ay dû sûkr'.
some noodles, coffee and sugar.

Chez la crémière, ell achète du lait,
Shay la kraim-yair, el ah-shett dû lay,
At the dairy store she buys some milk,

du beurre, de la crème et une douzaine d'oeufs.
dû berr, duh la kraim ay ûn doo-zayn' duh.
some butter, some cream and one dozen eggs.

Puis elle passe chez le marchand de poisson
Pwee zel pahs shay luh mar-shahn duh pwa-sohn
Then she goes to the fish seller's

pour acheter des truites,
poor ash-tay day trweet,
to buy trout,

des huîtres et un homard.
day zweetr' ay un oh-mahr.
some oysters and a lobster.

"C'est bien frais tout cela?"
"Say b'yen fray too suh-la?"
"Is all this quite fresh?"

demande-t-elle au marchand.
duh-mahn-duh-tel oh mar-shahn.
she asks the shopkeeper.

Enfin, chez le boulanger, elle demande:
Ahn-fen, shay luh boo-lahn-zhay, el duh-mahnd:
Finally, at the bakery she asks for:

> ### Les marchands du quartier (Neighborhood shopkeepers)
> *Chez* in the sense of *chez le boucher* — "at
> (to) the butcher's," *chez le boulanger* — "at
> (to) the baker's," so forth, is generally used
> in conversation. signs outside the shops
> generally end in *-ie*, and they are all feminine:
>
> | | |
> |---|---|
> | *boucherie* | butcher's shop |
> | *pâtisserie* | pastry shop |
> | *boulangerie* | bakery |
> | *pharmacie* | pharmacy, or drugstore |
> | *charcuterie* | sausage (cold cuts) shop |
> | *laiterie* | dairy store |
> | *teinturerie* | dry cleaner's |
> | *bijouterie* | jeweler's |
> | *papeterie* | stationery store |

"Une baguette bien fraîche, s'il vous plaît, Monsieur Dupin."
"Un bah-gett b'yen fraish, seel-voo-play, Muss-yuh Dů-pen."
"A very fresh loaf, please, Mr. Dupin."

Le boulanger répond:
Luh boo-lahn-zhay ray-pohn:
The baker answers:

"Nos baguettes sortent du four,
"Noh ba-ghett sohrt' dů foor,
"Our bread is just out of the oven,

elles sont encore toutes chaudes."
el sohn tahn-kohr toot shohd."
it is still quite warm."

La dame rentre chez elle
La dahm rahntr' shay zel
The lady returns home

avec la voiture chargée de provisions.
ah shar-zhay duh pru-vees yohn.
with her car loaded with foodstuffs.

Elle en a assez pour toute la semaine.
El en ah ah-say poor toot la suh-main.
She has enough (of them) for a whole week.

143

INSTANT CONVERSATION:
IN A RESTAURANT

UN CLIENT:
Uhn klee-yahn:
A CUSTOMER:

    Est-ce que cette table est libre?
    Ess-kuh sett tahbl' ay leebr'?
    Is this table free?

UNE SERVEUSE:
Üne sair-verrz:
A WAITRESS:

    Mais oui, monsieur. Asseyez-vous, s'il vous plaît.
    May wee, muss-yuh. Ah-say-yay-voo, seel voo play.
    Yes indeed, sir. Please sit down.

    Voici la carte.
    Vwa-see la kart.
    Here is the menu.

LE CLIENT:

    Merci. Pour commencer je voudrais
    Mair-see. Poor ko-mahn-say zhuh voo-dray
    Thank you. To begin I would like

    des hors-d'oeuvre variés.
    day ohr-duhvr' var-yay.
    some assorted appetizers.

LA SERVEUSE:
    Pas de potage?
    Pa duh po-tahzh?
    No soup?

Nous avons une excellente soupe à l'oignon.
Noo za-vohn ûne ex-say-lahnt soop ah l'ohn-yohn.
We have an excellent onion soup.

LE CLIENT:

Merci, pas de potage.
Mair-see, pa duh po-tahzh.
Thank you, no soup.

Quel est votre plat du jour?
Kel ay votr' pla dû zhoor?
What is your "today's special?"

LA SERVEUSE:

Aujourd'hui nous recommandons la sole meunière,
Oh-zhoor-dwee noo ruh-ko-mahn-dohn la sohl muhn-yair,
Today we recommend the sole meunière,

le coq au vin,
luh kohk oh ven,
the chicken with wine,

le gigot d'agneau aux flageolets,
luh zhee-go dan'yoh oh fla-zho-lay,
the leg of lamb with white beans,

ou le boeuf à la mode.
oo luh buhf ah la mohd.
or the beef à la mode.

LE CLIENT:

Qu'est-ce que c'est que le boeuf à la mode?
Kess kuh say kuh luh buhf ah la mohd?
What is beef à la mode?

À la mode

You will often see in menus *à la mode de*, which means "in the style of," such as *à la mode de Caen* — "in the style of Caen." Frequently, the *mode* is left out, and the expression becomes:

à la provençale — in the style of Provence
à l'alsacienne — in the Alsatian fashion
à l'américaine — in the American fashion

145

à l'anglaise   — English style
à la russe   — Russian style
or even names of famous people.

As France has such a tremendous tradition of *la haute cuisine*, it is not unusual even for French people to ask an explanation from the *maître d'hôtel*, such as: "what is it?" — *qu'est-ce que c'est que ça?*
or "how is it prepared?" — *comment est-ce préparé?*

LA SERVEUSE:

C'est du boeuf braisé
Say dŭ buhf bray-zay
It's braised beef

avec des champignons
ah-vek day shahn-peen-yohn
with mushrooms

et des légumes frais.
ay day lay-gŭme fray.
and fresh vegetables.

LE CLIENT:

Je crois que je préfère
Zhuh krwa kuh zhuh pray-fair
I think that I prefer

une entrecôte bordelaise
ŭn ahn tr'-koht bohr-duh-layz'
a steak bordelaise

avec des pommes de terre frites.
ah-vek day pohm duh tair freet.
with fried potatoes.

Potatoes or apples
Both words are expressed by *pommes*, although potatoes are really called *pommes de terre* —"apples of the earth." Of the many names for cooked potatoes note:
purée de pommes — mashed potatoes

pommes en robe de chambre — baked
potatoes

LA SERVEUSE:

Très bien, monsieur.
Tray b'yen, muss-yuh.
Very well, sir.

Comment désirez-vous l'entrecôte,
Koh-mahn day-zee-ray-voo lahn-tr'-koht,
How do you wish the steak,

bien cuite, à point ou saignante?
b'yen kweet', ah pwen oo sain-yahnt'?
well done, medium or rare?

LE CLIENT:

Plutôt saignante, s'il vous plaît.
Plŭ-toh sain-yahnt', seel voo play.
Rather rare, please.

LA SERVEUSE:

Désirez-vous des légumes ou une salade?
Day-zee-ray-voo day lay-gŭme oo ŭne sa-lahd?
Do you wish vegetables or a salad?

LE CLIENT:

Quels légumes avez-vous?
Kel lay-gŭme ah-vay-voo?
What vegetables have you?

LA SERVEUSE:

Des carottes, des petits pois, du chou-fleur,
Day ka-roht, day puh-tee pwa, dŭ shoo-fluhr,
Carrots, peas, cauliflower,

des asperges, des haricots verts.
day zahs-pairzh, day zah-ree-koh vair.
asparagus, green beans.

LE CLIENT:

Apportez-moi une salade verte
Ah-pohr-tay-mwa ŭne sa-lahd vairt
Bring me a green salad

147

avec de l'huile, du vinaigre et de la moutarde,
ah-vek duh lweel, dǔ vee-naigr' ay duh la moo-tard,
with oil, vinegar and mustard,

mais sans sel.
may sahn̹ sel.
but without salt.

LA SERVEUSE:

Et comme vin?
Ay kohm ven̹?
And as for wine?

LE CLIENT:

Du vin rouge — du Beaujolais.
Dǔ ven̹ roozh — dǔ Boh-zho-lay.
Some red wine — a Beaujolais.

LA SERVEUSE:

Parfaitement, monsieur. Tout de suite.
Par-fet-mahn̹, muss-yuh. Tood sweet.
Perfect, sir. Right away.

LA SERVEUSE:

Voulez-vous un dessert ou du fromage?
Voo-lay-voo un̹ day-sair oo dǔ fro-mazh?
Would you like a dessert or some cheese?

LE CLIENT:

Qu'est-ce que vous avez comme dessert?
Kess-kuh voo za-vay kohm day-sair?
What do you have for dessert?

LA SERVEUSE:

Crème au caramel,
Kraim oh ka-ra-mell,
Caramel custard,

des glaces à la vanille, au chocolat ou à la framboise,
day glahs ah la va-nee, oh sho-ko-la oo ah la frahn̹-bwaz',
vanilla ice cream, chocolate or strawberry,

LA SERVEUSE:

des fruits frais, de la pâtisserie;
day frwee fray, duh la pa-tees-ree;
fresh fruit, pastry;

nous avons aussi une salade de fruits au kirsch.
noo za-vohn zo-see ůn sa-lahd duh frwee oh Keersh.
we also have a fruit salad with Kirsch.

LE CLIENT:

C'est ça, j'ai envie d'une salade de fruits.
Say sa, zhay ahn-vee důn sa-lahd duh frwee.
That's it, I feel like having a fruit salad.

Mais avant, je voudrais du fromage . . .
May za-vahn, zhuh voo-dray dů fro-mahzh . . .
But before, I would like some cheese . . .

du camembert ou du roquefort.
dů Ka-mahn-bair oo dů rock-fohr.
Camembert or Roquefort.

LA SERVEUSE:

Je vous apporte le plateau de fromages.
Zhuh voo za-pohrt luh pla-toh duh fro-mahzh.
I'll bring you the cheese tray.

LE CLIENT:

Mademoiselle, un café filtre
Mad-mwa-zell, un ka-fay feeltr'
Miss, an espresso coffee

et l'addition, s'il vous plaît.
ay la-dees-yohn, seel voo play.
and the check, please.

Est-ce que le service est compris?
Ess-kuh luh sair-vees ay kohn-pree?
Is the service included?

LA SERVEUSE:

Oui monsieur.

Wee muss-yuh.

Yes sir.

Êtes-vous satisfait de votre déjeuner?

Ett-voo sa-tees-fay duh votr' day-zhuh-nay?

Are you satisfied with your lunch?

LE CLIENT:

Ah oui, un très bon déjeuner. Tenez.

Ah wee, un tray bohn day-zhuh-nay. Tuh-nay.

Oh yes, a very good lunch. Here.

LA SERVEUSE:

Je vous rapporte la monnaie dans un instant.

Zuh voo ra-pohrt la mohn-nay dahn zun nens-tahn.

I'll bring you back your change in an instant.

LE CLIENT:

Ce n'est pas la peine. C'est pour vous.

Suh nay pa la pain. Say poor voo.

Don't bother. It's for you.

LA SERVEUSE:

Merci, monsieur. Au plaisir de vous revoir.

Mair-see muss-yuh. Oh play-zeer duh voo ruh-vwahr.

Thank you sir. To the pleasure of seeing you again.

TEST YOUR FRENCH

Match these foods. Score 10 points for each correct answer. See answers below

1. des hors d'oeuvre variés	leg of lamb with white beans
2. soupe à l'oignon	frogs' legs
3. le coq au vin	calves' sweet breads
4. le gigot d'agneau aux flageolets	pastry
5. des cuisses de grenouilles	caramel custard
6. des escargots	chicken with wine
7. des ris de veau	cheese
8. crème au caramel	onion soup
9. du fromage	assorted appetizers
10. de la pâtisserie	snails

Answers: 4 5 7 10 8 3 9 2 1 6

SCORE _____%

step 15

HOW AND WHEN TO USE THE FAMILIAR FORM

Voici quelques exemples de l'emploi de tu:
Vwa-see kel-kuh-zek-zahn-pl' duh lahn-plwa duh tů:
Here are some examples of the use of *tu* (the familiar form):

The familiar word for "you"
Tu is another word for "you" and referred to generally as the familiar form. The present tense of the verb which goes with *tu* is the same as the form used for *je*, except for the first conjugation, where an *-s* is added, and "you are" and "you have," which are *tu es* and *tu as*. The object form of *tu* is *te*, and the possessive is *ton* for a masculine object, *ta* for a feminine one, and *tes* for the plural. When it stands alone it becomes *toi*. (Linguistically *tu* is equivalent to thou, little used in current English, but very alive in French.)

Tu s'emploie en famille:
Tů sahn-plwa ahn fa-mee':
Tu is used within the family:

UNE MÈRE:
Ůne mair:
A MOTHER:

Écoute-moi! Finis ton pain!
Ay-koot'-mwa! Fee-nee tohn pen!
Listen to me! Finish your bread!

SA FILLE:
Sa fee':
HER DAUGHTER:

Mais je n'ai pas faim, maman.
May zhuh nay pa fen, ma-mahn.
But I'm not hungry, mother.

LA MÈRE:

Alors, bois ton lait. Dépêche-toi!

Ah-lohr, bwa tohn lay. Day-pesh-twa!

Then, drink your milk. Hurry up!

> **The imperative for "tu"**
> The imperative form of *tu* is the same as its regular present form, except for the first conjugation, when the final -s is dropped. For the reflexive imperative *te* becomes *toi*, as in *dépêche-toi* — "hurry up," but in the case of the negative imperative as in *ne te dépêche pas* — "don't hurry," it reverts to *te*.

LA FILLE:

Je n'ai pas soif, non plus.

Zhuh nay pa swahf, nohn plŭ.

I'm not thirsty either.

LA MÈRE:

Fais ce que je te dis! Et tout de suite!

Fay suh kuh zhuh tuh dee! Ay tood sweet!

Do what I tell you! And right away!

LA FILLE:

Mais maman, pourquoi faut-il manger tellement?

May ma-mahn, poor-kwa foht-eel mahn-zhay tell-mahn?

But mother, why must I eat so much?

Je ne veux pas grossir.

Zuh nuh vuh pa gro-seer.

I don't want to get fat.

Les jeunes gens se tutoient:

Lay zhuhn zhahn suh tŭ-twa:

Young people use *tu* to each other:

> **On familiar terms**
> The verb *tutoyer* means for two people to use the familiar form to each other; in other words, to be on quite familiar terms.

— Salut, Gérard, ça va?
Sa-lü, Zhay-rahr, sa va?
Hi, Gerard, how's it going?

— Ça va pas mal, François, et toi?
Sa va pa mal, Frahn-swa, ay twa?
Not badly, Frank, and you?

— Oh, sans histoires.
Oh, sahn zees-twahr.
Oh, without problems.

— Dis donc!
Dee dohnk!
Say!

Tu sais qu'il y a une surprise-partie
Tü say keel ee ya üne sürprees-pahr-tee
Do you know that there's a surprise party

chez Robert ce soir?
shay Roh-bair suh swahr?
at Robert's this evening?

Tu y vas?
Tü ee va?
Are you going there?

— Non, je ne suis pas invité.
Nohn, zhuh nuh swee pa zen-vee-tay.
No, I'm not invited.

— Ça n'a pas d'importance,
Sa na pa den-pohr-tahns,
That's not important,

je t'invite.
zhuh ten-veet.
I invite you.

Viens-y avec moi.
V'yen-zee ah-vek mwa.
Come there with me.

Mais . . . apporte une bouteille!
May . . . ah-pohrt ûne boo-tay'!
But . . . bring a bottle!

Les amoureux se tutoient:
Lay za-moo-ruh suh tû-twa:
People in love use tu with each other:

ELLE:
El:
SHE:

Est-ce que tu m'aimes vraiment?
Ess-kuh tû maim' vray-mahn?
Do you really love me?

LUI:
Lwee:
HE:

Bien sûr. Je t'aime vraiment.
B'yen sûr. Zhuh taim vray-mahn.
Of course. I really love you.

ELLE:

Est-ce que tu vas m'aimer toujours?
Ess-kuh tû va may-may too-zhoor?
Are you going to love me always?

LUI:

Peut-être — qui sait?
Puh-tetr' — kee say?
Perhaps — who knows?

ELLE:

Pourquois dis-tu "peut-être"?
Poor-kwa dee-tû puh-tetr'?
Why do you say "perhaps"?

Tu es une brute.
Tu ay zûne brût'.
You are a brute.

Je te déteste!
Zhuh tuh day-test!
I hate you!

Tu s'emploie quand on parle aux enfants:
Tŭ sahn-plwa kahn tohn parl oh zahn-fahn:
Tu is used when one speaks to children:

UNE DAME:
Une dahm:
A LADY:

Bonjour, ma petite.
Bohn-zhoor, ma puh-teet.
Good morning, my little one.

Comment t'appelles-tu?
Koh-mahn ta-pell-tŭ?
What's your name?

UNE PETITE FILLE:
Une puh-teet fee':
A LITTLE GIRL:

Moi, je m'appelle Josette.
Mwa, zhuh ma-pell Zhoh-zett.
Me, I am called Josette.

> **Fille — jeune fille**
> The word *fille* means "girl" or "daughter." *Petite fille*, besides meaning "little girl" also means "granddaughter." *Jeune fille* is the regular word for "girl," as is *jeune personne*, literally "young person." Do not use *fille* by itself unless you mean "daughter," as it has a somewhat risqué connotation which might lead to a *faux-pas*.

LA DAME:
Et ce petit garçon . . . c'est ton frère?
Ay suh puh-tee gar-sohn . . . say tohn frair?
And that little boy . . . is he your brother?

156

LA PETITE FILLE:

Oui, c'est encore un bébé.

Wee, say tahṇ-kohr uṇ bay-bay.

Yes, he's still a baby.

Il peut marcher, mais il ne parle pas encore.

Eel puh mar-shay, may zeel nuh pahrl' pa zahṇ-kohr.

He can walk, but he doesn't speak yet.

LA DAME:

Mais toi, tu parles très bien.

May twa, tǔ pahrl tray b'yeṇ.

But you, you speak very well.

LA PETITE FILLE:

Oui, papa dit que je parle trop.

Wee, pa-pa dee kuh zuh parhl tro.

Yes, papa says that I speak too much.

LA DAME:

Tiens. Voilà un bonbon pour toi

T'yeṇ. Vwa-la uṇ bohṇ-bohṇ poor twa

Here. Here is a candy for you

et un autre pour ton petit frère.

ay uṇ nohtr' poor tohṇ p'tee frair.

and another for your little brother.

Tu s'emploie quand on parle aux animaux:

Tǔ **sahṇ-plwa kahṇ tohṇ pahrl' oh za-nee-moh:**

Tu is used when one speaks to animals:

Fifi, tais-toi!

Fee-fee, tay-twa!

Fifi, be quiet!

Descends de ce divan.

Day-sahṇ duh suh dee-vahṇ.

Get off that couch.

Laisse le chat tranquille.

Layss' luh sha trahṇ-keel.

Leave the cat alone.

Va-t'en! Tu es un vilain chien.
Va-tahn! Tŭ ay zun vee-len shyen.
Go away! You are a bad dog.

"Tu" with animals

As we have indicated the use of *tu* to animals, a student might ask whether animals would notice whether you were using the correct form — *tu* instead of *vous*. While the animals might not notice, you would get some odd looks from people nearby if you started to use the polite *vous* form with a dog, cat, horse, or even a child. This summarizes the whole concept of *tu*, which is that it is informal. Remember that *tu* does not necessarily mean that you like someone but just that you are on familiar and informal terms with them.

INSTANT CONVERSATION: AT A SIDEWALK CAFÉ

ELLE:

J'ai soif.
Zhay swahf.
I am thirsty.

LUI:

Est-ce que tu veux boire quelque chose dans ce café?
Ess-kuh tŭ vuh bwar kel-kuh shohz' dahn suh ka-fay?
Do you want to drink something at this café?

ELLE:

C'est une bonne idée. Entrons.
Say tŭne bonn ee-day. Ahn-trohn.
That's a good idea. Let's go in.

LUI:

Asseyons-nous là, à la terrasse.
Ah-say-yohn-noo la, ah la tay-rahss.
Let's sit down over there, on the terrace.

> **La terrasse**
> La terrasse refers to the open air part of a
> French restaurant — next to the sidewalk.

ELLE:

C'est ça!
Say sa!
That's it!

Tu veux voir passer les jolies filles.
Tŭ vuh vwar pa-say lay zho-lee fee'.
You want to see the pretty girls go by.

LUI:

Tu sais bien
Tŭ say b'yen
You know very well

que je ne regarde que toi. Garçon!
kuh zhuh nuh ruh-gahrd kuh twa. Gahr-sohn!
that I only look at you. Waiter!

LE GARÇON:
Le gahr-sohn:
THE WAITER:

Vous désirez, messieurs-dames?
Voo day-zeer-ay, mess-yuh-dahm?
(What) do you wish, ladies and gentlemen?

> **Messieurs — dames**
> The use of the plural by the waiter — *mes-sieurs-dames* — does not mean that the waiter cannot count, but is simply an easy formula used by waiters and others in addressing more than one person of different sexes.

LUI:

Qu'est-ce que tu prends, ma chérie?
Kees kuh tu prahn, ma shay-ree?
What are you going to take (have), my dear?

> **Compare the use of "tu"**
> This section shows how *tu* and *vous* are used in the same conversation, *vous* between the waiter and the married couple, and *tu* between the married couple when they speak to each other. As we now have presented the pronoun and verb forms for *tu*, all future verb forms and tenses introduced will show *tu* in its regular conjugational position, which is right after *je*.

ELLE:

Je ne sais pas.
Zhuh nuh say pa.
I don't know.

Peut-être une limonade.
Puh-tetr' ûne lee-mo-nahd.
Perhaps a lemonade.

LUI:

Et pour moi, un cognac à l'eau.
Ay poor mwa, uɲ kohn-yahk ah lo.
And for me, a cognac with water.

GARÇON:

Avec de l'eau minérale?
Ah-vek duh lo mee-nay-rahl?
With mineral water?

LUI:

Oui, et avec de la glace, s'il vous plaît.
Wee, ay ah-vek duh la glahss, seel voo play.
Yes, and with ice, please.

ELLE:

Attends, mon chéri. Commande-moi donc
Ah-tahɲ, mohɲ shay-ree. Koh-mahɲd-mwa dohɲk
Wait, my dear. Order for me then

un Dubonnet au lieu de la limonade.
uɲ Dû-boh-nay oh l'yuh duh la lee-moh-nahd.
a Dubonnet instead of the lemonade.

LUI:

Mais certainment.
May sair-tain-mahɲ.
But certainly.

Les femmes changent souvent d'avis,
Lay fahm shaɲzh soo-vahɲ da-vee,
Women often change their minds,

n'est-ce pas, ma chérie?
ness-pa ma shay-ree?
don't they, my darling?

Garçon! Pas de limonade pour Madame.
Gar-sohn̩! Pa duh lee-mo-nahd poor Ma-dahm.
Waiter! No lemonade for madam.

Elle désire un Dubonnet.
El day-zeer un̩ Dǔ-bo-nay.
She wants a Dubonnet.

ELLE:

Tu n'es pas fâché?
Tǔ nay pa fa-zhay?
You're not angry?

LUI:

Moi — fâché — pourquoi?
Mwa — fa-shay — poor-kwa?
Me — angry — why?

Tu sais bien que je fais toujours
Tǔ say b'yen̩ kuh zhuh fay too-zhoor
You know very well that I always do

tout ce que tu veux.
toos-kuh tǔ vuh.
everything that you wish.

ELLE:

Vraiment, toujours?
Vray-mahn̩, too-zhoor?
Really, always?

C'est vrai, tu es bien gentil.
Say vray, tǔ ay b'yen̩ zhahn̩-tee.
It's true, you are very nice.

GARÇON:

Voilà vos consommations.
Vwa-la vo kohn̩-so-mas-yohn̩.
Here are your drinks.

162

LUI:

    A ta santé!

    Ah ta sahɲ-tay!

    To your health!

ELLE:

    A la tienne, mon amour.

    Ah la t'yenn, mohɲ na-moor.

    To yours, my love.

TEST YOUR FRENCH

Translate these sentences into French, using the *familiar* form. Score 10 points for each correct answer. See answers below.

1. What's your name?

   _____

2. But you, you speak very well.

   _____

3. Are you going there?

   _____

4. Hurry up!

   _____

5. Do what I tell you!

   _____

6. Do you really love me?

   _____

7. I really love you.

   _____

8. You're not angry?

   _____

9. You are very nice.

   _____

10. I hate you!

   _____

Answers: 1. Comment t'appelles-tu? 2. Mais toi, tu parles très bien. 3. Tu y vas? 4. Dépêche-toi! 5. Fais ce que je te dis! 6. Est-ce que tu m'aimes vraiment? 7. Je t'aime vraiment. 8. Tu n'es pas fâché? 9. Tu es bien gentil. 10. Je te déteste!

SCORE _____%

step 16

DAYS, MONTHS, DATES, SEASONS, THE WEATHER

Les sept jours de la semaine sont:
Lay set zhoor duh la suh-main sohn:
The seven days of the week are:

lundi, mardi, mercredi,
lun-dee, mar-dee, mair-kruh-dee,
Monday, Tuesday, Wednesday,

jeudi, vendredi, samedi et dimanche.
zhuh-dee, vahn-druh-dee, sahm-dee ay dee-mahnsh.
Thursday, Friday, Saturday and Sunday.

Les douze mois de l'année s'appellent:
Lay dooz mwa duh la-nay sa-pell:
The twelve months of the year are called:

janvier, février, mars, avril,
zhahnv-yay, fay-vree-yay, mars, ah-vreel,
January, February, March, April,

mai, juin, juillet, août,
may, zhwen, zhwee-yay, oot,
May, June, July, August,

septembre, octobre, novembre et décembre.
sep-tahnbr', ok-tohbr' no-vahnbr' ay day-sahnbr'.
September, October, November and December.

Janvier est le premier mois de l'année.
Zhanv-yay ay luh pruhm-yay mwa duh la-nay.
January is the first month of the year.

Le premier janvier est le Premier de l'An.
Luh pruhm-yay jahnv-yay ay luh pruhm-yay duh lahn.
The first of January is the first of the year (New Year's Day).

Writing dates
The first of the month is the only date given an ordinal number; the other dates are given cardinal numbers.

February first — *le premier février*
February second — le 2 février

On dit à ses amis: "Bonne Année!"
Ohn dee ta say za-mee: "Bunn Ah-nay!"
One says to one's friends: "Happy New Year!"

"On" is the third person
The impersonal word *on* has the same pronoun form for the possessive as *il* and *elle*.

Février est le deuxième mois,
Fay-vree-yay ay luh duhz-yem mwa,
February is the second month,

Mars, le troisième, avril, le quatrième . . .
Mars, luh trwaz-yem, ah-vreel, luh ka-tree-yem . . .
March, the third, April, the fourth . . .

et décembre, le douzième
ay day-sahnbr', luh dooz-yem
and December, the twelfth

et dernier mois de l'année.
ay dairn-yay mwa duh la-nay.
and last month of the year.

Le 25 décembre est le Jour de Noël.
Luh vent-senk day-sahnbr' ay luh zhoor duh No-el.
The 25th of December is Christmas Day.

On dit: "Joyeux Noël!"
Ohn dee: "Zhwa-yuh No-el!"
One says: "Merry Christmas!"

et on fait des cadeaux aux enfants.
ay ohn fay day ka-doh oh zahn-fahn.
and presents are given to the children.

166

La fête nationale française
La fett nah-s'yohn-nahl frahn-sez
The French national holiday

est le quatorze juillet.
ay luh ka-tohrz zhwee-yay.
is the Fourteenth of July.

C'est l'anniversaire
Say la-nee-vair-sair
it is the anniversary

de la prise de la Bastille,
duh la prees duh la Bahs-tee',
of the taking of the Bastille,

pendant la Révolution Française.
pahn-dahn la Ray-vo-lu-s'yohn Frahn-sez.
during the French Revolution.

Same words — same meanings
Like *révolution*, there are hundreds of other words ending in -tion that have the same meaning in French and English. But remember that the "pronunciation" (*prononciation* in French) is not quite same. Here are just a few:

émotion	attraction
action	satisfaction
motion	construction
anticipation	réaction
section	occupation
opération	nation
attention	libération

Il y a des défilés de l'armée sur les boulevards;
Eel ee ya day day-fee-lay duh lar-may sur lay bool-var;
There are army parades on the boulevards;

le Président fait un discours et dit: "Vive la France!"
luh Pray-zee-dahn fay tun dess-koor ay dee: "Veev la Frahns!"
the President makes a speech and says: "Long live France!"

Le soir, il y a des feux d'artifice,
Luh swar, eel ee ya day fuh dahr-tee-feess,
At night, there are fireworks,

et on danse dans les rues.
ay ohṇ dahṇs' dahṇ lay rü.
and dancing in the streets.

———————

L'année se divise en quatre saisons:
La-nay suh dee-veez ahṇ katr' say-zohṇ:
The year is divided into four seasons:

> **The reflexive as the passive**
> *Se divise*, literally "divides itself," is a passive construction meaning "is divided."

le printemps, l'été, l'automne et l'hiver.
luh preṇ-tahṇ, lay-tay, lo-tonn ay lee-vair.
spring, summer, autumn and winter.

En hiver, il fait froid, et en été, il fait chaud.
Ahṇ nee-vair, eel fay frwa, ay ahṇ nay-tay, eel fay sho.
In the winter, it is cold, and in the summer, it is hot.

Au printemps, il fait beau temps mais il pleut assez souvent.
Oh preṇ-tahṇ, eel fay bo tahṇ may zeel pluh ah-say soo-vahṇ.
In the spring, there is good weather but it rains rather often.

En automne, il fait du vent
Ahṇ no-tonn, eel fay dü vahṇ
In the autumn, there is wind

et les feuilles tombent des arbres.
ay lay foy' tohṇb day zarbr'.
and the leaves fall from the trees.

— Quel temps fait-il généralement en France?
Kel tahṇ fay-teel zhay-nay-ral-mahn ahṇ Frahṇs?
How is the weather generally in France?

Quel temps fait-il?
The third person form of *faire* is used to describe certain aspects of the weather and temperature . . .

> *il fait froid* — it is cold
> *il fait chaud* — it is hot
> *il fait mauvais temps* — it is bad weather
> *il fait beau* — it is nice weather

But remember, when a person is hot, cold, thirsty, etc. *avoir* is used instead of *faire*.

— Le temps est plus ou moins semblable
Luh tahṇ ay plǔ zoo mweṇ sahṇ-blabl'
The weather is more or less like

à celui des États-Unis.
ah suh-lwee day zay-ta-zǔ-nee.
that of the United States.

Mais il n' y fait ni si froid, ni si chaud.
May zeel nee fay nee see frwa, nee see sho.
But there it is neither so hot nor so cold.

> **Ni . . . ni = neither . . . nor**
> The expression *ni . . . ni* means "neither . . . nor," *ou . . . ou* means "either . . . or."

— Est-ce qu'il neige beaucoup à Paris?
Ess keel nehzh bo-koo ah Pa-ree?
Does it snow much in Paris?

— Non, pas beaucoup. Il y neige quelquefois,
Nohṇ, pa bo-koo. Eel ee nehzh kel-kuh-fwa,
No, not much. There it snows sometimes,

— mais à Cannes, il ne neige presque jamais.
may za Kahnn, eel nuh nezh pres-kuh zha-may.
but in Cannes, it almost never snows.

> **The double negative is correct (in French)**
> Note the double negative. *Jamais* means
> "never" when used alone and when used in a
> sentence, it must be preceded by *ne*, which is
> correct in French but translates as "not never"
> in English.

Dans les autres pays de langue française,
Dahn laz zohtr' pay-ee duh lahng frahn-sez
In the other French speaking countries,

le climat est moins modéré:
luh klee-ma ay mwen mo-day-ray:
the climate is less moderate:

au Canada, il fait très froid en hiver
oh Ka-na-da, eel fay tray frwa ahn nee-vair
in Canada, it is very cold in the winter

> **"En" meaning "in" or "to"**
> Most countries are feminine and use the word
> *en* for "in" or "to:" *en France* — "in France,"
> *en Italie* — "in Italy," *en Chine* — "in China,"
> *en Amérique* — "in America." When the coun-
> try is masculine, then *à* is used with the definite
> article: *au Mexique* — "in Mexico," *au
> Japon* —"in Japan," and in the case of mascu-
> line plural, *aux États-Unis* — "in the United
> States." You will find the names of the principal
> countries in the dictionary section of this book.

et il y neige souvent.
ay eel ee nezh soo-vahn.
and it often snows there.

En Afrique Centrale il fait toujours chaud
Ahn na-freek sahn-trahl eel fay too-zhoor sho
In Central Africa it is always hot

et il y pleut beaucoup.
ay eel ee pluh bo-koo.
and it rains a lot there.

Dans les déserts, comme le Sahara,
Dahn lay day-zair, kohm luh Sa-ah-ra,
In the deserts, such as the Sahara,

il fait très chaud dans la journée,
eel fay tray sho dahn la zhoor-nay,
it is very hot in the day,

et souvent froid la nuit.
ay soo-vahn frwa la nwee.
and often cold at night.

À Tahiti, le climat est merveilleux,
Ah Ta-ee-tee, luh klee-ma ay mair-vay-yuh,
In Tahiti, the climate is marvellous,

il y fait toujours un temps très agréable.
eel ee fay too-zhoor un tahn tray za-gray-ahbl'.
the weather there is always very pleasant.

INSTANT CONVERSATION:
TALKING ABOUT THE WEATHER

Tout le monde parle du temps.
Tool' mohnd parl' dü tahn.
Everybody speaks about the weather.

Au printemps, quand le soleil brille,
Oh pren-tahn, kahn luh so-lay' bree',
In the spring, when the sun shines,

et quand souffle une brise agréable,
ay kahn soofl' üne breez ah-gray-ahbl',
and when a pleasant breeze is blowing,

> on dit: 'Comme il fait beau! Quelle belle journée!"
> **ohn dee: "Kohm eel fay bo! Kel bel zhoor-nay!"**
> one says: "How beautiful the weather is! What a beautiful day!"

Et quand la nuit est claire,
Ay kahn la nwee ay klair,
And when the night is clear,

quand on voit la lune et les étoiles,
kahn tohn vwa la lüne ay lay zay-twahl,
when one sees the moon and the stars shine,

> on dit: "Quelle nuit merveilleuse!"
> **ohn dee: "Kel nwee mair-vay-yuhz!"**
> one says: "What a marvelous night!"

En été, l'après-midi, en plein soleil:
Ahn nay-tay, la-pray-mee-dee, ahn plen so-lay':
In the summer, in the afternoon, with full sunshine:

> "Il fait terriblement chaud, n'est-ce pas?"
> **"Eel fay tay-reebl'-mahn sho, ness pa?"**
> "It is terribly hot, isn't it?"

172

Quand on entend dehors le vent et la pluie,
Kahn tohn nahn-tahn duh-ohr luh vahn ay la plwee,
When one hears outside the wind and the rain,

On dit: 'Quel mauvais temps! Il pleut à verse."
Ohn dee: "Kel mo-vay tahn! Eel pluh ta vairss."
One says: "What bad weather! It's pouring rain."

On demande souvent: "Est-ce qu'il pleut toujours?"
Ohn duh-mahnd' soo-vahn: "Ess keel pluh too-zhoor?"
One often asks: "Is it still raining?"

En automne, quand il commence à faire froid,
Ahn no-tonn, kahn teel ko-mahns ah fair frwa,
In the autumn, when the weather starts getting cold,

On dit: "Il fait assez froid aujourd'hui."
Ohn dee: "Eel fay ta-say frwa oh-zhoor-dwee."
One says: "It is rather cold to-day."

L'hiver, la radio annonce souvent:
Lee-vair, la rahd-yo ah-nohns soo-vahn:
In the winter, the radio often announces:

"Froid très vif et chute de neige.
"Frwa tray veef ay shûte duh nezh.
"Very cold and snowfall.

La glace et la neige rendent la circulation difficile.
La glahss ay la nehzh rahnd' la seer-kû-lass-yohn dee-fee-seel.
Ice and snow are making traffic difficult.

Il y a de la glace sur les lacs."
Eel ee ya duh la glass sûr lay lahk."
There is ice on the lakes."

Parfois, l'été, les titres des journaux indiquent:
Par-fwa, lay-taz, lay teetr' day zoor-no en-deek:
Sometimes, in the summer, the newspapers' headlines indicate:

"Violents orages sur toute la France.
"Vee-oh-lahn zo-rahzh sûr toot la Frahnss.
"Heavy storms over all of France.

173

Vents très forts. Pluies abondantes
Vahn tray fohr. Plwee za-bohn-dahnt
Very strong winds. Heavy rains

avec du tonnerre et des éclairs."
ah-vek dů toh-nair ay day zay-clair."
with thunder and lightning."

> An example of the staccato weather or news style of radio and TV announcements is given here for your consideration. Incidentally, you should try to listen to French radio stations frequently, as well as to go to French movies without reading the subtitles.

Après la pluie, il fait souvent du brouillard.
Ah-pray la plwee, eel fay soo-vahn dů broo-yahr.
After the rain, there is often fog.

On dit: "Quel brouillard! On n'y voit rien.
Ohn dee: "Kel broo-yahr! Ohn nee vwa r'yen.
One says: "What a fog! One does not see anything.

Impossible de conduire.
En-poh-seebl' duh kohn-dweer.
Driving is impossible.

C'est trop dangereux.
Say tro dahn-zhuh-ruh.
It is too dangerous.

Restons ici et regardons la télévision."
Res-tohn zee-see ay ruh-gar-dohn la tay-lay-veez-yohn."
Let us stay here and look at television."

> The first person plural of any verb can be used by itself without the *nous* as a way of saying "let's:" "let's talk" — *parlons!* If the verb is reflexive, *nous* comes after the verb:
> "let's sit down" — *asseyons-nous!*

TEST YOUR FRENCH

Translate these comments on the weather into English. Score 10 points for each correct answer. See answers below.

1. Comme il fait beau!

2. Quelle belle journée!

3. Quelle nuit merveilleuse!

4. Il fait terriblement chaud, n'est-ce pas?

5. Quel mauvais temps!

6. Il pleut à verse.

7. Est-ce qu'il pleut toujours?

8. Il fait assez froid aujourd'hui.

9. Il fait souvent froid la nuit.

10. Quel brouillard! On n'y voit rien!

SCORE _____%

HOW TO FORM THE FUTURE TENSE

Le temps futur est très facile.
Luh tohn̯ fŭ-tŭr ay tray fa-seel.
The future tense is very easy.

Pour former là première personne du futur avec "je,"
Poor for-may la pruhm-yair pair-sohn dŭ fŭ-tŭr ah-vek "zhuh,"
To form the first person of the future with "I,"

Prenez l'infinitif et ajoutez -ai.
Pruh-nay len̯-fee-nee-teef ay ah-zhoo-tay -ai.
Take the infinitive and add -ai.

You build on the infinitive
Most verbs form their future by adding the future ending for each person, of which you have already learned the one for je, to the infinitive of the first and second conjugations. In the case of the third conjugation, verbs like vendre drop the -e and add the future endings — je vendrai ("I will sell") while verbs ending in -oir, such as recevoir, drop the -oi- and the appropriate endings are added — je recevrai ("I will receive"). Some of the more common verbs have special forms for the future and these you should learn by heart. Here are the more important ones, given in the infinitive first, followed by the form for je in the future.

être (je serai), avoir (j'aurai)
aller (j'irai), faire (je ferai)
pouvoir (je pourrai), vouloir (je voudrai)
voir (je verrai), savoir (je saurai)
venir (je viendrai)

Demain je me lèverai de bonne heure.
Duh-men zhuh muh lay-vuh-ray duh bunn err.
Tomorrow I shall get up early.

J'irai chez le médecin.
Zhee-ray shay luh mayd-sen.
I shall go to the doctor.

Je lui demanderai quelque chose pour ma toux.
Zhuh lwee duh-mahn-duh-ray kel-kuh shohz poor ma too.
I'll ask him for something for my cough.

Et j'aurai l'occasion de lui parler de mon foie.
Ay zho-ray lo-kahz-yohn duh lwee pahr-lay duh mohn fwa.
And I'll have a chance to talk to him about my liver.

> **Les organes**
> Speaking of doctors, some of the more important internal organs include "the heart" — *le coeur,* "the lungs" — *les poumons,* "the stomach" — *l'estomac,* "the kidneys" — *les reins,* "the liver" — *le foie,* this last one being famous in conversation as in *crise de foie* — "crisis of the liver," thought sometimes to be caused by rich and delicious French food which one cannot help eating in excess.

Je vous téléphonerai de chez lui,
Zhuh voo tay-lay-fo-nuh-ray duh shay lwee,
I'll phone you from his office,

et je vous dirai à quelle heure je reviendrai.
ay zhuh voo dee-ray ah kel err zhuh ruhv-yen-dray.
and I'll tell you at what time I shall come back.

Pour la deuxième personne "vous," ajoutez *-ez.*
Poor la duhz-yom pair-sonn "voo," ah-zhoo-tay *-ez.*
For the second person "you," add *-ez.*

Oui, vous ferez bien d'y aller.
Wee, voo fuh-ray b'yen dee yahl-lay.
Yes, you'll do well to go there.

Et pendant que vous y serez,
Ay pahn-dahn kuh voo zee suh-ray,
And while you'll be there,

pourrez-vous prendre rendez-vous pour moi?
poo-ray-voo prahndr' rahn-day-voo poor mwa?
will you be able to make an appointment for me?

Chez le médecin
When visiting or being visited by a doctor, note the following constructions for indicating where you feel discomfort:

I have a headache — *J'ai mal à la tête*
I have a sore throat — *J'ai mal à la gorge*
I have a stomach ache — *J'ai mal à l'estomac*
I'm dizzy — *J'ai des vertiges*
It hurts here — *Ça me fait mal ici*

A "prescription" is *une ordonnance* and things the doctor will say to you will include:

You have a fever — *Vous avez de la fièvre*
You must stay in bed — *Il faut rester au lit*
Take this three times a day — *Prenez ceci trois fois par jour*
You will feel better — *Vous vous sentirez mieux*
Come back in two days — *Revenez dans deux jours*

Je crois que je pourrai y aller la semaine prochaine.
Zhuh krwa kuh zhuh poo-ray ce ya-lay la suh-main pro-shain.
I think that I'll be able to go there next week.

Je serai libre lundi ou mardi.
Zhuh suh-ray leebr' lun-dee oo mar-dee.
I'll be free Monday or Tuesday.

Et pour "il," "elle" et "on" ajoutez -*a.*
Ay poor eel, el et ohn ah-zhoo-tay -*a.*
And for "he," "she" and "one" add -a.

— Armand, quand reviendra-t-il?

Ahr-mahn, kahn ruhv-yen-dra-teel?

Armand, when will he come back?

> **Compounds follow the pattern**
> If a basic verb is irregular, as is the case of *venir* in the future, all its compounds, such as *revenir*, follow exactly the same pattern.

— Il sera de retour demain matin.

Eel suh-ra duh ruh-toor duh-men ma-ten.

He'll be back tomorrow morning.

— Aura-t-on l'occasion de le voir?

Oh-ra-tohn lo-kahz-yohn duh luh vwar?

Shall we have a chance to see him?

> **La liaison**
> Note the use of the -*t*- between *reviendra* and *il*, and between *aura* and *on*. The -*t*- is an example of liaison and separates the two vowels. One could also use *est-ce que* without inversion and this would be *est-ce qu'on aura l'occasion de le voir?*

— Non, il repartira le soir même pour Milan.

Nohn, eel ruh-par-tee-ra luh swar mem poor Mee-lahn.

No, he'll leave that same night for Milan.

Il y signera les contrats et visitera les usines.

Eel ee seen-yuh-ra lay kohn-tra ay vee-zee-tuh-ra lay zŭ-zeen.

There he'll sign the contracts and visit the plants.

— Croyez-vous qu'il y fera de bonnes affaires?

Krwa-yay-voo keel ee fuh-ra duh bunn za-fair?

Do you think that he'll do a good business there?

> **"De" before adjectives**
> In a partitive construction, and where there is already an adjective in front of the noun, *de* is used without the article, as in *de bonnes affaires*.

Pour la forme familière "tu" ajoutez -*as*
Poor la form fa-meel-yair "tǔ" ah-zhoo-tay -*as*
For the familiar form "tu" add -*as*

— Est-ce que tu me téléphoneras demain?
Ess kuh tǔ muh tay-lay-fohn-ra duh-men?
Will you call me tomorrow on the phone?

— Oui, mais à quelle heure est-ce que tu seras chez toi?
Wee, may zah kel err ess-kuh tǔ suh-ra shay twa?
Yes, but at what time will you be home?

Pour "nous" ajoutez la terminaison "-*ons*":
Poor "noo" ah-zhoo-tay la tair-mee-nay-zohn "-*ons*":
For "nous" add the ending "-*ons*":

Samedi prochain nous irons tous à la campagne.
Sam-dee pro-shen noo zee-rohn toos ah la kahn-pine.
Next Saturday we shall all go to the country.

Nous prendrons le train et nous descendrons à Nancy.
Noo prahn-drohn luh tren ay noo day-sahn-drohn ah Nahn-see.
We shall take the train and we shall get off at Nancy.

Puis nous irons en voiture jusqu'au château de mon oncle.
Pwee noo zee-rohn ahn vwa-tǔr zhǔss-ko sha-toh duh mohn nohnkl'.
Then we'll go by car to my uncle's country estate.

Un château en France
Château originally meant "castle" but now is used for any large country estate — especially if it has a large central house. The word for the medieval castle is *château-fort*.

Nous monterons à cheval et nous visiterons les environs.
Noo mohn-tuh-rohn za shuh-vahl ay noo vee-zee-tuh-rohn lay
                                        zahn-vee-rohn.
We'll ride horseback and we'll visit the surroundings.

Nous pourrons aller nager dans le lac.
Noo poo-rohn zah-lay na-zhay dahn luh lahk.
We shall be able to go swimming in the lake.

Le soir, si le temps le permet, nous dînerons
Luh swar, see luh tahṇ luh pair-may, noo dee-nuh-rohṇ
At night, weather permitting, we'll have dinner

et nous danserons sur la terrasse.
ay noo dahṇ-suh-rohṇ sůr la tair-rass.
and we'll dance on the terrace.

Je crois que nous nous amuserons bien.
Zhuh krwa kuh noo noo za-můz-rohṇ b'yeṇ.
I believe that we'll have a good time.

> **Bon amusement!**
> The reflexive verb *s'amuser,* literally "to amuse
> oneself," is the regular word for "to have a
> good time." When wishing one a pleasant eve-
> ning's diversion, one says *amusez-vous bien —*
> "have a good time," or simply *bon amusement.*

Pour "ils-elles" ajoutez la terminaison — *"ont"*
Poor "ils-elles" ah-zhoo-tay la tair-mee-nay-zohṇ — *"ont"*
For "ils-elles" (they), add the ending — *"ont"*

UN JEUNE HOMME:
Uhn zhuhn ohm:
A YOUNG MAN:

> Pensez-vous qu'un jour les hommes vivront sur la lune?
> **Pahṇ-say-voo kuhṇ zhoor lay zohm veev-rohṇ sur la lůne?**
> Do you think that one day men will live on the moon?

UN VIEIL HOMME:
Uhn v'yay ohm:
AN OLD MAN:

> Bien sûr. Bientôt il y aura des bases et, sans doute, un service de vols
> quotidiens.
> **B'yeṇ sůr. B'yeṇ-toh eel ee aw-ra day bahz ay sahṇ doot uhṇ
> sair-vees duh vohl ko-teed-yeṇ.**
> Of course, soon there will be bases there and, doubtlessly, a
> daily flight service.

181

LE JEUNE HOMME:

Et les habitants de notre terre,
Ay lay za-bee-tahɲ duh notr' tair,
and the inhabitants of our earth,

iront-ils aussi jusqu'aux planètes?
ee-rohɲ-teel oh-see zhuhz-ko pla-nett?
will they also go to the planets?

LE VIEIL HOMME:

Certainement. Une fois sur la lune
Sair-tayn-mahɲ. Une fwa sur la lŭne
Certainly, once on the moon

les voyages futurs seront plus faciles
lay vwa-yahzh fŭ-tŭr suh-rohɲ plŭ fa-seel
future trips will be easier

et on continuera jusqu'aux planètes.
ay ohɲ kohn-teen-wair-ah zhuhz-ko pla-nett.
and they will continue to the planets.

Pourtant, moi je crois que les astronautes
Poor-tahɲ, mwa zhuh krwa kuh lay zahs-tro-noht
However, I think the astronauts

n'arriveront pas aux étoiles très bientôt.
na-reev-rohɲ pa zo zay-twahl tray b'yeɲ-toh.
will not get to the stars very soon.

Moi, je ne verrai pas cet événement-là.
Mwa, zhuh nuh vair-ray pa set tay-vain-mahɲ-la.
(As for) me, I won't see that event.

Peut-être vous autres, les jeunes, le verrez.
Puh-tetr' voo-zohtr', lay zhuhn, luh vair-ray.
Maybe you young people will see it.

Idiomatic usage
autre — other
un autre — another
vous autres Français — you French (people)

INSTANT CONVERSATION: PLANNING A TRIP TO FRANCE

— Vous partirez pour la France le mois prochain, n'est-ce pas?
Voo par-tee-ray poor la Frahnss luh mwa pro-shen, ness pa?
You will leave for France next month, won't you?

— Oui, mon mari et moi nous irons à Paris.
Wee, mohn ma-ree ay mwa noo zee-rohn za Pa-ree.
Yes, my husband and I will go to Paris.

Nous y passerons l'été.
Noo zee pa-sair-rohn lay-tay.
We will spend the summer there.

— Les enfants iront-ils avec vous?
Lay zahn-fahn ee-rohn teel ah-vek voo?
Will the children go with you?

— Non, ils ne pourront pas.
Nohn, eel nuh poor-rohn pa.
No, they won't be able to.

Ils devront aller en classe.
Eel duhv-rohn ah-lay ahn klahss.
They'll have to attend class.

Ma soeur se chargera d'eux.
Ma serr suh shar-zhair-ra duh.
My sister will take care of them.

— Qu'est-ce que vous ferez pendant votre séjour en France?
Kess kuh voo fuh-ray pahn-dahn votr' say-zhoor ahn Frahnss?
What will you do during your stay in France?

— D'abord nous visiterons Paris,
Da-bohr noo vee-zeet-rohn Pa-ree,
First we shall visit Paris,

les musées, les monuments, les magasins, les églises.
lay mŭ-zay, lay mo-nŭ-mahṇ, lay ma-ga-zeṇ, lay zay-gleez.
the museums, monuments, shops, churches.

— Il faudra aussi visiter les environs:
Eel fo-dra oh-see vee-zee-tay lay zahṇ-vee-rohṇ:
You should also visit the surroundings:

le Palais de Versailles, Fontainebleau, la Malmaison ...
luh Pa-lay duh Vair-sye', Fohṇ-tain-blo, la Mal-may-zohṇ ...
the Palace of Versailles, Fontainebleau, the Malmaison ...

— Oui, certainement. Mais je ne sais pas si nous aurons le temps
Wee, sair-tain'-mahṇ. May zhuh nuh say pa see noo zo-rohṇ luh tahṇ
Yes, certainly. But I don't know whether we shall have time

d'aller jusqu'à Chartres voir la cathédrale.
da-lay zhŭss-ka Chartr' vwar la ka-tay-drahl.
to go as far as Chartres to see the cathedral.

De toute façon, nous ferons le tour des Châteaux de la Loire.
Duh toot fa-sohn, noo fuh-rohṇ luh toor day Sha-toh duh la Lwahr.
Anyway, we shall tour the Chateaux de la Loire.

— J'espère que vous ne manquerez pas les spectacles Son et Lumière.
Zheh-spair kuh voo nuh mahn-kuh-ray pa lay spek-tahkl' Sohṇ ay
                                                          Lum-yair.
I hope you won't miss the "Sound and Light" shows.

Je suis sûr que vous en serez enchantés.
Zhuh swee sŭr kuh voo zahṇ sur-ray zahṇ-shaṇ-tay.
I am sure that you will be delighted with them.

— Nous passerons une nuit à Chenonceaux.
Noo pass-rohṇ ŭne nwee ah Shuh-nohṇ-so.
We shall spend a night in Chenonceaux.

— Et où irez-vous ensuite?
Ay oo ee-ray-voo zahṇ-sweet?
And where will you go next?

— Nos amis les Arnault viendront nous chercher en voiture.
No za-mee lays Ar-no v'yen-drohṇ noo shair-say ahṇ vwa-tur.
Our friends the Arnaults will come and get us in their car.

184

On se retrouvera à Chenonceaux
Ohn suh ruh-troo-vra ah Shuh-nohn-so
We will meet in Chenonceaux

et nous irons tous les quatre à Cannes,
ay noo zee-rohn too lay katr' ah Kahnn,
and we'll all four go to Cannes,

où nous prendrons de vraies vacances.
oo noo prahn-drohn duh vray va-kahns.
where we'll have a real vacation.

> **Les vacances**
> "Vacation" — *vacances* — is singular in English but plural in French.

Nous nagerons dans la mer,
Noo nazh-rohn dahn la mair,
We'll swim in the sea,

nous ferons de la voile,
noo fuh-rohn duh la vwahl,
we'll go sailing,

et nous nous reposerons sur la plage.
ay noo noo ruh-pohz-rohn sûr la plazh.
and we'll relax on the beach.

— Oui, car vous ne vous reposerez pas beaucoup la nuit.
Wee, kahr voo nuh voo ruh-pohz-ray pa bo-koo la nwee.
Yes, for you'll not rest much at night.

Vous y serez pour le Festival,
Voo zee suh-ray poor luh Fes-tee-vahl,
You will be there for the Festival,

Cannes sera très animée à ce moment-là.
Kahnn suh-ra tray za-nee-may ah suh mo-mahn-la.
Cannes will be very lively at that time.

Vous serez sans doute invités dans beaucoup d'endroits.
Voo suh-ray sahn doot en-vee-tay dahn bo-koo dahn-drwa.
No doubt you'll be invited to many places.

185

Et il faudra voir le Casino de Monte-Carlo . . .
Ay eel fo-dra vwar luh Ka-see-no duh Mohn-ta Kar-lo . . .
And you'll have to see the Casino in Monte-Carlo . . .

J'espère que vous gagnerez aux jeux.
Zhes-pair kuh voo gan-yuh-ray oh zhuh.
I hope that you'll win at the games.

— Oh, moi, je serai contente si Richard n'y perd pas sa chemise.
    Oh, mwa, zhu suh-ray kohn-tahnt see Ree-shar nee pair pa sa
                                         zhuh-meez.
Oh, as for me, I'll be happy if Richard doesn't lose his shirt
                                           there.

N'oubliez pas!
To fix the future in your mind, here is a chart of
the future endings of the principal verb groups.

	parler	finir	rendre	recevoir
je	parler ai	finir ai	rendr ai	recevr ai
tu	-as	-as	-as	-as
il	-a	-a	-a	-a
nous	-ons	-ons	-ons	-ons
vous	-ez	-ez	-ez	-ez
ils	-ont	-ont	-ont	-ont

TEST YOUR FRENCH

Translate into French, using the future tense. Score 10 points for each correct answer. See answers below.

1. Tomorrow I shall get up early. _____

2. I shall go to Paris. _____

3. I'll phone you. _____

4. I'll be free Monday and Tuesday. _____

5. When will he come back? _____

6. We'll go by car. _____

7. We'll have dinner at eight o'clock. _____

8. What will you do? _____

9. He will stop a few days in Cannes. _____

10. Cannes will be very lively. _____

Answers: 1. Demain je me lèverai de bonne heure. 2. J'irai à Paris. 3. Je vous téléphonerai. 4. Je serai libre lundi et mardi. 5. Quand reviendra-t-il? 6. Nous irons en voiture. 7. Nous dînerons à huit heures. 8. Qu'est-ce que vous ferez? 9. Il s'arrêtera quelques jours à Cannes. 10. Cannes sera très animée.

SCORE _____%

HOW TO FORM THE PAST PARTICIPLE

Quand on se promène dans une ville française,
Kahn tohn suh pro-main' dahn zůne veel frahn-sez,
When one walks about a French city,

on voit souvent écrit:
ohn vwa soo-vahn tay-kree:
one often sees written:

> FERMÉ LE DIMANCHE.
> **Fair-may luh dee-mansh.**
> CLOSED ON SUNDAYS.
>
> FERMÉ POUR RÉPARATIONS.
> **Fair-may poor ray-pa-ras-yohn.**
> CLOSED FOR REPAIRS.
>
> OUVERT JUSQU'À 22 HEURES.
> **Oo-vair zhůs-ka ven-duh-zerr.**
> OPEN TILL 10 P.M.

> **24 hour system**
> Note the frequent use of the 24 hour system in French.

> SENS INTERDIT
> **Sahns en-tair-dee**
> ENTRY FORBIDDEN
>
> INTERDIT AUX PIÉTONS
> **En-tair-dee toh pee-ay-tohn**
> FORBIDDEN TO PEDESTRIANS
>
> STATIONNEMENT AUTORISÉ
> **Stahs-yohn'-mahn oh-toh-ree-zay**
> PARKING PERMITTED

RUE BARRÉE — DÉTOUR
Rǔ ba-ray — Day-toor
STREET BLOCKED — DETOUR

et dans les jardins publics:
ay dahn̯ lay zhahr-den̯ pǔ-bleek:
and in the city parks:

IL EST DÉFENDU DE MARCHER SUR LE GAZON.
Eel ay day-fahn̯-dǔ duh mahr-shay sǔr luh ga-zohn̯.
IT IS FORBIDDEN TO WALK ON THE GRASS.

Les mots *fermé, ouvert, interdit, autorisé, barré* et *défendu*
Lay mo *fair-may, oo-vair, en̯-tair-dee, oh-toh-ree-zay* ay *day-fahn̯-dǔ*
The words "closed," "open," "forbidden," "permitted," "blocked," and
"prohibited"

sont les participes passés des verbes
sohn̯ lay par-tee-seep pa-say day vairb
are the past participles of the verbs

fermer, ouvrir, interdire, autoriser, barrer et *défendre.*
fair-may, oo-vreer, en̯-tair-deer, oh-toh-ree-zay, ba-ray* ay *day-fahn̯dr'.
"to close," "to open," "to forbid," "to permit," "to block (off)" and "to
prohibit."

Et puis, quand on entre dans un magasin,
Ay pwee, kahn̯ tohn̯ nahn̯tr' dahn̯ zun̯ ma-ga-zen̯,
And then, when one enters a shop,

on voit ou on entend des expressions comme
ohn̯ vwa oo ohn̯ nahn̯-tahn̯ day zex-press-yohn̯ kohm
one sees or hears expressions such as

PRIX RÉDUITS
Pree ray-dwee
PRICES REDUCED

TOUS NOS PRIX SONT MARQUÉS.
Too no pree sohn̯ mar-kay.
ALL OUR PRICES ARE MARKED.

"C'est payé. Voilà votre reçu."
"Say pay-yay. Vwa-la, vohtr' ruh-sǔ."
"It's paid. Here is your receipt."

French Step by Step

Et quelquefois:
Ay kel-kuh-fwa:
And sometimes:

"Je regrette. C'est vendu."
"Zhuh ruh-gret. Say vahn-dû."
"I regret. It is sold."

Ce sont les participes passés de
Suh sohn lay par-tee-seep pa-say duh
These are the past participles of

réduire, marquer, payer, recevoir et *vendre.*
ray-dweer, mar-kay, pay-yay, ruh-suh-vwar ay vahndr'.
"reduce," "mark," "pay," "receive," and "sell."

The past participle
The past participle corresponds in use to the English past participle, such as "taken," "included," "forbidden," "sold," "finished," "closed," "served," etc. The past participle of French verbs is formed the following way:

First conjugation verbs form their past participle in *-é:*
 fermer ("to close") — *fermé* ("closed")
Second conjugation verbs have a final *-i:*
 finir ("to finish") — *fini* ("finished")
Third conjugation verbs, those ending in *-re* or *-oir,* form the past participle in *-u:*
 vendre ("to sell") — *vendu* ("sold")
 recevoir ("to receive") — *reçu* ("received")

Past participles ending in different letters from those indicated above include:

 faire (to do) — *fait* (done) *être* (to be) — *été* ("been")
 asseoir (to sit) — *assis* (seated)
 courir (to run) — *couru* (run)
 dire (to say) — *dit* (said)
 écrire (to write) — *écrit* (written)
 mettre (to put) — *mis* (put)
 mourir (to die) — *mort* (dead)

190

ouvrir (to open) — *ouvert* (opened)
prendre (to take) — *pris* (taken)
rire (to laugh) — *ri* (laughed)
tenir (to hold) — *tenu* (held)
vivre (to live) — *vécu* (lived)
venir (to come) — *venu* (come)

Les participes passés sont employés partout.
Lay par-tee-seep pa-say sohn tahn-plwa-yay par-too.
The past participles are used everywhere.

Au cinéma:
Oh see-nay-ma:
At the movies:

RECOMMANDÉ AUX ADULTES
Ruh-ko-mahn-day oh za-dült
RECOMMENDED FOR ADULTS

INTERDIT AUX MOINS DE SEIZE ANS
En-tair-dee toh mwen duh sez ahn
FORBIDDEN TO (THOSE) UNDER SIXTEEN

"C'est commencé?"
"Say ko-mahn-say?"
"Has it started?"

"Non, c'est fini dans cinq minutes."
"Nohn, say fee-nee dahn sen mee-nüt."
"No, it is finished in five minutes."

Au Bureau de Poste:
Oh Bü-ro duh Pohst:
At the Post Office:

LETTRES ET PAQUETS RECOMMANDÉS.
Lettr' zay pa-kay ruh-ko-mahn-day.
REGISTERED LETTERS AND PACKAGES.

Dans les gares et dans les trains:
Dahn lay gahr' ay dahn lay tren:
In railroad stations and trains:

191

BAGAGES ENREGISTRÉS
Ba-gahzh ahɲ-ruh-zhees-tray
BAGGAGE CHECKED

OBJETS PERDUS
Ob-zhay pair-dů
LOST OBJECTS (LOST AND FOUND)

PLACE RÉSERVÉE
Plahss ray-zair-vay
RESERVED SEAT

— Pardon, est-ce que cette place est occupée?
Par-dohɲ, ess-kuh set plahss ay tohk-ků-pay?
Is this seat taken?

— Oui, elle est prise.
Wee, el ay preez'.
Yes, it's taken.

> **The pasticiple as adjective**
> The past participle *pris* is used as an adjective here, so it must be feminine to agree with *la place.*

— Est-il permis de fumer?
Ay-teel pair-mee duh fů-may?
Is smoking allowed?

— Non, c'est défendu. Regardez. C'est écrit là.
Nohɲ, say day-fahɲ-dů. Ruh-gahr-day. Say-tay-kree la.
No, it's forbidden. Look. It's written here.

Et au wagon-restaurant:
Ay oh va-gohɲ-res-toh-rahɲ:
And in the dining-car:

Premier service — Le dîner est servi.
Pruhm-yay sair-vees — Luh dee-nay ay sair-vee.
First sitting — Dinner is served.

> **The passive**
> The past participle can be used with *être* ("to be") to form the passive, the same as in English.

These seats are reserved — *Ces places sont réservées.*

— Est-ce que le service est compris?
Ess-kuh luh sair-veess ay kohn-pree?
Is the service included?

À la campagne on voit souvent:
Ah la kahn-pine ohn vwa soo-vahn:
At the country one often sees:

CHASSE GARDÉE — PÊCHE RÉSERVÉE
Shahss gahr-day — Pesh ray-zair-vay
HUNTING PROTECTED — FISHING RESTRICTED

ACCÈS INTERDIT
Ak-say en-tair-dee
ACCESS FORBIDDEN

Le participe passé employé au passif:
Luh pahr-tee-seep pahs-say ahn-plwa-yay oh pahs-seef:
The past participle employed in the passive:

Le français est parlé en France, en Suisse et en Belgique.
Luh Frahn-say ay pahr-lay ahn Frahns', ahn Sweess' ay ahn Bel-zheek.
French is spoken in France, Switzerland and Belgium.

The passive or "on"
In conversational French, there is a tendency to avoid the passive by using the impersonal *on*. "French is spoken in Haiti" can be equally rendered by *on parle français en Haïti* or by *le français est parlé en Haïti.*

Il est parlé aussi au Canada
Eel ay pahr-lay oh-see oh Ka-na-da
It is also spoken in Canada

et dans divers pays d'Afrique et d'Asie.
ay dahn dee-vair pay-ee dahf-reek ay da-zee.
and in various countries of Africa and Asia.

Il est employé aux Nations Unies.
Eel ay tahn-plwa-yay oh Nahs-yohn Zůnee.
It is used in the United Nations.

Il est étudié dans le monde entier,
Eel ay tay-tůd-yay dahn luh mohnd ahnt-yay,
It is studied throughout the world,

parce que la littérature, l'histoire et la culture françaises
par-suh kuh la lee-tay-ra-tůr, lees-twar ay la kůl-tůr frahn-sez
because French literature, history and culture

sont tellement appréciées.
sohn tell-mahn ah-pray-s'yay.
are so (widely) appreciated.

Remember
Note how *appréciées* is feminine plural because it refers to three feminine words. But if one of the words were masculine, then the adjective would take the masculine form.

Les écriteaux (signs)
Step 18 has dealt with past participles you may see written on signs, as well as other uses of this form of the verb. However, as all signs don't necessarily include past participles, here are some others which you should know the meaning of:

défense d'afficher	— no posting (of signs)
défense d'entrer	— no admittance
renseignements	— information
attention	— caution
sens unique	— one way
passage à niveau	— railroad crossing
ralentissez	— slow down
carrefour dangereux	— dangerous crossroads
passage pour piétons	— passage for pedestrians
voie sans issue	— dead-end street
dames	— ladies
hommes	— men
lavabos	— lavatories

TEST YOUR FRENCH

Match these signs. Score 10 points for each correct answer. See answers below.

1.	FERMÉ LE DIMANCHE	PRICES REDUCED
2.	OUVERT JUSQU'À 22 HEURES	CLOSED FOR REPAIRS
3.	SENS UNIQUE	RECOMMENDED FOR ADULTS
4.	FERMÉ POUR RÉPARATIONS	RESERVED SEAT
5.	RUE BARRÉE	LOST AND FOUND
6.	STATIONNEMENT AUTORISÉ	CLOSED ON SUNDAYS
7.	PRIX RÉDUITS	STREET CLOSED
8.	PLACE RÉSERVÉE	OPEN TILL 10 P.M.
9.	OBJETS PERDUS	PARKING PERMITTED
10.	RECOMMANDÉ AUX ADULTES	ONE WAY

Answers: 7 4 10 8 9 1 5 2 6 3

SCORE _____%

195

step 19

HOW TO FORM THE PAST TENSE WITH *AVOIR* —

Le participe passé est employé
Luh par-tee-seep pa-say ay tahn̯-plwa-yay
The past participle is used.

pour former le passé des verbes.
poor fohr-may luh pa-say day vairb.
to form the past (tense) of the verbs.

Voicí comment on fait le passé avec *avoir:*
Vwa-see ko-mahn̯ tohn̯ fay luh pa-say ah-vek *ah-vwar:*
Here is how you make the past with *avoir* ("to have"):

On prend le présent d'avoir
Ohn̯ prahn̯ luh pray-zahn̯ da-v'war
One takes the present of *avoir*

et on le met devant le participe passé.
ay ohn̯ luh may duh-vahn̯ luh par-tee-seep pa-say.
and one puts it before the past participle.

Et voilà! Vous avez le passé.
Ay vwa-la! Voo za-vay luh pa-say.
And, there you are! You have the past tense.

Use the past participle

One of the principal uses of the past participle which you have just learned in Step 18 is to form the past tense of other verbs. This is done by combining the past participle with the present tense of *avoir* for some verbs and with the present tense of *être* for some others. In Step 19, we are taking up those which use *avoir*, and in Step 20, we will take up verbs which form their past with *être*. Here is the past of *trouver*, a regular verb of the first conjugation:

196

j'ai trouvé	— I found
tu as trouvé	— you found (fam.)
il (elle) a trouvé	— he (she) found
nous avons trouvé	— we found
vous avez trouvé	— you found
ils (elles) ont trouvé	— they found

In French, there is no difference between "I found," etc., and "I have found," etc., as they are both expressed by this past tense, which in French is called *le passé composé.*

Voilà des exemples du passé avec *j'ai:*
Vwa-la day zek-zahŋpl dů luh pa-say ah-vek *zhay:*
Here are some samples of the past with *j'ai:*

Hier, j'ai visité le Musée des Beaux-Arts.
Ee-yair, zhay vee-zee-tay luh Mů-zay day Bo-zahr.
Yesterday, I visited the Museum of Fine Arts.

J'ai regardé les statues et les tableaux.
Zhay ruh-gahr-day lay sta-tů ay lay ta-blo.
I looked at the statues and paintings.

J'ai parlé longtemps avec le guide.
Zhay par-lay lohŋ-tahŋ ah-vek luh gheed.
I spoke a long time with the guide.

J'ai écouté ses explications avec intérêt.
Zhay ay-koo-tay say zex-plee-kahs-yohŋ ah-vek eŋ-tay-ray.
I listened to his explanations with interest.

Je l'ai remercié et je lui ai donné un bon pourboire.
Zhuh lay ruh-mairs-yay ay zhuh lwee ay doh-nay uŋ bohŋ poor-bwahr.
I thanked him and I gave him a good tip.

Remember
There is no difference between the past and the perfect. The foregoing verbs are also equivalent to "I have visited," "I have looked at," "I have spoken," etc.

Le passé avec *il a, elle a, on a:*
Luh pa-say ah-vek *il a, elle a, on a:*
The past with *il a, elle a, on a:*

— Est-ce que quelqu'un a téléphoné?
Ess-kuh kel-kun ah tay-lay-fo-nay?
Did anyone phone?

— Oui, Mme Albert a appelé.
Wee, Ma-dahm Al-bair ah ah-puh-lay.
Yes, Mrs. Albert called.

— A-t-elle laissé un message?
Ah-tel lay-say un may-sahzh?
Did she leave a message?

— Non, elle n'a pas laissé de message.
Nohn, el na pa lay-say duh may-sazh.
No, she didn't leave a message.

L'apostrophe — (the apostrophe)
When the past is negative, the ne . . . pas is put around *avoir* and the *-e* dropped before the *a-* of *avoir*, since both are vowels. Here is the negative past of the verb *parler*, a first conjugation verb:

> *je n'ai pas parlé*
> *tu n'as pas parlé*
> *il (elle) n'a pas parlé*
> *nous n'avons pas parlé*
> *vous n'avez pas parlé*
> *ils (elles) n'ont pas parlé*

— Est-ce qu'on a commencé?
Ess kohn ah ko-mahn-say?
Have they begun?

— Oui, on a déjà fermé les portes.
Wee, ohn na day-zhah fair-may lay port.
Yes, they have already closed the doors.

Le passé avec *nous avons:*
Luh pa-say ah-vek *nous avons:*
The past with *nous avons:*

Nous avons cherché un appartement partout.
Noo za-vohn̥ shair-shay un ah-part-mahn̥ par-too.
We have looked everywhere for an apartment.

Nous en avons parlé à beaucoup de gens.
Noo zahn̥ na-vohn̥ par-lay ah bo-koo duh zhahn̥.
We have spoken about it to many people.

Mais nous n'avons rien trouvé.
May noo na-vohn̥ r'yen̥ troo-vay.
But we haven't found anything.

Hier nous avons placé une annonce dans le journal.
Ee-yair noo za-vohn̥ pla-say ůne ah nohn̥ss dahn̥ luh zhoor-nahl.
Yesterday we placed an ad in the paper.

Le passé avec *vous avez:*
Luh pa-say ah-vek *vous avez:*
The past with *vous avez:*

Avez-vous passé un bon été?
Ah-vay-voo pa-say un bohn̥ ay-tay?
Did you spend a good summer?

On m'a dit que vous avez beaucoup voyagé.
Ohn ma dee kuh voo za-vay bo-koo vwa-ya-zhay.
I was told that you traveled a lot.

Quel pays avez-vous aimé le mieux?
Kel pay-ee ah-vay voo-zay-may luh m'yuh?
What country did you like the best?

Le passé avec *ils ont* ou *elles ont:*
Luh pah-say ah-vek *ils ont* oo *elles ont:*
The past with *ils ont* or *elles ont:*

Les Bernard ont été invités chez nous pour samedi.
Lay Bair-nahr ohn̥ tay-tay en-vee-tay shay noo poor sahm-dee.
The Bernards have been invited to our house for Saturday.

Mais ils n'ont pas accepté.
May zeel nohn̥ pa zahk-sep-tay.
But they did not accept.

J'espère qu'ils n'ont pas oublié.
Zhess-pair keel nohn pa zoo-blee-ay.
I hope that they did not forget.

Voilà quelques examples avec des
Vwa-la kel-kuh zek-zahnpl ah-vek day
Here are some examples with

participes passés finissant en -*i*, -*s* et -*t:*
par-tee-seep pa-say fee-nee-sahn ehn -*i*, -*s*, ay -*t:*
past participles ending in -*i*, -*s* and -*t:*

> ### Past participles -i, -s, or -t
> The examples of the past participles we have
> given up to now have been of verbs ending with
> -*e* which are the majority of French verbs, those
> of the first (-*er*) conjugation. Among the other
> conjugations, the past participles of the most
> frequently used verbs are often irregular, so it is
> therefore better to learn them individually,
> through use. In general, the past participles of
> the second conjugation (-*ir*) end in -*i*, and those
> of the third conjugation (-*re* or -*oir*) and in -*u*.

— Avez-vous fini de lire la lettre d'Hélène?
Ah-vay voo fee-nee duh leer la lettr' day-lain?
Did you finish reading Helen's letter?

Qu'est-ce qu'elle vous a dit?
Kess kel voo za dee?
What did she tell you?

— Elle a dit qu'elle a pris une décision importante.
El ah dee kel ah pree ûne day-seez-yohn en-pohr-tahnt.
She said that she made an important decision.

Elle et son amie Marthe ont ouvert une boutique.
El ay sohn na-mee Mart ohn too-vair ûne boo-teek.
She and her friend Martha opened a shop.

— Quand ont-elles fait cela?
Kahn ohn-tel fay suh-la?
When did they do that?

— Il y a deux semaines.
Eel ee ya duh suh-main.
Two weeks ago.

Ago

Il y a is also the translation for "ago":

> *il y a dix minutes* — ten minutes ago
> *il y a dix ans* — ten years ago
> *il y a longtemps* — a long time ago

Elle a dit qu'elle a écrit des invitations
El ah dee kel ah ay-kree day zen-vee-tahs-yohn
She said that she wrote invitations

à tout le monde — et à vous aussi.
ah tool' mohnd — ay ah voo zo-see.
to everyone — and to you too.

Sans doute avez vous mis l'invitation
Sahn doot za-vay voo mee len-vee-tahs-yohn
Doubtlessly you have put the invitation

de côté sans la lire.
duh ko-tay sahn la leer.
aside without reading it.

Des participes passés finissant en "u":
Day par-tee-seep pa-say fee-nee-sahn tahn-nů:
Past participles ending in "u":

Excusez-nous! Nous n'avons pas pu venir plus tôt.
Ex-ků-zay-noo! Noo na-vohn pa pů vuh-neer plů toh.
Excuse us! We could not come earlier.

J'ai dû attendre ma femme.
Zhay dů ah-tahndr' ma fahm.
I had to wait for my wife.

Il lui a fallu une heure pour s'habiller.
Eel lwee ah fa-lů ůn err poor sa-bee-yay.
She needed an hour to get dressed.

To be necessary = to need
Fallu is the past participle of *falloir* — "to be necessary." When used with an indirect object pronoun, it means "to need."
Il me faut de l'argent — I need money.

Avez-vous lu l'article sur Henri Lamoureux?
Ah-vay-voo lǔ lahr-teekl' sǔr Ahṇ-ree La-moo'ruh?
Have you read the article on Henry Lamoureux?

Je l'ai vu dans le journal de ce matin.
Zhuh lay vǔ dahṇ luh zhoor-nahl duh suh ma-teṇ.
I saw it in this morning's paper.

Mais je ne l'ai pas encore lu.
May zhuh nuh lay pa zahṇ-kohr lǔ.
But I haven't read it yet.

J'ai entendu parler de lui.
Zhay ahṇ-tahṇ-dǔ par-lay duh lwee.
I've heard him spoken about.

J'en ai entendu parler.
entendre dire — to hear (something said)
entendre parler — to hear (something talked about)
J'ai entendu parler d'elle — I've heard about her.
J'ai entendu dire que . . . — I've heard it said that . . .
J'en ai entendu parler — I've heard about it.

Pensez donc! On dit qu'il a eu cinq femmes.
Pahṇ-say dohnk! Ohṇ dee keel ah ǔ seṇk fahm.
Just think! They say that he has had five wives.

Imagine!
"To imagine" is translated by *se figurer* or by *s'imaginer.*

Formidable! On peut dire qu'il a beaucoup vécu, n'est-ce pas?
Fohr-mee-dahbl'! Ohṇ puh deer keel ah bo-koo vay-kǔ, ness pa?
Remarkable! One can say that he's lived a lot, don't you think?

Le verbe *avoir* lui-même
Luh vairb *ah-vwar* lwee-mem
The verb *avoir* itself

forme le passé avec *avoir*.
fohrm luh pa-say ah-vek *ah-vwar*.
forms the past with *avoir*.

> **Soi-même = oneself**
> *Même* means "same" and also "self," when combined with the disjunctive pronouns, as follows:
>
> | | |
> |---|---|
> | *moi-même* | — myself |
> | *toi-même* | — yourself (fam.) |
> | *lui-même* | — himself |
> | *elle-même* | — herself |
> | *soi-même* | — oneself, itself |
> | *nous-mêmes* | — ourselves |
> | *vous-même* | — yourself |
> | *vous-mêmes* | — yourselves |
> | *eux-mêmes* | — themselves (mas.) |
> | *elles-mêmes* | — themselves (fem.) |

Hier j'ai eu un entretien avec le directeur.
Ee-yair, zhay ǔ un nahntr-t'yen ah-vek luh dee-rek-terr.
Yesterday I had a talk with the director.

Vraiment? Vous avez eu de la chance.
Vray-mahn? Voo zah-vay zǔ duh la shanss.
Really? You were lucky.

Même le verbe *être* forme le passé avec *avoir*.
Maim luh verb *etr'* fohrm luh pa-say ah-vek *ah-vwar*.
Even the verb *être* (to be) forms the past with *avoir*.

Avez-vous été à Marseille?
Ah-vay-voo zay-tay ah Mar-say?
Did you go to Marseilles?

Oui, j'y ai été au mois de mai.
Wee, zhee ay ay-tay oh mwa duh may.
Yes, I was there in the month of May.

Avez-vous été chez Antoine?
Ah-vay-voo zay-tay shay zahn-twahn?
Have you been to Antoine's house?

Oui. Il a été très étonné de me voir.
Wee. Eel ah ay-tay tray-zay-toh-nay duh muh vwar.
Yes. He was very surprised to see me.

INSTANT CONVERSATION:
WHAT HAPPENED AT THE OFFICE

LA SECRÉTAIRE:
La Suh-kray-tair:
THE SECRETARY:

Bonjour, Monsieur le Directeur. Avez-vous fait bon voyage?
Bohn-zhoor, Muss-yuh luh Dee-rek-terr. Ah-vay-voo fay bohn
vwa-yahzh?
Good morning, sir (Mr. Director). Did you have a good trip?

LE PATRON:
Luh Pa-trohn:
THE EMPLOYER:

Assez bon. Merci. Dites-moi, est-ce qu'il y a eu quelque chose de
nouveau?
Ah-say bohn. Mair-see. Deet'-mwa, ess keel ee ya ů kel-kuh
shohz duh noo-voh?
Quite good. Thank you. Tell me, has there been anything
new?

LA SECRÉTAIRE:

M. Gautier a vendu six voitures pendant votre voyage.
Muss-yuh Goht-yay ah vahn-dů see vwa-tůr pahn-dahn vo-truh
vwa-yahzh.
Mr. Gautier sold six cars during your trip.

LE PATRON:

Très bien. Et les autres vendeurs, qu'est-ce qu'ils ont fait?
Tray b'yen. Ay lay zohtr' vahn-derr, kess keel zohn fay?
Very well. And the other salesmen, what did they do?

LA SECRÉTAIRE:

Ils ont vendu quatre de nos nouveaux modèles,
Eel zohn vahn-dů kahtr' duh no noo-vo mo-del,
They sold four of our new models,

205

deux camions, sept camionettes et dix motocyclettes.
duh kahm-yohn, set kahm-yo-nett ay dee mo-toh-see-klett.
two trucks, two light trucks and ten motorcycles.

LA PATRON:

Qui a fait les dépôts en banque?
Kee ah fay lay day-po ehn bahnk?
Who made the bank deposits?

LA SECRÉTAIRE:

Moi-même. Je les ai portés tous les jours avant midi.
Mwa-mem'. Zhuh lay zay pohr-tay too lay zhoors ah-vahn mee-dee.
Myself. I took them every day before noon.

LE PATRON:

Eh bien, je vois qu'on n'a pas perdu de temps
Ay b'yen, zhuh vwa kohn na pa pair-dü duh tahn
Well, I see that no time has been lost

pendant mon absence.
pahn-dahn mohn nab-sahns.
during my absence.

LA SECRÉTAIRE:

Je crois bien. Tous les soirs, j'ai dû rester
Zhuh krwa b'yen. Too lay swahr, zhay dü ress-tay
I should say so. Every evening, I had to stay

pour terminer le courrier.
poor tair-mee-nay luh koor-yay.
to finish the mail.

LA PATRON:

Et Michèle, est-ce qu'elle vous a été utile?
Ay Mee-shell, ess kel voo za ay-tay ü-teel?
And Michèle, has she been useful to you?

LA SECRÉTAIRE:

Elle a été absente pendant trois jours
El ah ay-tay ab-sahnt' pahn-dahn trwa zhoor
She was absent for three days

à cause d'un rhume, rien de grave.
ah kohz dun rŭme, r'yen duh grahv.
because of a cold, nothing serious.

LE PATRON:

Et la nouvelle réceptionniste
Ay la noo'vel ray-seps-yo-neest
And the new receptionist

a-t-elle bien travaillé?
ah-tel b'yen tra-va-yay?
has she worked well?

LA SECRÉTAIRE:

Eh bien, à vrai dire, elle n'a pas fait grand-chose.
Ay b'yen, ah vray deer, el na pa fay grahn shohz.
Well, to tell the truth, she did not do much.

> ### The disappearing "e"
> With some words, the -e for the feminine adjec-
> tive is dropped. Note it in the case of
>
> *grand-chose* — much (as in "not much")
> *grand-mère* — grandmother

Elle a passé la plus grande partie de son temps
El ah pahs-say la plŭ grahnd' pahr-tee duh sohn tahn
She spent most of her time

à bavarder au téléphone.
ah ba-vahr-day oh tay-lay-fohn.
chatting on the phone.

LE PATRON:

Tiens! A propos de téléphone
T'yen! Ah pro-po duh tay-lay-fohn
Well! Speaking of the telephone

y a-t-il eu des messages pour moi?
ee-ya-teel ŭ day may-sazh poor mwa?
have there been any messages for me?

Un message pour vous
Many words ending in -age are the same in spelling, though not in pronunciation, in both French and English. They are mostly masculine gender.

le message	le courage
le passage	l'âge
le voyage	les bagages (plural only)

Several other words retain their French pronunciation even in English.

le ménage	le massage
le mirage	le garage
le corsage	

LE SECRÉTAIRE:

Oui, et nous avons gardé une liste
Wee, ay noo za-vohɲ gahr-day ŭne leest
Yes, and we kept a list

des appels téléphoniques.
day za-pell tay-lay-fo-neek
of the telephone calls.

Une dame, Mademoiselle Renée Latour,
Ŭne dahm, Mahd-mwa-zel Ruh-nay La-toor,
A lady, Miss Renée Latour,

vous a appelé plusieurs fois.
voo za ap-lay plŭz-yerr fwa.
called you several times.

Elle n'a pas voulu laissé son numéro.
El na pa voo-lŭ lay-say sohɲ nŭ-may-ro.
She did not want to leave her number.

LE PATRON:

Voyons . . . Ah oui, je crois que je sais qui c'est.
Vwa-yohɲ . . . Ah wee, zhuh krwa kuh zhuh say kee say.
Let's see . . . Ah yes, I think that I know who it is.

Où avez-vous mis mes messages?
Oo ah-vay-voo mee may may-sazh?
Where did you put my messages?

LA SECRÉTAIRE:

Dans le tiroir de votre bureau.
Dahn luh tee-rwar duh vohtr' bů-ro.
In your desk drawer.

Je l'ai fermé à clé. Voilà la clé.
Zhuh lay fair-may ah klay. Vwa-la la klay.
I locked it. Here is the key.

Locked up
Fermer is "to close." But to express "to lock"
you must say *fermer à clé* — "to close with a
key."

LE PATRON:

Mes compliments, mademoiselle, vous avez été discrète.
May kohn-plee-mahn, mad-mwa-zel, voo za-vay zay-tay dees-kret.
My congratulations, mademoiselle, you have been discreet.

A propos,
Ah pro-po,
By the way,

j'ai décidé de vous donner cette augmentation
zhay day-see-day duh voo doh-nay set ohg-mahn-tahs-yohn
I have decided to give you that raise

dont nous avons déjà parlé.
dohn noo za-vohn day-zha pahr-lay.
about which we have already spoken.

Dont
Dont is another one of the well-known short
words in French which mean so many things.
Dont is equivalent to "about which," "of
which," "about whom," "of whom," "whose,"
"from whom," according to the context.

LA SECRÉTAIRE:

Je vous remercie, Monsieur le Directeur.
Zhuh voo ruh-mair-see, Muss-yuh luh Dee-rek-terr.
I thank you, Mr. Director.

TEST YOUR FRENCH

Translate these sentences into French. Using the past tense with *avoir*. Score 10 points for each correct answer. See answers below.

1. Yesterday I visited the Museum.

2. I looked at the paintings.

3. Did anyone phone?

4. Renée called.

5. Did she leave a message?

6. Did you have a good trip?

7. What city did you like the best?

8. They did not forget.

9. What did she tell you?

10. We could not come earlier.

Answers: 1. Hier, j'ai visité le musée. 2. J'ai regardé les tableaux. 3. Est-ce que quelqu'un a téléphoné? 4. Renée a appelé. 5. A-t-elle laissé un message? 6. Avez-vous fait bon voyage? 7. Quelle ville avez-vous aimée le mieux? 8. Ils n'ont pas oublié. 9. Qu'est-ce qu'elle vous a dit? 10. Nous n'avons pas pu venir plus tôt.

SCORE _____%

210

HOW TO FORM THE PAST TENSE WITH *ÊTRE*

Certains verbes forment leur passé avec *être,*
Sair-ten vairb fohrm lerr pa-say ah-vek *etr',*
Certain verbs form their past with *être,* (*to be*)

Des verbes comme *aller, venir, entrer, sortir.*
Day vairb kohm *ah-lay, vuh-neer, ahn-tray, sohr-teer.*
Verbs such as "to go," "to come," "to go in," "to go out."

arriver, partir, monter, descendre, rester, etc.
***ah-ree-vay, pahr-teer, mohn-tay, day-sahndr', res-tay,* et-say-tay-ra.**
"to arrive," "to leave," "to go up," "to go down," "to stay'" etc.

Going, coming, remaining
An important group of verbs which form their past with *être* include those of motion, including those expressing the idea "going to," "arriving at," "coming from," and "staying."

Nous sommes arrivés en retard à cause d'un embouteillage.
Noo sohm za-ree-vay ahn ruh-tahr ah kohz dun nahn-boo-tay-yahzh.
We arrived late because of a traffic jam.

Traffic
The word for "traffic jam" is *embouteillage,* which means "putting into a bottle" (*bouteille*), with the implication that it is stopping at the neck — rather a good word for traffic jam. The regular word for "traffic" is *circulation.*

Nous sommes partis de chez nous très en avance.
Noo sohm pahr-tee duh shay noo tray zahn na-vahnse.
We left home much ahead of time.

Nous sommes montés dans un taxi, Place de l'Opéra,
Noo sohm mohn-tay dahn zun tahk-see, Plahss duh Lo-pay-ra,
We got into a taxi, (at the) Place de l'Opéra,

211

et le taxi est allé jusqu'à la Place Vendôme,
ay luh tahk-see ay ta-lay zhǔs-ka la Plahss Vahn̥-dohm,
and the taxi went as far as the Place Vendôme,

mais il y est resté une demi-heure sans bouger . . .
may zeel ee yay res-tay ǔn duh-mee-err sahn̥ boo-zhay . . .
but it stayed there a half-hour without budging . . .

alors nous sommes descendus du taxi,
ah-lohr noo sohm day-sahn̥-dǔ dǔ tahk-see,
so then we got out of the taxi,

et nous sommes venus par le métro!
ay noo sohm vuh-nǔ pahr luh may-tro!
and we came by subway!

Agreement with subject

Verbs that form their past with *être* agree with the subject in number and gender; that is why *nous sommes venus* has an -s on the past participle. If the people who came were exclusively females, then it would be *nous sommes venues*.

Tous les verbes réfléchis comme
Too lay vairb ray-flay-shee kohm
All the reflexive verbs such as

se lever, se laver, s'habiller, s'amuser, etc.,
suh luh-vay, suh la-vay, sa-bee-yay, sa-mǔ-zay, et-say-tay-ra,
"to get up," "to wash," "to dress," "to have fun," etc.,

forment aussi leur passé avec *être.*
fohrm oh-see lerr pa-say ah-vek *etr.*
also form their past with *être* ("to be").

Arriving and learning

There are two other verbs which form the past with *être: naître* — "to be born," and *mourir* — "to die," which, in a way, are certainly connected with arriving and leaving a place. Here is an example of the past:

Napoléon est né en Corse et il est mort à Sainte-Hélène à l'âge de 52 ans. — Napoleon was born in Corsica and died in St. Helena at the age of 52 years.

Ce matin, je me suis levé de bonne heure.
Suh ma-ten, zhuh muh swee luh-vay duh bunn err.
This morning, I got up early.

Je me suis habillé en vitesse.
Zhuh muh swee za-bee-yay ahn vee-tess.
I got dressed quickly.

Je me suis dit: Pour une fois je ne serai pas en retard.
Zhuh muh swee dee: Poor ûne fwa, zhuh nuh suh-ray pa zahn ruh-tar.
I told myself: For once, I shall not be late.

Et je me suis dépêché pour partir à l'heure.
Ay zhuh muh swee day-pay-shay poor pahr-teer ah lerr.
And I hurried up in order to leave on time.

Au moment où je me suis assis
Oh mo-mahn too zhuh muh swee zas-see
The moment I sat down

pour prendre mon petit déjeuner,
poor prahndr' mohn puh-tee day-zhuh-nay,
to take my breakfast,

Marie s'est coupée en coupant le pain.
Ma-ree say koo-pay ahn koo-pahn luh pen.
Marie cut herself while cutting the bread.

En la soignant, je me suis mis en retard.
Ahn la swan-yahn, zhuh muh swee mee zahn ruh-tahr.
In taking care of her, I made myself late.

En

Note how *en*, certainly one of the most important words in French, is used in different expressions:

> *En le soignant* — (used for *by* or *in* with the present participle)
> *En retard* — late ("in delay")
> *En avance* — early ("in advance")
> *Il ne s'en est pas aperçu* — he didn't notice it (substitutes for *it*)

213

En is also used to give a special meaning to some verbs:

s'en aller — to go off, to leave
s'en faire — to worry
en vouloir à — to have something against (someone)

Heureusement, quand je suis arrivé au bureau,
Uh-ruhz'-mahn', kahn zhuh swee za-ree-vay oh bŭ-ro,
Fortunately, when I arrived at the office,

le patron ne s'en est pas aperçu.
luh pa-trohn nuh sahn nay pa za-pair-sŭ.
the boss did not notice it.

Reflexive verbs in the past
All reflexive verbs are conjugated in the past with the present tense of *être*. The reflexive also includes verbs which are reciprocal, such as *se voir* — "to see each other," *s'entendre* — "to understand each other," and *se parler* — "to speak to each other."
   Nous nous sommes vus hier. — We saw each other yesterday.

Le participe passé avec *être* s'accorde avec le sujet:
Luh par-tee-seep pa-say ah-vek *aitr'* sah-kord' ah-vek luh sŭ-zhay:
The past participle with *être* ("to be") agrees with the subject:

Monsieur est sorti. — Madame est sortie aussi.
Muss-yuh ay sohr-tee. — Ma-dahm ay sohr-tee oh-see.
Mr. _____ is out. Mrs. _____ is out also.

Monsieur — Madame
The titles *monsieur* and *madame* are often used by themselves, without the proper name, like "sir" or "madam," not only in direct address, but even in indirect reference when the name is already known.

Ils ne sont pas encore revenus.
Eel nuh sohn pa zahn-kohr ruhv-nŭ.
They have not come back yet.

Past Participle
As you have seen in Step 18, the past participle, when used as an adjective, agrees in
gender and number with the noun it refers to.
Here, as part of a verbal construction with a
form of *être*, it agrees with the subject. But
when verbs form their past tense with *avoir* the
past participle becomes feminine or plural only
when the object precedes the verb. See examples below.

— Qui a pris la lettre que j'ai mise sur la table?
Kee ah pree la lettr' kuh zhay meez sûr la tahbl'?
Who took the letter that I put on the table?

— Personne ne l'a prise.
Pair-sohn nuh la preez.
Nobody took it.

— Vous l'avez mise dans votre poche.
Voo la-vay meez dahṇ vohtr' pohsh.
You put it into your pocket.

— Et les autres lettres, vous les avez écrites?
Ay lay zohtr' lettr', voo lay za-vay zay-kreet?
And the other letters, did you write them?

— Oui, et on les a déjà mises à la poste.
Wee, ay ohṇ lay za day-zha meez ah la post.
Yes, and they have already been mailed.

Now you hear it
Most of the time you will not note this agreement of the past participle in conversation, although you will notice it in writing, but you will
definitely hear it when the past participle ends
in -s or -t:
The things that I saw — *Les choses que j'ai
vues* — (here, you do not hear it
pronounced).
The things that I said — *Les choses que j'ai
dites* — (here, you hear it, because the past
participle ends in -t).

215

INSTANT CONVERSATION:
WHAT HAPPENED AT THE PARTY

PIERRE:
P'yair:
PETER:
> Est-ce que tu t'es bien amusé hier soir?
> **Ess kuh tu tay b'yeŋ na-mŭ-zay ee-yair swar?**
> Did you have fun last night?

FRANÇOIS:
Frahŋ-swa:
FRANCIS:
> Plus ou moins. Je suis sorti avec Marcelle.
> **Plŭ zoo mweŋ. Zhuh swee sohr-tee ah-vek Mar-sel.**
> More or less. I went out with Marcelle.

PIERRE:
> Et qu'est-ce qui est arrivé?
> **Ay kess kee ay ta-ree-vay?**
> And what happened?

FRANÇOIS:
> Elle s'est fâchée avec moi.
> **El say fa-shay ah-vek mwa.**
> She became angry with me.

PIERRE:
> Tiens, pourquoi? Qu'est-ce qui s'est passé?
> **T'yeŋ, poor-kwa? Kess kee say pa-say?**
> Well why? What went on?

FRANÇOIS:
> Nous sommes allés chez Léon.
> **Noo sohm za-lay shay Lay-ohŋ.**
> We went to Leon's.

FRANÇOIS:

On a dansé, chanté et on s'est bien amusé.
Ohn na dahn-say, shan-tay ay ohn say b'yen na-mů-zay.
We danced, sang and we had a good time.

Tout a très bien marché
Too ta tray b'yen mahr-shay
Everything went fine

Ça marche?
Marcher, literally "to march," is used the same as *aller* to show that things are going or are not going well.

Ça marche — It is going well
Ça ne marche pas — It is not going well

jusqu'à l'arrivée de Béatrice.
zhůs-ka la-ree-vay duh Bay-ah-treess.
until Beatrice arrived.

Elle m'a fait les yeux doux.
El mah fay lay zyuh doo.
She gave me the eye.

Les yeux doux
Colloquial expressions can be approximately but not exactly translated as here when in the case of *faire les yeux doux à quelqu'un* — literally "to make sweet eyes at someone," but idiomatically "to give someone the eye."

J'ai dansé un peu avec elle.
Zhay dahn-say un puh ah-vek el.
I danced a little with her.

Et nous avons bavardé un moment.
Ay noo za-vohn ba-vahr-day un mo-mahn.
And we chatted for a while.

PIERRE:

Je vois! Et Marcelle s'est mise en colère.
Zhuh vwa! Ay Mahr-sel say meez ahn ko-lair.
I see! And Marcelle got angry.

FRANÇOIS:

Exactement. Et elle a voulu rentrer tout de suite.
Ek-zak-tuh-mahṇ. Ay el ah voo-lǚ rahṇ-tray tood' sweet.
Exactly. And she wanted to go home right away.

Je n'ai pas pu la calmer.
Zhuh nay pa pǚ la kahl-may.
I could not calm her down.

J'ai dû appeler un taxi pour la ramener chez elle.
Zhay dǚ ahp-lay uṇ tahk-see poor la rahm-nay shay zel.
I had to call a taxi to take her home.

Quand je l'ai quittée, elle ne m'a dit ni merci ni au revoir.
Kahṇ zhuh lay kee-tay, el nuh ma dee nee mair-see nee ohr-vwar.
When I left her, she did not say either thank you or good by.

PIERRE:

Et ce matin, tu lui as parlé?
Ay suh ma-teṇ, tǚ lwee ah pahr-lay?
And this morning, did you talk to her?

FRANÇOIS:

Bien sûr. Je lui ai téléphoné.
B'yeṇ sǚ. Zhuh lwee ay tay-lay-fo-nay.
Surely. I called her on the phone.

J'ai essayé de lui parler.
Zhay ay-say-yay duh lwee pahr-lay.
I tried to talk to her.

"De" followed by the infinitive

Essayer — "to try," is another verb which takes *de* before the infinitive.
   Essayez de le faire! — Try to do it!

Other important verbs that take *de* before a following infinitive include:

essayer de	— to try (to)
cesser de	— to cease (to)
se dépêcher de	— to hurry (to)
dire de	— to tell (to)
promettre de	— to promise (to)

refuser de	— to refuse (to)
remercier de	— to thank (for)
finir de	— to finish (doing something)
permettre de	— to permit (to)
oublier de	— to forget (to)
avoir peur de	— to be afraid (to) (of)
venir de	— to have just (done something)

Mais elle a raccroché
May zel ah ra-kro-shay
But she hung up

dès qu'elle a reconnu ma voix.
day kel ah ruh-ko-nǔ ma vwa.
as soon as she recognized my voice.

> **Dès que**
> *Dès que* means "from the moment that" or "as soon as."

PIERRE:

Que veux-tu? Marcelle a toujours été jalouse.
Kuh vuh-tǔ? Mahr-sel ah too-zhoor ay-tay zha-looz.
What can you do? Marcelle has always been jealous.

> **Que voulez-vous?**
> *Que veux-tu,* or the more formal, *que voulez-vous?* is literally "What do you want?"' but idiomatically means "What can you do?" or "That's how it is."

Pour avoir la paix, envoie-lui donc des fleurs,
Poor ah-vwar la pay, ahn-vwa lwee dohnk day flerr,
To have peace, send her some flowers then,

si tu ne l'as pas encore fait.
see tǔ nuh la pa zahn-kohr fay.
if you have not yet done so.

219

TEST YOUR FRENCH

Fill in the past participles for the following constructions with *être*. Score 10 points for each correct answer. See answers below.

1. Nous sommes _____ en retard. (fem.)
   (arrived)

2. Nous sommes _____ du taxi. (mas.)
   (got out)

3. Nous sommes _____ par le métro. (mas.)
   (came)

4. Je me suis _____ de bonne heure. (mas.)
   (got up)

5. Je me suis _____ en vitesse. (fem.)
   (got dressed)

6. Je me suis _____. (mas.)
   (hurried)

7. Qu'est-ce qui est _____?
   (happened)

8. Nous sommes _____ chez Léon. (mas.)
   (went)

9. Monsieur Durand est _____.
   (left)

10. Madame Albert n'est pas encore _____.
    (arrived)

Answers: 1. arrivées 2. descendus 3. venus 4. levé 5. habillée 6. dépêché 7. arrivé 8. allés 9. parti 10. arrivée

SCORE _____%

step 21

On se sert souvent du conditionnel
Ohṇ suh sair soo-vahṇ dŭ kohṇ-deess-yo-nell
We often use the conditional

dans des invitations et des suggestions.
dahṇ day zeṇ-vee-tahs-yohṇ ay day sug-zhest-yohṇ,
In invitations and suggestions.

Voudriez-vous quelque chose à boire?
Voo-dree-yay-voo kel-kuh shohz ah bwar?
Would you like something to drink?

Est-ce que votre femme pourrait se joindre à nous?
Ess-kuh vohtr' fahm poo-ray suh zhweṇdr' ah noo?
Could your wife join us?

The conditional

The conditional is not a tense but a mood. It corresponds to several uses of the English "would." *Je voudrais* — "I would like," which you have learned as a special expression in previous Steps, is simply the conditional of "to want," that is more indirect than the blunt "I want." It is more polite to say "what would you like . . ." than "What do you want?," in English as well as in French.

The conditional is formed in exactly the same way as the future, except that the endings are different. Note the present conditional of *parler:* — *je parlerais, tu parlerais, il* (*elle*) *parlerait, nous parlerions, vous parleriez, ils* (*elles*) *parleraient.* As you can see, all the endings sound the same, except the ones for *nous* and *vous*, which are *-ions* and *-iez* respectively. The

221

verbs that have irregular stems in the future,
which we examined in Step 17, retain the same
stems for the conditional, with, of course, the
conditional endings.

Voilà un court dialogue avec le conditionnel:
Vwa-la un koor dee-a-log ah-vek luh kohn-dees-yo-nell:
Here is a short dialogue with the conditional:

— Est-ce que je pourrais prendre une photo de vous?
Ess kuh zhuh poo-ray prahndr'ûn fo-toh duh voo?
Could I take a photograph of you?

— En prendriez-vous une de moi?
Ahn prahn-dree-yay-voo zûne duh mwa?
Would you take one of me?

— Par ce beau temps, ne voudriez-vous pas
Pahr suh bo tahn, nuh voo-dree-yay-voo pa
With this fine weather, wouldn't you like

faire une promenade en voiture?
fair ûne prohm-nahd ahn vwa-tûr?
to take a ride in the car?

On pourrait aller au Restaurant
Ohn poo-ray ta-lay oh Res-toh-rahn
We could go to the Restaurant

du Bois pour déjeuner.
dû Bwa poor day-zhuh-nay.
of the Woods for lunch.

Est-ce que ça vous plairait?
Ess kuh sa voo play-ray?
Would you like that?

— J'aimerais bien, mais pas aujourd'hui.
Zhaim-ray b'yen, may pa zo-zhoor-dwee.
I would like to, but not today.

— Alors, est-ce que ce serait possible demain?
Ah-lohr, ess-kuh suh suh-ray po-seebl' duh-men?
Then, would it be possible tomorrow?

— Oui, je crois que demain je pourrais.
Wee, zhuh crwa kuh duh-men zhuh poo-ray.
Yes, I think that tomorrow I might be able to.

Could and might
The present tense of *pouvoir* means "can" or
"may," and the conditional means "could" or
"might." There is no special word for "might."

Voilà comment on se sert du conditionnel
Vwa-la ko-mahn tohn suh sair dů kohn-dees-yo-nell
Here is how the conditional is used

pour demander quelque chose poliment.
poor duh-mahn-day kel-kuh shohz po-lee-mahn.
to request something politely.

— Pourriez-vous me rendre un service?
Poor-yay-voo muh rahndr'un sair-vees?
Could you do me a favor?

Vous serait-il possible
Voo suh-ray-teel po-seebl'
Would it be possible for you

de me prêter cinquante francs?
duh muh preh-tay sen-kahnt frahn?
to lend me fifty francs.

Je pourrai vous les rendre dans une semaine.
Zhuh poo-ray voo lay rahndr' dahn zůn suh-main.
I will be able to give them back to you within a week.

— Je voudrais bien, mais je n'ai pas d'argent sur moi.
Zhuh voo-dray b'yen, may zhuh nay pa dahr-zhan sůr mwa.
I would like to, but I don't have any money with me.

— N'auriez-vous pas au moins vingt francs?
Nohr-yay-voo pa zo mwen ven frahn?
Wouldn't you have at least twenty francs?

On se sert aussi du conditionnel pour raconter
Ohn suh sair oh-see dů kohn-dees-yo-nell poor ra-kohn-tay
The conditional is also used to tell

223

ce qui a été dit au passé sur des projets futurs.
suh kee ah ay-tay dee toh pa-say sûr day pro-zhay fû-tûr.
what has been said in the past about future plans.

— Le directeur, vous a-t-il demandé
Luh dee-rek-terr voo za-teel duh-mahn-day
Did the director ask you

quand vous prendriez vos vacances?
kahn voo prahn-dree-yay vo va-kahnss?
when you would take your vacation?

> **Re future plans**
> Another important use of the conditional is to recount what someone said in the past about his future plans. Compare:
>
> *Il dit qu'il vous verra demain.*
> He says that he'll see you tomorrow.
> and *Il a dit qu'il vous verrait demain.*
> He said that he would see you tomorrow.

— Non, mais il m'a dit qu'il serait absent en juillet
Nohn, may zeel ma dee keel suh-ray-tab-sahn ahn zhoo'ee-yay
No, but he told me that he would be away in July

et qu'en août il aurait un congrès en Amérique.
ay kahn noo eel oh-ray tun kohn-gray ahn na-may-reek.
and that in August he would have a conference in America.

— En ce cas, il vaudrait mieux
Ahn suh ka, eel vo-dray m'yuh
In that case, it would be better

prendre les vôtres plus tard.
prahn-dr' lay vohtr' plû tar.
to take yours later.

Vous devriez lui demander
Voo duh-vree-yay lwee duh-mahn-day
You should ask him

Ought to and should

Devoir is "must," "to be obliged," "to owe," but, in its conditional form, it means "ought" or "should" in the sense of obligation, of something that you should really do.

Vous devriez voir ce film. —
You ought to see that movie.
Je devrais vraiment partir maintenant. —
I really should leave now.

si vous pourriez les prendre en septembre.
see voo poor-yay lay prahndr' ahn sep-tahnbr'.
if you could take it in September.

Ainsi vous n'auriez pas de difficulté
En-see voo nor-yay pa duh dee-fee-kůl-tay
That way you wouldn't have any difficulty

à trouver une chambre dans les hôtels.
ah troo-vay ůne shahmbr' dahn lay zo-tell.
in finding a room in a hotel.

INSTANT CONVERSATION:
LEAVING A TELEPHONE MESSAGE

— Allô! Est-ce que je pourrais parler avec Mme. Jolivet?
Ah-lo! Ess kuh zhuh poo-ray pahr-lay ah-vek Ma-dahm Zho-lee-vay?
Hello! Could I speak with Mrs. Jolivet?

— Elle n'est pas là, monsieur; elle est sortie.
El nay pa la, muss-yuh; el ay sohr-tee.
She isn't in, sir; she went out.

— Mais elle m'a dit qu'elle serait chez elle à six heures!
May zel ma dee kel suh-ray shay zel ah see-zerr!
But she told me that she would be at home at six o'clock!

Elle ne vous a pas dit quand elle reviendrait?
El nuh voo za pa dee kahn tel ruhv-yen-dray?
She didn't say when she would come back?

— Elle a dit qu'elle serait peut-être en retard,
El a dee kel suh-ray puh-tetr' ahn ruh-tahr,
She said that she would probably be late,

qu'elle aurait des courses à faire,
kel oh-ray day koor sa fair,
that she would first do some shopping,

et qu'après elle irait prendre le thé avec une amie,
ay ka-pray el ee-ray prahndr' luh tay ah-vek ůn ah-mee,
and that after that she would have tea with a friend,

et qu'elle rentrerait chez elle à six heures environ.
ay kel rahn-truh-ray shay zel ah see zerr ahn-vee-rohn.
and that she would come home at about six o'clock.

Auriez-vous la bonté de rappeler plus tard?
Ohr-yay-voo la bohn-tay duh rahp-lay plů tar?
Would you be kind enough to call later?

— Bien entendu. Mais voudriez-vous bien lui dire
B'yen nahn-tahn-dů. May voo-dree-yay-voo b'yen lwee deer
Of course. But would you please tell her

que M. Blanchard a téléphoné?
kuh Muss-yuh Blahn-shahr ah tay-lay-fo-nay?
that Mr. Blanchard telephoned?

Allô?

Here are some other telephone expressions that you might find useful:

Ne quittez pas. — Hold the line.
La ligne est occupée. — The line is busy.
À quel numéro est-ce que je peux l'atteindre? — At what number can I get him (her)?
Vous vous êtes trompé de numéro. — You have the wrong number. (literally, You made a mistake in the number.)
Je m'excuse. (or) *Excusez-moi.* — Excuse me.

TEST YOUR FRENCH

Translate the following. Score 10 points for each correct answer. See answers below.

1. You should visit Montmartre.

   _____

2. He said that he would come at eight.

   _____

3. How much time would it take?

   _____

4. Would you have something to drink?

   _____

5. I would like to buy some stamps.

   _____

6. Could I take a picture?

   _____

7. It would be better to leave right now. (use *valoir*)

   _____

8. We would like to see Versailles.

   _____

9. Could I speak to Marcelle? (use "Est-ce que . . .")

   _____

10. Could you do it?

   _____

SCORE _____%

step 22

THE IMPERFECT — A TENSE TO USE WHEN TELLING A STORY

Quand on emploie des expressions comme:
Kahn tohɲ nahɲ-plwa day zex-press-yohɲ kohm:
When we use expressions like:

> "mon père disait toujours . . ."
> **"mohɲ pair dee-zay too-zhoor . . ."**
> "my father always used to say . . ."

> ou "quand j'étais jeune . . ."
> **oo "kahɲ zhay-tay zhuhn . . ."**
> or "when I was young . . ."

> ou "lorsque nous vivions en Provence . . ."
> **oo "lohrs-kuh noo veev-yohɲ zahɲ Pro-vahɲss . . ."**
> or "when we used to live in Provence . . ."

> ou "quand nous étions au lycée . . ."
> **oo "kahɲ noo zayt-yohɲ zo lee-say . . ."**
> or "when we were in high school . . ."

ou d'autres phrases décrivant des actions
oo dohtr' frahz day-kree-vahɲ day zaks-yohɲ
or other phrases describing actions

répétées ou continuées dans le passé
ray-pay-tay zoo kohɲ-tee-nway dahɲ luh pa-say
repeated or continued in the past

nous employons l'imparfait.
noo zahɲ-plwa-yohɲ leɲ-par-fay.
we use the imperfect.

Uses of the imperfect
The imperfect is equivalent to the English "used to" in the sense of a continued action in the past, whether or not "used to" is specifically

229

used. For instance, to say that you were living somewhere over a period of time, use the imperfect. This tense is also used to describe something that happened often, or to describe a scene as it was when something else happened.

At that time we were living in Paris.
À cette époque nous habitions Paris.
He used to go skiing every winter,
Il faisait du ski tous les hivers,
    but last winter he broke his leg.
    mais l'hiver passé il s'est cassé la jambe.

Pour reconnaître l'imparfait
Poor ruh-ko-netr' len-par-fay
To recognize the imperfect

dans la conversation, remarquez
dahn la kohn-vair-sahs-yohn, ruh-mar-kay
in conversation, note

le son -ais àla fin du verbe
luh sohn ay **ah la fen dů vairb**
the sound ais at the end of the verb

pour la plupart des personnes,
poor la plů-pahr day pair-sohn,
for most of the persons,

le son final -ions pour nous
luh sohn fee-nahl yohn **poor noo**
the final sound -ions for nous

et le son final -iez pour vous,
ay luh sohn fee-nahl yay **poor** voo,
and the final sound -iez for vous,

comme pour le conditionnel.
kohm poor luh kohn-dees-yoh-nell.
as for the conditional.

Endings for the imperfect
The endings of the imperfect tense are exactly the same as those of the conditional. The key

230

sound is *ais* (or *ait* or *aient,* which sound the
same), but in the case of the imperfect they are
added not to the infinitive of the verb, but to the
stem.

I would speak　— *je parlerais*
I was speaking
(or)
I used to speak — *je parlais*

On emploie l'imparfait pour raconter des souvenirs:
Ohṇ nahṇ-plwa leṇ-pahr-fay poor ra-kohṇ-tay day soov-neer:
The imperfect is used to tell remembrances:

La vie était très difficile pendant la guerre.
La vee ay-tay tray dee-fee-seel pahṇ-dahṇ la gair.
Life was very difficult during the war.

Vous n'étiez pas ici.
Voo net-yay pa zee-see.
You were not here.

Vous ne savez pas ce que c'était.
Voo nuh sa-vay pa suh kuh say-tay.
You do not know what it was.

Il n'y avait pas d'essence.
Eel nee ah-vay pa day-sahṇs.
There was no gasoline.

On ne pouvait pas se servir de sa voiture.
Ohṇ nuh poo-vay pa suh sair-veer duh sa vwa-tůr.
One could not use one's car.

Quand on voulait aller quelque part,
Kahṇ tohṇ voo-lay ah-lay kel-kuh pahr,
When one wanted to go somewhere,

on devait y aller à bicyclette ou à pied,
ohṇ duh-vay-tee ah-lay ah bee-see-klett oo ah p'yay,
one had to go there on a bicycle or on foot,

ou par le métro . . . quand il marchait.
oo pahr luh may-tro . . . kahṇ teel mahr-shay.
or by subway . . . when it was working.

Il y avait des cartes d'alimentation,
Eel ee ah-vay day kahrt' da-lee-mahn-tass-yohn,
There were ration cards,

et il n'y avait pas grand-chose dans les magasins.
ay eel nee ah-vay pa grahn-shohz dahn lay ma-ga-sen.
and there was not much in the stores.

Heureusement nous avions des parents à la campagne.
Uh-ruhz-mahn noo zav-yohn day pa-rahn ah la kahn-pine'.
Fortunately we had relatives in the country.

Une fois par semaine, nous allions les voir à bicyclette.
Ůne fwa pahr suh-main, noo zahl-yohn lay vwar ah bee-see-klett.
Once a week, we would go and see them on a bicycle.

Ils nous donnaient des oeufs, du beurre et du fromage.
Eel noo doh-nay day zuh, dů berr ay dů fro-mahzh.
They used to give us eggs, butter and cheese.

Quand on raconte l'histoire ou des histoires,
Kahn tohn rah-kohnt lees-twar oo day zees-twar,
When one tells history or stories,

on se sert souvent de l'imparfait:
ohn suh sair soo-vahn duh len-pahr-fay:
one often uses the imperfect:

Marie-Antoinette, reine de France, avait dans son boudoir
Ma-ree-Ahn-twa-net, rain duh Frahns, ah-vay dahn sohn boo-dwar
Marie-Antoinette, queen of France, had in her dressing-room

> **Pourquoi "boudoir?"**
> the word *boudoir* comes from the verb
> *bouder* — "to pout."
> In other words a "a place (for a lady) to pout."

un miroir où elle se regardait
un mee-rwar oo el suh ruh-gahr-day
a mirror where she would look at herself

pendant qu'on l'habillait.
pahn-dahn kohn la-bee-yay.
while she was being dressed.

Ce miroir était attaché au mur, et,
Suh mee-rwar ay-tay ta-ta-shay oh mǔr, ay,
This mirror was attached to the wall, and,

à cause d'une imperfection dans le verre,
ah kohz dǔn en-pair-feks-yohn dahn luh vair,
because of an imperfection in the glass,

la reine pouvait y voir quelquefois son corps mais pas sa tête.
la rain poo-vay-tee vwar kel-kuh-fwa sohn kohr may pa sa tet.
the queen could sometimes see her body in it but not her head.

Peut-être était-ce l'annonce
Puh-tetr' ay-tess la-nohnss
Maybe this was the announcement

du destin qui l'attendait.
dǔ dess-ten kee la-tahn-day.
of the fate that was waiting for her.

Heureusement, elle n'en savait rien.
Uh-ruhz'-mahn, el nahn sa-vay r'yen.
Happily, she didn't know anything about it.

L'imparfait exprime aussi l'interruption au passé:
Len-pahr-fay ex-preem oh-see len-tay-rups-yohn oh pah-say:
The imperfect expresses also an interruption in the past:

J'étais tranquillement en train de dormir,
Zhay-tay trahn-keel-mahn ahn tren duh dohr-meer,
I was sleeping peacefully,

quand le téléphone a sonné.
kahn luh tay-lay-fohn ah so-nay.
when the telephone rang.

> Here is a good example of the imperfect used to set the descriptive stage for something that was going on when something else happened, as in the case of the sleeping man awakened by the telephone.

C'était Raymond, cet imbécile;
Say-tay Ray-mohn, set en-bay-seel;
It was Raymond, that imbecile;

Il voulait savoir le numéro de Chantal.
Eel voo-lay sa-vwar luh nŭ-may-ro duh Shahn-tahl.
He wanted to know Chantal's number.

Je lui ai dit que je n'aimais pas répondre
Zhuh lwee ay dee kuh zhuh nay-may pa ray-pohndr'
I told him that I did not like answering

au téléphone quand je dormais.
oh tay-lay-fohn kahn zhuh dohr-may.
the telephone when I was asleep.

INSTANT CONVERSATION: A FAMILY REUNION — RECALLING THE PAST

LUI:
Lwee:
HE:

> Nous allons dîner chez mes grands-parents.
> **Noo za-lohn dee-nay shay may grahn-pa-rahn.**
> We are going to have dinner at my grandparents.

> Ils vous parleront beaucoup de moi. Ils raconteront
> **Eel voo parl'-rohn bo-koo duh mwa. Eel ra-kohnt-rohn**
> They will talk much about me. They will tell you

> comment j'étais et tout ce que je faisais
> **ko-mahn zhay-tay ay too suh kuh zhuh fuh-zay**
> how I was and all that I was doing

> quand j'étais petit . . .
> **kahn zhay-tay puh-tee . . .**
> when I was a child . . .

LA GRAND-MÈRE:
La grahn-mair:
THE GRANDMOTHER:

> Vous savez, Richard passait tous les étés chez nous en Savoie.
> **Voo sa-vay, Ree-shar pa-say too lay zay-tay shay noo ahn Sa-vwa.**
> You know, Richard used to spend every (lit. "all the") summer with us in
> Savoy.

> C'était un beau petit garçon.
> **Say-tay tun bo puh-tee gar-sohn.**
> He was a beautiful little boy.

> Il était très intelligent
> **Eel ay-tay tray zen-tay-lee-zhan**
> He was very smart

235

mais il nous donnait du mal.
may zeel noo doh-nay du mahl.
but he used to give us trouble.

LE GRAND-PÈRE:
Luh grahn-pair:
THE GRANDFATHER:

Il partait sans dire où il allait.
Eel par-tay sahn deer oo eel ah-lay.
e used to leave without saying where he was going.

Parfois, il faisait tout seul des promenades en montagne.
Pahr-fwa, eel fuh-say too suhl day pro-muh-nahd zahn mohn-tine.
Sometimes, he would take a walk alone in the mountains.

LA GRAND-MÈRE:

Nous ne savions jamais où il pouvait être.
Noo nuh sav-yohn zha-may oo eel poo-vay tetr'.
We never knew where he could be.

Il inventait des jeux violents.
Eel en-vahn-tay day zhuh v'yo-lahn.
He used to invent violent games.

Il avait sa bande de garçons qui jouaient à la guerre
Eel ah-vay sa bahnd' duh gar-sohn kee zhoo-ay ta la gair'
He had his boys' gang who used to play war

et se jetaient des pierres et des pétards.
ay suh zhuh-tay day p'yair ay day pay-tar.
and throw stones and firecrackers at each other.

Les voisins protestaient ...
Lay vwa-zen pro-tes-tay ...
The neighbors used to protest ...

LE GRAND-PÈRE:

Au cinéma, il aimait surtout les Westerns;
Oh see-nay-ma, eel ay-may sûr-too lay Wes-tairn;
At the movies, he used to like best the Westerns;

Il voulait aller en Amérique voir les cow-boys et les peaux-rouges.
Eel voo-lay ta-lay ahn̪ na-may-reek vwar lay cow-boys ay lay po-roozh.
He wanted to go to America to see the cowboys and the redskins.

LA GRAND-MÈRE:
Mais avec nous il était toujours si affectueux.
May ah-vek noo eel ay-tay too-zhoor see ah-fek-twuh.
But with us he was always so affectionate.

Quand il est parti pour les Etats-Unis,
Kahn̪ teel ay par-tee poor lay zay-ta-zů-nee,
When he left for the United States,

nous pensions qu'il allait simplement visiter le pays
noo pahn̪s-yohn̪ keel ah-lay sen̪-pluh-mahn̪ vee-zee-tay luh pay-ee
we thought that he was simply going to visit the country

et qu'il devait bientôt revenir.
ay keel duh-vay b'yen̪-toh ruhv-neer.
and that he was to come back soon.

Nous ne savions pas naturellement
Noo nuh sahv-yohn̪ pa na-tů-rell-mahn̪
We did not know naturally

qu'il allait épouser une Américaine.
keel ah-lay-tay-poo-zay ůna-may-ree-kain̪'.
that he was going to marry an American girl.

LE GRAND-PÈRE:
Mais une Américaine très charmante.
May zůn Ah-may-ree-kain' tray shar-mahn̪t'.
But a very charming American.

Nous voulions beaucoup faire votre connaissance.
Noo vool-yohn̪ bo-koo fair vohtr' ko-nay-sahn̪s.
We wanted very much to meet you.

LA GRAND-MÈRE:
Venez, mes enfants. Le dîner est servi.
Vuh-nay, may zahn̪-fahn̪. Luh dee-nay ay sair-vee.
Come on, my children. Dinner is served.

237

La politesse
When dining at people's homes, don't forget to say — *Ceci est delicieux.* "This is delicious." Also, when you visit people, they will often say to you *Faites comme chez vous* — "Make yourself at home." A polite formula for you to use when you leave is *Je vous remercie de votre hospitalité* — "I thank you for your hospitality."

Nous avons un civet de lapin. Richard l'aimait tant
Noo za-vohṇ zun see-vay duh la-pen. Ree-shar lay-may-tahṇ
We have rabbit stew. Richard used to like so much

quand il était petit.
kahṇ teel ay-tay puh-tee.
when he was a boy.

———

ELLE:
El:
SHE:

Tiens, j'ai appris bien des choses sur toi
T'yeṇ, zhay ah-pree b'yeṇ day shohz sŭr twa
Well, I learned many things about you

Les exceptions
Generally, adverbs of quantity are followed by *de* without the article. However, there are three exceptions: *bien* "many," *encore* "still more," and *la plupart* "most." These three retain the definite article with *de*.
Encore des choses à faire — Still more things to do.

que je ne savais pas auparavant.
kuh zhuh nuh sa-vay pa oh-pa-ra-vahṇ.
that I did not know before.

Mais dis donc, est-ce que je dois apprendre à faire du civet de lapin?
May dee dohṇk, ess kuh zhuh dwa za-prahṇdr' ah fair dŭ see-vay duh la-peṇ?
But tell me then, must I learn to make rabbit stew?

TEST YOUR FRENCH

Translate the following sentences into French using the Imperfect Tense (Imparfait) in each case. Score 10 points for each correct answer. See answers below.

1. My mother always used to say . . .

   _____

2. Life was very difficult then.

   _____

3. We had relatives in town.

   _____

4. When I was young . . .

   _____

5. I used to read many books.

   _____

6. She was looking at herself in the mirror.

   _____

7. He was sleeping peacefully.

   _____

8. We never knew where he was.

   _____

9. He used to like to go to the movies.

   _____

10. We wanted so much to see that play.

   _____

Answers: 1. Ma mère disait toujours . . . 2. La vie était alors très difficile. 3. Nous avions des parents en ville. 4. Quand j'étais jeune . . . 5. Je lisais beaucoup de livres. 6. Elle se regardait dans la glace. 7. Il dormait tranquillement. 8. Nous ne savions jamais où il était. 9. Il aimait aller au cinéma. 10. Nous voulions tellement voir cette pièce.

SCORE _____%

239

step 23

HOW TO USE THE PAST PERFECT AND THE FUTURE PERFECT

L'imparfait d'*avoir* ou d'*être*
Len-par-fay da-vwar oo detr'
The imperfect of *avoir* or *être*

se combine avec le participe passé
suh kohn-been ah-vek luh par-tee-seep pa-say
combines with the past participle

pour former le plus-que-parfait.
poor fohr-may luh plǔ-kuh-par-fay.
to form the pluperfect tense.

The "pluperfect"

The *plus-que-parfait* ("the past perfect") is quite simple to form, because all you have to do is to combine the imperfect of *avoir* or *être* with the past participle of the verb. The result is equivalent to the English construction: "had gone," "had seen," "had heard," "had come," etc. To refresh your recollection about which verbs take *être* and which *avoir* to form their compound tenses, take another look at Steps 19 and 20. Here are examples for each auxiliary:

> *j'avais vu, etc.* — I had seen, etc.
> *j'étais arrivé, etc.* — I had arrived, etc.

Celui-ci sert à indiquer une action passée
Suhl-wee-see sair ah en-dee-kay ǔne aks-yohn pa-say
This one is used to refer to a past action

avant une autre action passée.
ah-vahn-tǔn ohtr' aks-yohn pa-say.
before another past action.

240

Je m'étais déjà couché
Zhuh may-tay day-zha koo-shay
I had already gone to bed

quand Victor et Marie sont arrivés avec du champagne.
kahŋ Veek-tohr ay Ma-ree sohŋ ta-ree-vay ah-vek du shaŋ-pine.
when Victor and Marie arrived with champagne.

Quand je suis arrivé à la banque
Kahŋ zhuh swee za-ree-vay ah la bahŋk
When I arrived at the bank

je me suis aperçu
zhuh muh swee za-pair-sŭ
I noticed

que j'avais perdu mon carnet de chèques.
kuh zha-vay pair-dŭ mohŋ kar-nay duh shek.
that I had lost my checkbook.

Nous avions juste fini de dîner,
Noo zav-yohŋ zhŭst fee-nee duh dee-nay,
We had just finished having supper,

mais nous étions encore à table,
may noo zet-yohŋ zahŋ-kohr ah tahbl',
but we were still at the table,

quand nous avons entendu un coup de revolver . . .
kahŋ noo za-vohŋ zahŋ-tahŋ-dŭ uŋ koo duh ray-vohl-vair . . .
when we heard a revolver shot . . .

Il paraît qu'un voleur avait cassé
Eel pa-ray kuŋ vo-lerr ah-vay ka-say
It appears that a burglar had broken

la vitrine d'un bijoutier,
la vee-treen duŋ bee-zhoot-yay,
a jeweler's shop window,

et qu'il était parti avec des bijoux;
ay keel ay-tay pahr-tee ah-vek day bee-zhoo;
and that he had left with some jewels;

mais des gens, qui l'avaient vu,
may day zhahn kee la-vay vũ,
but some people who had seen him,

avaient appelé la police,
ah-vay-tahp-lay la po-leess,
had called the police,

qui était arrivée très vite.
kee ay-tay ta-ree-vay tray veet.
who had arrived very quickly.

Comme nous sortions du restaurant,
Kohm noo sohrt-yohn dũ res-toh-rahn,
As we were coming out of the restaurant,

on nous a dit qu'on l'avait emmené au commissariat de police.
ohn noo za dee kohn la-vay tahn-muh-nay oh ko-mee-sahr-ya duh po-leess.
we were told that he had been taken to the police station.

Le coup de revolver
This small scene illustrates the relationship between the different past tenses: the imperfect sets a stage for what is going on in the past; the revolver shot happened once only at a definite time, and is therefore the regular past — *le passé composé.*

Au secours!
Speaking of emergencies, here are some key words:

Help! — *Au secours!*
Fire! — *Au feu!*
Look out! — *Attention!*
There has been an accident — *Il y a eu un accident*
Quickly! — *Vite!*

> Call an ambulance! — *Appelez une ambulance!*
> Stop, thief! — *Au voleur!*
> There he goes! — *Le voilà!*
> Police! — *Police!*
> Stop! — *Arrêtez!*
> Stop him! — *Arrêtez-le!*
> Stop her! — *Arrêtez-la!*

Comme le plus-que-parfait indique
Kohm luh plǔ-kuh pahr-fay eɲ-deek
As the past perfect indicates

une action déjà terminée au passé,
ǔn aks-yohɲ day-zha tair-mee-nay oh pa-say,
an action already finished in the past,

le futur antérieur indique une action
luh fǔ-tǔr ahɲ-tair-yerr eɲ-deek ǔne ahk-s'yohɲ
the future perfect indicates an action

> ### The future perfect
> To form the future perfect, the past participle is used with the future of *avoir* or *être,* according to which one the verb requires. The future perfect corresponds exactly to the English concept — "will have gone," "will have seen," "will have heard," "will have come," etc.

déjà terminée dans l'avenir.
day-zha tair-mee-nay dahɲ lahv-neer.
already finished in the future.

Croyez-vous qu'ils auront fini de dîner?
Krwa-yay-voo keel-zo-rohɲ fee-nee duh dee-nay?
Do you think that they will have finished having dinner?

La semaine prochaine, j'aurai reçu
La suh-main pro-shain, zho-ray ruh-sǔ
Next week, I will have received

la réponse de mes parents à ma lettre.
la ray-pohɲs' duh may pa-rahɲ ah ma lettr'.
my parent's reply to my letter.

Dites donc! Le mois prochain,
Deet dohnk! Luh mwa pro-shen,
Think of it! Next month,

ils auront terminé l'autoroute.
eel zo-rohn tair-mee-nay lo-toh-root.
they will have completed the expressway.

Le paragraphe suivant montre
Luh pa-ra-grahf swee-vahn mohntr'
The next paragraph shows

comment on emploie ce temps pour exprimer
ko-mahn tohn nahn-plwa suh tahn poor ex-pree-may
how this tense is used to express

ce qui aura eu lieu dans l'avenir.
suh kee oh-ra ü l'yuh dahn lahv'-neer.
what will have taken place in the future.

— Qu'est-ce qu'on aura découvert dans cent ans?
Kess kohn no-ra day-koo-vair dahn sahn tahn?
What will have been discovered in a hundred years?

— Sans doute bien des gens auront fait
Sahn doot b'yen day zhahn oh-rohn fay
Without a doubt many people will have taken

des voyages interplanétaires.
day vwa-yahzh en-tair-pla-nay-tair.
interplanetary trips.

Nous aurons établi des bases sur les autres planètes.
Noo zo-rohn ay-ta-blee day bahz sür lay zohtr' pla-net.
We shall have established bases on the other planets.

Les savants auront découvert
Lay sa-vahn oh-rohn day-koo-vair
Scientists will have discovered

de nouvelles sources d'alimentation.
duh noo-vel soors da-lee-mahn-tahs-yohn.
new sources of food.

Les progrès de la médecine auront prolongé encore
Lay pro-gray duh la maid-seen oh-rohn pro-lohn-zhay ahn-kor
The progress of medicine will have lengthened still more

la durée moyenne de la vie.
la du-ray mwa-yenn duh la vee.
the average span of life.

Et les ordinateurs auront complètement
Ay lay zohr-dee-na-terr oh-rohn kohn-plet-mahn
And computers will have completely

changé l'enseignement.
sahn-zhay lahn-sain-yuh-mahn.
changed teaching.

— Qui sait? Peut-être aura-t-on trouvé
Kee say? Puh-tetr' oh-ra-tohn troo-vay
Who knows? Perhaps one will have found

aussi un moyen de réduire les impôts?
oh-see un mwa-yen duh ray-dweer lay zen-po?
also a way of reducing taxes?

> **Verb patterns "réduire"**
> *Réduire* ("to reduce") is an irregular verb
> whose part participle is *réduit* and whose pre-
> sent participle is *réduisant.* Its present tense is
> the following: *je réduis, tu réduis, il (elle) réduit,
> nous réduisons, vous réduisez, ils (elles) rédui-
> sent.* Other verbs which follow this pattern in-
> clude *produire* "to produce," *introduire*, "to
> introduce," *séduire* "to charm" or "to seduce,"
> *construire* "to construct," *reconstruire* "to re-
> construct," and *détruire* "to destroy."

TEST YOUR FRENCH

Write the proper form of the Past Perfect or Future Perfect (Auxiliary and Past Participle) of the verb in parenthesis in the space underlined. Score 10 points for each correct answer. See answers below.

1. Quand je suis arrivé, ils _____ _____ _____.
      (had   already   left)

2. Mais on m'a téléphoné pour me dire qu'un agent de police l'_____
      (had
_____ dans la rue.
   found)

3. Je pensais que j'_____ _____ mon portefeuille.
      (had   lost)

4. Il est allé la voir, mais on lui a dit qu'elle _____ _____.
      (had   gone out)

5. Nous voulions faire sa connaissance parce que nous _____
      (had
_____ son dernier livre.
   read)

6. Il ne savait pas que j'_____ _____ en France.
      (had   lived in)

7. Dans quatre ans, ils _____ _____ leurs diplômes.
      (will have received)

8. Bientôt, je pense, les astronautes _____ _____ des
      (will have established)
   bases sur une autre planète.

9. Dès que (As soon as) vous _____ _____ ce livre, rendez-le
      (will have finished)
   moi.

10. Avant la semaine prochaine, il _____ _____ son chèque.
      (will have sent)

SCORE ____%

Des phrases comme:
Day frahz kohm:
Sentences like:

S'il pleut demain, nous n'irons pas à la plage.
Seel pluh duh-men, noo nee-rohn pa za la plahzh.
If it rains tomorrow, we won't go to the beach.

S'il arrive, je lui donnerai votre message.
Seel ah-reev, zhuh lwee dohn-ray vohtr' may-sahzh.
If he arrives, I'll give him your message.

sont des conditions simples.
sohn day kohn-dess-yohn senpl'.
are simple conditions.

Quelquefois, la supposition est plus évidente, comme:
Kel-kuh-fwa, la sû-po-zees-yohn ay plû zay-vee-dahnt, kohm:
Sometimes, the supposition is more evident, like:

Si vous étiez à ma place, qu'est-ce que vous feriez?
See voo zet-yay za ma plahss, kess kuh voo fur-yay?
If you were in my place, what would you do?

Si j'étais à votre place, je consulterais un avocat.
See zhet-yay ah vohtr' plahss, zhuh kohn-sûl-tray zun na-vo-ka.
If I were in your place, I would consult a lawyer.

Pour ce genre de supposition
Poor suh zhahnr duh sû-po-zees-yohn
For this kind of supposition

il faut employer l'imparfait après *si*
eel fo tahn-plwa-yay len-par-fay ah-pray *see*
we must use the imperfect after *si*

et mettre l'autre verbe au conditionnel.
ay mettr' lohtr' vairb oh kohṇ-dees-yo-nell.
and put the other verb in the conditional.

Les suppositions imaginaires
When you say ''If you were in my place'' or ''If you were I,'' you are supposing something that isn't true, and it is for this sort of condition that you use *si* with the imperfect for the ''if'' clause, and the conditional in the other.

L'histoire suivante, qui pourrait se passer
Lees-twar swee-vahṇt', kee poo-ray suh pa-say
The following story, which could take place

entre Marseillais, fait appel au conditionnel.
ahn-truh Mar-say-yay, fay ta-pell oh kohṇ-dees-yo-nell.
between people from Marseille, calls for the conditional.

The allusion to Marseille is a reference to the imaginative stories told about the well-known French anecdotal characters Marius and Olive, the typical *Marseillais*.

The adjective form of a dweller of a city usually ends in *-ais*, *-ien*, *-in*, *-ois*, and in many other ways, while the feminine endings are *-aise*, *-ienne*, *-ine*, and *-oise*. In general, these endings must be learned by practice, since every city and village has its own form.

— Si vous étiez à la chasse en Afrique
See voo-zet-yay za la shahs ahṇ na-freek
If you were hunting in Africa

et que vous rencontriez un lion, que feriez-vous?
ay kuh voo rahṇ-kohṇ-tree-ay zun lee-ohṇ, kuh fur-yay voo?
and you met a lion, what would you do?

— Si je rencontrais un lion, je le tuerais avec mon fusil.
See zhuh rahṇ-kohṇ-tray zuṇ lee-ohṇ, zhuh luh tǔ-ray za-vek mohṇ
                                                              fǔ-zee.
If I met a lion, I would kill him with my rifle.

— Et si vous n'aviez pas de fusil?
Ay see voo nav-yay pa duh fǔ-zee?
And if you didn't have a rifle?

— Si je n'avais pas de fusil, je me servirais de mon sabre.
See zhuh na-vay pa duh fŭ-zee, zhuh muh sair-vee-ray duh mohṇ sahbr'.
If I didn't have a rifle, I would use my saber.

— Et si vous n'aviez pas de sabre?
Ay see voo nav-yay pa duh sahbr'?
And if you didn't have a saber?

— Si je n'en avais pas, je grimperais sur un arbre.
See zhuh nahṇ na-vay pa, zhuh greṇ-puh-ray sŭr uṇ nahbr'.
If I didn't have any, I would climb up a tree.

— Et s'il n'y avait pas d'arbre tout près?
Ay seel nee ya-vay pa dahbr' too pray?
And if there were no tree near at hand?

— S'il n'y avait pas d'arbre tout près,
Seel nee ya-vay pa dahbr' too pray,
If there were no tree near at hand,

je courrais le plus vite possible.
zhuh koorray luh plŭ veet po-seebl'.
I'd run as fast as possible.

— Hm . . . je crois que le lion vous rattraperait facilement.
Uhm . . . zhuh crwa kuh luh lee-ohṇ voo rat-tra-puh-ray fa-seel-mahṇ.
Hm . . . I think that the lion would catch up with you easily.

— Mais dites donc, vous! Êtes-vous de mon côté
May deet dohṇk, voo! Ett-voo duh mohṇ ko-tay
Now you look here! Are you on my side

Dites donc
Dites donc is literally ''say, then'' but is really a
conversational stop for calling attention. The
repetition of *vous* gives a note of remonstrance.

ou êtes-vous du côté du lion?
oo ett-voo du ko-tay du lee-ohṇ?
or are you on the side of the lion?

Il y a encore des suppositions
Eel ee ya ahṇ-kohr day su-po-zees-yohṇ
There are other suppositions

qui se rapportent à des choses qui ne se sont jamais passées.
kee se ra-pohrt' ah day shohz' kee nuh suh sohn̈ zha-may pa-say
which refer to things that never happened.

Si Napoléon avait conquis la Russie,
See Na-po-lay-ohn̈ ah-vay kohn̈-kee la Rů-see,
If Napoleon had conquered Russia,

le cours de l'histoire aurait été très différent.
luh koor duh lees-twar oh-ray tay-tay tray dee-fay-rahn̈.
the course of history would have been very different.

Si Lafayette n'avait pas aidé Washington,
See La-fa-yett na-vay pa zay-day Va-shin̈g-ton,
If Lafayette had not helped Washington,

est-ce que les Américains
ess-kuh lay za-may-ree-ken̈
would the Americans

auraient obtenu leur indépendance quand même?
oh-ray ob-tuh-nů lerr en̈-day-pahn̈-dahn̈s kahn̈ mem?
have obtained their independence anyway?

Things that never happened
There is an even more pronounced supposition referring to things that never happened, such as wondering how things would have been had other things never happened, or happened, as the case may be.

The above examples illustrate this, as Napoleon, to his sorrow, never conquered Russia, while Lafayette, aided by Rochambeau, (who seldom gets credit,) definitely *did* help the struggling colonists. In such cases, the past perfect is used with *si*, while the conditional perfect is used in the other clause, that is the conditional of *être* or *avoir* with the past participle. Compound tenses are really quite easy, inasmuch as you already know the past participles as well as the forms of *avoir* and *être*, which combine with them to express certain concepts.

INSTANT CONVERSATION:
WHAT WOULD YOU DO IF YOU WON
THE LOTTERY?

— Que feriez-vous si vous gagniez
Kuh fur-yay-voo see voo gahn-yay
What would you do if you won

le gros lot à la Loterie Nationale?
luh gro lo ah la Loht-ree Nahs-yo-nahl?
the big prize in the National Lottery?

— Tout d'abord, on déménagerait
Too da-bohr, ohn day-may-nahzh-ray
The very first thing, we would move

dans une maison plus grande.
dahn zŭne may-zohn plŭ grahnd'.
to a bigger house.

Cela ferait plaisir à ma femme.
Suh-la fur-ray play-zeer ah ma fahm.
That would please my wife.

Ensuite j'achèterais une nouvelle voiture.
Ahn-sweet, zha-shet-ray zŭn noo-vell vwa-tŭr.
Then I would buy a new car.

Cela me ferait plaisir à moi.
Suh-la muh fuh-ray play-zeer ah mwa.
That would please me.

Puis nous ferions un voyage dans le Midi,*
Pwee noo fur-yohn zun vwa-yahzh dahn luh Mee-dee,
Then we would take a trip to the Midi,

* *The south of France.*

et nous rendrions visite à mes parents.
ay noo rahn-dree-ohn vee-zeet ah may pa-rahn.
and we would visit my parents.

Je leur offrirais des machines modernes pour leurs vignobles,
Zhuh lerr oh-free-ray day ma-sheen' mo-dairn' poor lerr veen-yohbl',
I would offer them some modern machinery for their vineyards,

et ainsi ils doubleraient leurs bénéfices
ay en-see eel doo-bluh-ray lerr bay-nay-fees
and they therefore would be able to double their profits

et ils n'auraient pas à travailler si dur.
ay eel no-ray pa za tra-va-yay see dûr.
and they wouldn't have to work so hard.

— Et après ça, qu'est-ce que vous feriez?
Ay ah-pray sa, kess kuh voo fur-yay?
And after that, what would you do?

Continueriez-vous à travailler?
Kohn-tee-nûr-yay voo za tra-va-yay?
Would you continue to work?

> **Verbs followed by ''à''**
> *Continuer* is followed by à when used in conjunction with a second verb. Other verbs that use à this way include:
>
> | | |
> |---|---|
> | *apprendre à* | — to learn (to) |
> | *consentir à* | — to consent (to) |
> | *commencer à* | — to begin (to) |
> | *réussir à* | — to succeed (in) |
> | *hésiter à* | — to hesitate (to) |
> | *aider à* | — to help (to) |
> | *inviter à* | — to invite (to) |
> | *chercher à* | — to try (to) |

— Bien sûr! Il faudrait travailler.
B'yen sûr! Eel fo-dray tra-va-yay.
Of course! One would have to work.

L'argent de la loterie ne durerait pas toujours.
Lahr-zahn duh la loht-ree nuh dû-ruh-ray pa too-zhoor.
The lottery money wouldn't last forever.

— Mais ce serait agréable tant qu'il durerait, pas vrai?
May, suh suh-ray-ta-gray-ahbl' tahn keel dů-ruh-ray, pa vray?
But it would be nice while it would last, not so?

— D'accord. Sortons maintenant pour acheter un billet.
Da-kohr. Sohr-tohn ment-nahn poor ash-tay un bee-yay.
Agreed. Let's go out now to buy a ticket.

(La semaine suivante)
(La suh-main' swee'vahnt)
(The following week)

— Ah, je n'ai pas de veine! Je n'ai rien gagné du tout.
Ah! zhuh nay pa duh vain! Zhuh nay r'yen gahn-yay dů too.
Ah, I have no luck! I didn't win anything at all.

— De toute façon, si vous aviez gagné,
Duh toot fa-sohn, see voo zav-yay gahn-yay,
Anyway, if you had won,

vous auriez tout dépensé.
voo-zohr-yay too day-pahn-say.
you would have spent all of it.

— Peut-être, mais du moins j'aurais eu le plaisir de l'avoir dépensé.
Puh-tetr', may dů mwen zho-ray-zů luh play-zeer duh la-vwar
day-pahn-say.
Perhaps, but at least I would have had the pleasure of having
spent it.

"Avoir" + the past participle
Here is an example of the infinitive of *avoir* with
the past participle. Compare:

> I'm happy to do it. —
> *Je suis content de le faire.*
> I'm happy to have done it. —
> *Je suis content de l'avoir fait.*

TEST YOUR FRENCH

Translate the following simple conditions. Score 10 points for each correct answer. See answers below.

1. If he comes, I'll tell him.

2. If it snows, I won't go.

3. If you wish, I'll do it.

Translate the following using the imperfect and the conditional

4. If I were in your place, I would not do it.

5. If we were free today, we would accompany you. (accompagner)

6. If he met a lion, he would run as fast as possible.

7. What (Que) would he do if he won?

8. If you had a lot of money would you continue to work?

9. What (Que) would you do the very first thing?

10. I would buy a pearl necklace (un collier de perles) for my wife.

SCORE _____%

step 25   HOW TO USE THE SUBJUNCTIVE

On emploie le subjonctif après le mot *que,*
Ohn nahn-plwa luh sŭb-zhohnk-teef ah-pray luh mo *kuh*
The subjunctive is used after the word *que,*

The subjunctive mood
The subjunctive is not a tense but a mood which includes several tenses. In the following examples of the principal verb groups, you will find the subjunctive endings for the present.

First conjugation: parler
> *que je parle*
> *que tu parles*
> *qu'il parle*
> *que nous parlions*
> *que vous parliez*
> *qu'ils parlent*

Second conjugation:

finir	partir
que je finisse	*que je parte*
que tu finisses	*que tu partes*
qu'il finisse	*qu'il parte*
que nous finissions	*que nous partions*
que vous finissiez	*que vous partiez*
qu'ils finissent	*qu'ils partent*

Third conjugation:

rendre	recevoir
que je rende	*que je reçoive*
que tu rendes	*que tu reçoives*
qu'il rende	*qu'il reçoive*
que nous rendions	*que nous recevions*
que vous rendiez	*que vous receviez*
qu'ils rendent	*qu'ils reçoivent*

quand on veut ou désire qu'une autre personne
kahn tohn vuh oo day-zeer kûne no-truh pair-sohn
when one wishes or desires that another person

fasse quelque chose.
fahs kel-kuh shohz.
do something.

Je voudrais que vous acceptiez mon invitation.
Zhuh voo-dray kuh voo zak-sept-yay mohn nen-vee-tahs-yohn.
I would like you to accept (or, that you accept) my invitation.

Il veut que nous revenions demain.
Eel vuh kuh noo ruh-vuhn-yohn duh-men.
He wants us to come back (or, that we come back) tomorrow.

You must keep the "that"
The reason the subjunctive is important in French is because you must use it in places where, in English, you can use the infinitive as in expressions such as "I want him to come," which changes when translated to "I want that he come." In fact, to express anything that you want, desire or wish another person to do (or vice versa), you must use the subjunctive. The key word of the subjunctive is *que*, which functions as a signal indicating that the following verb must be in the subjunctive. This *que*, of course, only indicates the subjunctive where it is necessary, namely in the second verb after expressions of wish, doubt, emotion, uncertainty, and after certain conjunctions.

Notez le subjonctif dans des phrases exprimant des émotions,
No-tay luh sub-zohn-teef dahn day frahz ex-pree-mahn day zay-mohs-yohn,
Note the subjunctive in sentences expressing emotion,

ou des sentiments, après le mot *que*.
oo day sahn-tee-mahn, ah-pray luh mo *kuh*.
or sentiments, after the word *that*.

Je suis content que vous soyez ici,

Zhuh swee kohn-tahṇ kuh voo swa-yay zee-see,

I am happy that you are here,

mais je regrette que votre femme soit malade.

may zhuh ruh-grett kuh vohtr' fahm swa ma-lahd.

but I regret that your wife is sick.

The first form gives the key

The present subjunctive of *être* and *avoir* are irregular. Here they are:

être	avoir
que je sois	*que j'aie*
que tu sois	*que tu aies*
qu'il soit	*qu'il ait*
que nous soyons	*que nous ayons*
que vous soyez	*que vous ayez*
qu'ils soient	*qu'ils aient*

You should familiarize yourself with the first person subjunctive of the following irregular verbs as it gives the key to the other forms:

aller	*— que j'aille*
savoir	*— que je sache*
venir	*— que je vienne*
dire	*— que je dise*
pouvoir	*— que je puisse*
vouloir	*— que je veuille*
faire	*— que je fasse*

Oui, c'est dommage qu'elle n'ait pas pu venir,

Wee, say doh-mahzh kel nay pa pǔ vuh-neer,

Yes, it's a pity that she couldn't come,

The past in the subjunctive

Note the difference between "It's a pity she can't come" — *C'est dommage qu'elle ne puisse pas venir,* and "It's a pity she couldn't come" — *C'est dommage qu'elle n'ait pas pu venir.* The second example is in the past subjunctive, which is formed by the present of *avoir* plus the past participle, or by the present of *être,* if it is a verb that takes *être.*

mais le médecin ne veut pas qu'elle sorte.
may luh maid-sen nuh vuh pa kel sohrt'.
but the doctor doesn't want her to go out.

On emploie le subjonctif avec *il faut que:*
Oh ah-plwa luh sŭb-zhohnk-teef ah-vek *eel fo kuh:*
One uses the subjunctive with *it is necessary that* (or *must*):

Il faut que je lui parle.
Eel fo kuh zhuh lwee pahrl.
I must speak to him.

Il faut que vous visitiez Fontainebleau.
Eel foh kuh voo vee-zeet-yay Fohn-tain-blo.
You must visit Fontainebleau.

Il faut que nous partions maintenant.
Eel foh kuh noo pahrt-yohn ment-nahn.
We must go now.

Le subjonctif s'emploie après d'autres expressions
Luh sŭb-zhohnk-teef sahn-plwa ah-pray dohtr' zex-press-yohn
The subjunctive is used after other expressions

indiquant la nécessité et après certaines conjonctions.
en-dee-kahn la nay-say-see-tay ay ah-pray sair-tain kohn-zhohnks-yohn.
indicating necessity and after certain conjunctions.

— Il vaudrait mieux qu'on nous réveille à sept heures,
Eel vo-drai m'yuh kohn noo ray-vay ah set err,
It would be better that they call us at seven o'clock,

pour que nous ayons le temps de faire nos valises.
poor kuh noo zay-yohn luh tahn duh fair no va-leez.
so that we may have the time to pack our bags.

Il est important que nous arrivions
Eel ay ten-por-tahn kuh noo za-reev-yohn
It is important that we arrive

une heure en avance, car
ŭn err ah na-vahnss, kahr
one hour ahead of time, because

avant que nous puissions monter en avion,
ah-vahn̦ kuh noo pwees-yohn̦ mohn̦-tay ahn̦ nahv-yohn̦,
before we can get on the plane,

il faut qu'on fasse peser les bagages
eel fo kohn̦ fahss puh-zay lay ba-gahzh
we have to have the luggage weighed

et il est nécessaire qu'on examine les billets et passeports.
ay eel ay nay-sess-sair ko-neg-za-meen lay bee-yay ay pahss-por.
and it is necessary to check the tickets and passports.

— Pourquoi se presser? Il y aura bien un autre avion.
Poor-kwa suh press-say? Eel ee yo-ra b'yen̦ un̦ nohtr' av-yon̦.
Why hurry? There will be another plane.

— Je ne crois pas que nous puissions
Zhuh nuh crwa pa kuh noo pwees'yohn̦
I don't think that we will be able

changer nos réservations.
shahn̦-zhay no ray-zair-vahss-yohn̦.
to change our reservations.

D'ailleurs, autant que je sache,
Da-yerr, oh-tahn̦ kuh zhuh sash,
Moreover, as far as I know,

c'est le seul vol direct.
say luh suhl vohl dee-rekt.
it's the only direct flight.

INSTANT CONVERSATION:
THE GENERATION GAP

LE PÈRE:
La pair:
THE FATHER:

> Ca m'ennuie que Maurice n'ait pas
> **Sa mahn-nwee kuh Mo-reess nay pa**
> It bothers me that Maurice does not have
>
> de meilleures notes en classe.
> **duh may-yerr not ahn klahss.**
> better grades in class.
>
> J'ai peur qu'il ne puisse pas
> **Zhay puhr keel nuh pweess pa**
> I am afraid that he cannot
>
> réussir à ses examens.
> **ray-ŭ-seer ah say zeg-za-men.**
> pass his examinations.
>
> Il ne faut pas qu'il sorte si souvent
> **Eel nuh fo pa keel sohrt see soo-vahn**
> He must not go out so often
>
> ni qu'il aille trop au cinéma.
> **nee keel eye tro po see-nay-ma.**
> nor go too much to the movies.

LA MÈRE:
LA MARE:
THE MOTHER:

> Mais il faut tout de même bien qu'il s'amuse, cet enfant.
> **Ma, zeel fo tood maim b'yen keel sa-mŭz, set ahn-fahn.**
> But he still must have some fun, the (poor) child.

LE PÈRE:

Quoi qu'il en soit, je tiens à ce qu'il fasse de sérieux efforts
Kwa keel ahɳ swa, zhuh t'yeɳ-za suh keel fahss duh sair-yuh zay-fohr
However that may be, I want him to make some serious efforts

> **Special "subjunctive" expressions**
> However, whenever, whoever, and like con-
> structions also must be followed by the
> subjunctive:
> > Whatever may happen. — *Quoi qu'il arrive.*

et qu'il obtienne de meilleures notes.
ay keel obt-yenn duh may-yerr not.
and that he gets better grades.

LA MÈRE:

Personnellement, je ne pense pas que
Pair-so-nell-mahɳ, zhuh nuh pahɳs pa kuh
Personally, I do not think that

ses notes soient insuffisantes.
say not swa teɳ-sŭ-fee-zahɳt'.
his grades are inadequate.

Pourvu qu'il travaille un peu plus
Poor-vŭ keel trahv-eye uɳ puh plŭ
Provided he works a little more

et qu'on le laisse tranquille, tout ira bien.
ay kohɳ luh less trahɳ-keel, too tee-ra b'yeɳ.
and that he is left alone, all will go well

LE PÈRE:

Eh bien non. Je n'admets pas qu'il ait d'aussi mauvaises notes,
Ay b'yeɳ nohɳ. Zhuh nahd-may pa keel ay-doh-see mo-vayz noht,
Absolutely not. I won't allow him to have such bad grades,

ni qu'il soit si paresseux.
nee keel swa see pa-ray-suh.
nor that he be so lazy.

Qu'il vienne me voir. J'ai à lui parler.
Keel v'yehn muh vwar. Zhay ah lwee pahr-lay.
Let him come to see me. I have to talk to him.

261

When the subjunctive is used by itself — with the third person — it has the sense of "let ...!"

Let him leave! — Qu'il parte!

LA MÈRE:

Maurice, ton père veut que tu ailles le voir tout de suite.
Mo-rees, tohn pair vuh kuh tŭ eye luh vwar tood sweet.
Maurice, your father wants you to go and see him right now.

Don't forget "tu"

Although we have given the form for *tu* in the different tenses and roots, it is not used very often in the dialogues, as the *vous* form is much more useful to you as a student of French. Here, however, it is the natural form for mother and son to use when they speak to each other.

LA MÈRE:

Je crains qu'il ne soit en colère.
Zhuh cren keel nuh swa ahn ko-lair.
I am afraid he is angry.

MAURICE:

Oui, je sais ce qu'il va me dire.
Wee, zhuh say suh keel vam' deer.
Yes, I know what he is going to tell me.

Il me dira ce qu'il veut que je fasse,
Eel muh dee-ra suh keel vuh kuh zhuh fahss,
He will tell me what he wants me to do,

ce qu'il faut que je fasse dans la vie,
suh keel fo kuh zhuh fahss dahn la vee,
what I must do with my life,

la profession qu'il veut que je choisisse . . .
la pro-fess-yohn keel vuh kuh zhuh shwa-zeess . . .
the profession that he wants me to choose . . .

Et comme moi, je veux être directeur de films,
Ay kohm mwa, zhuh vuh zetr' dee-rek-terr duh feelm,
And since I, I want to be a film director,

Je ne veux pas qu'on s'occupe de mes affaires
Zhuh nuh vuh pa kohn̦ so-kũp duh may za-fair
I don't want anybody to interfere with my business

et je ne veux pas qu'on m'embête.
ay zhuh nuh vuh pa kohn̦ mahn̦-bet.
and I don't want people to bother me.

LA MÈRE:

Mais, Maurice, tu sais bien que ton père
May, Mo-rees, tu sas b'yen̦ kuh tohn̦ pair
But, Maurice, you know well that your father

veut faire pour le mieux pour ton frère et pour toi.
vuh fair poor luh m'yuh poor tohn̦ frair ay poor twa.
wants to do the best for your brother and yourself.

Il veut que vous finissiez vos études,
Eel vuh kuh voo fee-neess-yay vo zay-tũd,
He wants you to finish college,

que vous ayez des diplômes,
kuh voo zay-yay day dee-plohm,
that you get degrees,

qu'Edouard devienne médecin comme son grand-père
kay-dwar duh-v'yenn maid-sen̦ kohm sohn̦ grahn̦-pair
that Edward become a physician like his grandfather

et que tu sois avocat comme lui.
ay kuh tũ swa za-vo-ka kohm lwee.
and that you be a lawyer like him.

MAURICE:

Et voilà! Entre ce qu'il veut que je fasse,
Ay vwa-la! Ahn̦tr' suh keel vuh kuh zhuh fahss,
Here we are! Between what he wants me to do,

et ce que moi j'ai envie de faire,
ay suh kuh mwa zhay ahn-vee duh fair,
and what I do want to do,

Relative phrases
Remember the uses of these relative phrases.

Ce qui — That which, what (subject)
Ce que — That which, what (object)
Ce dont — That of which (what), That about
which, (what)

What I want is . . . — *Ce que je veux,
c'est . . .*
What I spoke about — *Ce dont j'ai parlé*
What is important in this matter is
— *Ce qui est   important dans cette affaire,
c'est . . .*

il y a un abîme.
eel ee ya un na-beem.
there is an abyss.

Qu'il cesse de m'embêter!
Keel sess duh mohn-bet-tay!
Let him stop annoying me!

LA MÈRE:

Ciel! Que la vie était différente
S'yel! Kuh la vee ay-tay dee-fay-rahnt'
Heavens! How different life was

quand j'étais jeune. On ne parlait jamais
kahn zhay-tay zhuhn. Ohn nuh par-lay zha-may
when I was young. One never spoke

comme ça à ses parents.
kohm sa ah say pa-rahn.
like that to one's parents.

Imperfect
Note how the mother, in her aside, shifts to the
imperfect, which is the tense that is used to
speak of things that were, or used to be.

Emotions — and a short cut

The emotional scene you have just examined includes most of the constructions, many concerned with emotions or wishes, which require the use of the subjunctive. While knowledge of the subjunctive is essential for a complete grasp of French, it is frequently possible "to get around it," especially in the case of *il faut,* by using the infinitive. *Il faut partir,* for example, could mean "I, you, she, he, we, they must leave," depending on the context. Also, although the imperfect subjunctive exists, it is rarely used in conversation, and the present is used instead.

He wanted me to come. — *Il voulait que je vienne.*

TEST YOUR FRENCH

PART I — Fill in the blank with the correct subjunctive form of the verb given in parenthesis. Score 10 points for each correct answer. See answers below.

1. Il faut que nous (partir) _____.

2. Elle est contente que vous (être) _____ ici.

3. Avant que vous ne (quitter) _____ la France, il faut voir Versailles.

4. Il est important qu'il le (savoir) _____.

5. Je veux qu'il (venir) _____ me voir.

PART II — Read the last dialogue about Maurice and answer the following questions by checking True or False. Score 10 points for each correct answer. See answers below.

	Vrai (True)	Faux (False)
6. Le père de Maurice veut que son fils devienne architecte.	( )	( )
7. Maurice a déjà obtenu son diplôme.	( )	( )
8. Le père et le fils sont d'accord sur la carrière de Maurice.	( )	( )
9. Maurice a bien travaillé cette année.	( )	( )
10. Son père veut qu'il obtienne de meilleures notes.	( )	( )

Answers: 1. partions 2. soyez 3. quittiez 4. sache 5. vienne 6. F 7. F 8. F 9. F 10. T

SCORE _____%

step 26 HOW TO READ FRENCH

Voilà quelques conseils pour faciliter
Here is some advice to make easier

vos lectures en français.
your reading in French.

Dans la correspondance commerciale
In business correspondence

vous trouverez souvent
you will often find

qu'on emploie le conditionnel et le subjonctif.
that the conditional and the subjunctive are used.

Par exemple:
For example:

Cher Monsieur:
Dear Sir:

Nous voudrions que vous nous fassiez parvenir
We would appreciate your sending us

le plut tôt possible la marchandise
as soon as possible the merchandise

que nous avons commandée.
that we ordered.

Il faudrait que nous la recevions
It would be necessary for us to receive it

avant la fin de novembre.
before the end of November.

Si vous étiez dans l'impossibilité d'expédier
Should you be unable to ship

267

cette marchandise, nous vous serions reconnaissants
this merchandise, we would be grateful

de nous le faire savoir par retour du courrier,
your letting us know by return mail,

car nous devrions alors nous adresser
for we would then have to apply

sans délai à un autre fournisseur.
without delay to another supplier.

Veuillez agréer, cher Monsieur, l'assurance
Please accept, my dear sir, the assurance

de notre parfaite considération.
of our highest regard.

Letter endings

French greetings at the end of a business letter tend to be rather long, the echo, perhaps, of a more polite epoch. In a personal letter, one can end with "cordially" or "sincerely," by saying *meilleures amitiés, bien cordialement,* or *bien à vous.*

Quand vous lisez les journaux, vous vous apercevrez
When you read newspapers, you will notice

qu'on emploie surtout le présent et le passé.
that the present and the past are mostly used.

"Le président de la République a fait un discours hier à Rennes
"The President of the Republic made a speech in Rennes yesterday

qui a été fort applaudi. Il a terminé par ces mots:
which was greatly applauded. He finished with these words:

Mes chers concitoyens,
My dear fellow citizens,

je suis sûr que nous sommes d'accord
I am sure that we are in agreement

pour nous féliciter des progrès qui ont été accomplis."
to congratulate ourselves on the progress that has been accomplished."

En lisant les livres, toutefois,
In reading books, however,

on découvre un autre temps des verbes: le passé défini.
one discovers another verb tense: the definite past.

Ce temps est employé presque uniquement
This tense is used almost solely

dans la littérature.
in literature.

A literary tense: le passé simple
You should learn to recognize *le passé défini* "the past definite," or *le passé simple* "the simple past," as it is often called, because you will need it when you read French books. Here are the endings for the three conjugations.

donner	finir
je donnai	*je finis*
tu donnas	*tu finis*
il donna	*il finit*
nous donnâmes	*nous finîmes*
vous donnâtes	*vous finîtes*
ils donnèrent	*ils finirent*

rendre	recevoir
je rendis	*je reçus*
tu rendis	*tu reçus*
il rendit	*il reçut*
nous rendîmes	*nous reçûmes*
vous rendîtes	*vous reçûtes*
ils rendirent	*ils reçurent*

Here are the forms for the past definite of

être	and	avoir
je fus		*j'eus*
tu fus		*tu eus*
il fut		*il eut*
nous fûmes		*nous eûmes*
vous fûtes		*vous eûtes*
ils furent		*ils eurent*

The first forms for some of the most important
irregular verbs are as follows:
Those that end in -is:

faire	— *je fis*
dire	— *je dis*
prendre	— *je pris*

Those that end in -us:

vouloir	— *je voulus*
pouvoir	— *je pus*
savoir	— *je sus*
devoir	— *je dus*
taire	— *je tus*

Voilà un exemple
Here is an example

du passé défini employé avec d'autres temps.
of the past definite past used with other tenses.

Pendant le régne de Louis XIV
During the reign of Louis XIV

l'ambassadeur d'un petit état allemand
the ambassador from a small German state

allait être présenté à la cour de France.
was about to be presented to the French court.

Comme il ne parlait pas bien le français
As he did not speak French well

on lui donna un interprète.
he was given an interpreter.

Alors, quand il fut présenté à Sa Majesté Louis XIV
So, when he was presented to His Majesty, Louis XIV

l'ambassadeur parla d'abord en allemand
the ambassador spoke first in German

puis il se tut et laissa la parole à l'interprète.
then fell silent and left the word to the interpreter.

Celui-ci fit un noble discours
The latter made a noble speech

plein d'allusions à la grandeur du Roi Soleil.
full of allusions to the greatness of the Sun King.

Quand il cessa de parler,
When he stopped speaking,

l'ambassadeur le prit à part et lui dit:
the ambassador took him aside and said to him:

"J'ai compris votre traduction
"I understood your translation

mais ce n'était pas du tout ce que j'avais dit."
however, it wasn't at all what I had said."

"Non, Monseigneur, répondit l'interprète,
"No, my lord, replied the interpreter,

ce n'est pas ce que vous avez dit
it wasn't what you said

mais c'est bien ce que vous auriez dû dire."
but it was certainly what you ought to have said."

N'hesitez pas à lire les grandes oeuvres littéraires françaises,
Don't hesitate to read the great French literary works,

non seulement pour améliorer votre français,
not only to improve your French,

mais pour le plaisir et l'amusement que vous y trouverez.
but for the pleasure and amusement that you will find in them.

Notez comment la scène suivante,
Note how the following scene,

choisie du grand maître Molière,
chosen from the great master Molière,

est facile à comprendre.
is easy to understand.

LE MAÎTRE DE PHILOSOPHIE:
THE MASTER OF PHILOSOPHY:

Sont-ce des vers que vous lui voulez écrire?
Are they verses that you want to write to her?

MONSIEUR JOURDAIN:
> Non, non point de vers.
> No, no verses.

LE MAÎTRE:
> Vous ne voulez que de la prose?
> You want only prose?

M. JOURDAIN:
> Non, je ne veux ni prose ni vers.
> No, I want neither prose nor verse.

LE MAÎTRE:
> Il faut bien que ce soit l'un ou l'autre.
> It must be one or the other.

M. JOURDAIN:
> Pourquoi?
> Why?

LE MAÎTRE:
> Par la raison, monsieur, qu'il n'y a,
> For the reason, monsieur, that there is only,
>
> pour s'exprimer, que la prose ou les vers.
> to express oneself, prose or verse.

M. JOURDAIN:
> Il n'y a que la prose ou les vers?
> There is only prose or verse?

LE MAÎTRE:
> Non, monsieur. Tout ce qui n'est point
> No, monsieur. Everything which isn't
>
> prose est vers, et tout ce qui n'est point
> prose is verse, and everything which isn't
>
> vers est prose.
> verse is prose.

M. JOURDAIN:
> Et comme l'on parle, qu'est-ce que c'est donc que cela?
> And when one speaks, what's that then?

LE MAÎTRE:

De la prose.

Prose.

M. JOURDAIN:

Quoi! quand je dis: Nicole, apportez-moi
What! when I say: Nicole, bring me

mes pantoufles, et me donnez mon bonnet de nuit,
my slippers and give me my night cap,

c'est de la prose?
that's prose?

LE MAÎTRE:

Oui, monsieur.
Yes, monsieur.

M. JOURDAIN:

Par ma foi, il y a plus de quarante ans
By my faith, for more than forty years

que je dis de la prose, sans
then I've been saying prose without

que j'en susse rien; et je vous suis
knowing anything about it; and I am

Even though the selection from Molière was written hundreds of years ago, you will note that the only word that would present any difficulty to you as a student would be the imperfect subjunctive of *savoir* — *je susse*, which is no longer used in conversation anyway. To help you recognize this construction in literature, remember that it uses the same base as the past definite, with the result that the imperfect ending for the first person of the type verbs *parler, finir, rendre* and *recevoir* are *que je parlasse, que je finisse, que je rendisse* and *que je reçusse*, and follow with the regular endings except that the third person singular ends with *-ât, -ît,* or *-ût.*

le plus obligé du monde
the most obliged person in the world to you

de m'avoir appris cela.
for having taught me that.

Tout ce que vous lisez en français,
Everything that you read in French,

que ce soit des pièces, des romans,
whether it is plays, novels,

des livres d'histoire ou d'art,
books of history or art,

augmentera votre connaissance du français
will increase your knowledge of French

et sera une inépuisable source de distraction.
and will be an inexhaustible source of entertainment.

Pourtant, le plus important, c'est de parler
However, the most important thing is to speak

et d'entendre parler les autres, parce que,
and to listen to others speak, because,

pour bien apprendre une langue,
to learn a language well,

il faut la pratiquer à toute occasion.
one must practice it at every opportunity.

UN DERNIER MOT

While you have learned up to now the essential elements for speaking and understanding French, you will encounter, when reading French books, magazines, and newspapers, many words not included in this book. You will be aided, however, in your understanding and use of new words by the fact that more than 40% of all English words are French in origin and will therefore be easy for you to use, especially since you already know how to pronounce French syllables.

The reason for the existence of so many basic French words in English goes back to the Norman conquest of England in 1066 and the fact that the rulers — and eventually the ruled — communicated in French. When English surfaced again, it was not the same as before, as it contained a host of French words, and, even though their pronunciation is different in English, many thousands of these words, happily for students of French, are still with us.

When you read French, therefore, do not use the dictionary, except in rare cases. Let the meaning and construction become evident to you through context and your own intuition — And above all, read *aloud* at every chance you get. One good plan is for you to read French material onto cassettes, or copy spoken material in your own voice and compare your entries from day to day. As you progress, you will be surprised at how soon it will sound as if French were your own language, or at least a very well acquired one.

DICTIONARY
ENGLISH — FRENCH

This dictionary contains numerous words not in the preceding text, but which will complete your ability to use current French. It is an interesting linguistic fact that most people use less than 2,000 words in their daily conversation in any language. In this dictionary, you have over 2,600 words chosen especially for frequency of use.

N.B.   1. Masculine and feminine gender of nouns is shown by (*m*) or (*f*) after the noun.

2. Nouns usually form the plural in *s*. When *x* is used for the plural, it is so indicated.

3. Adjectives must agree in number and gender with the nouns they describe. Adjectives are given in the masculine form, while the feminine ending is shown as *-e,* or other feminine endings according to the word, such as *-ère, -ille, -euse, -ienne, -aise,* etc. When adjectives remain the same for masculine and feminine, no alternate form is given.

4. Only the most important adverbs are given. But remember that most adjectives become adverbs by adding *-ment* to the feminine form of the adjective.
Adjective: *heureux — happy*
Adverb: *heureusement — happily*

5. When a choice of meaning is approximately equal between two frequently used words or expressions, both are given, separated by a comma. This will help to increase your comprehension of the words you will hear or see in French.

A

a, an   un, (*m*) une (*f*)
about (*concerning*)   concernant
about (*approximately*)   environ
absent   absent (*m*), -e (*f*)
above   au-dessus de
absolutely   absolument
accent   accent (*m*)
(*to*) accept   accepter
accident   accident (*m*)
account   compte (*m*)
across   à travers
actor   acteur (*m*)
actress   actrice (*f*)
(*to*) add   ajouter
address   adresse (*f*)
(*to*) admire   admirer
adjective   adjectif (*m*)
(*to*) advance   avancer
adventure   aventure (*f*)
advertisement   annonce (*f*)
adverb   adverbe (*m*)
advice   conseil (*m*)
(*to be*) afraid   avoir peur
Africa   Afrique (*f*)
after   après

afternoon   après-midi (*m*)
again   encore
against   contre
age   âge (*m*)
agency   agence (*f*)
agent   agent (*m*)
ago   il y a
agreeable   agréable
agreed   entendu
ahead   en avant
air   air (*m*)
(*by*) air mail   par avion
airplane   avion (*m*)
airport   aéroport (*m*)
all   tout
that's all   c'est tout
(*to*) allow   permettre
all right   très bien
almost   presque
alone   seul
alphabet   alphabet (*m*)
already   déjà
also   aussi
always   toujours
ambulance   ambulance (*f*)
America   Amérique (*f*)
American   américain (*m*), -e (*f*)

among parmi
amount montant (*m*)
amusing amusant (*m*), -e (*f*)
and et
angel ange (*m*)
angry fâché
animal animal (*m*)
ankle cheville (*f*)
anniversary anniversaire (*m*)
annoying ennuyeux (*m*), -euse (*f*)
another un autre (*m*), une autre (*f*)
answer réponse
(*to*) **answer** répondre
ant fourmi (*f*)
any (*adj.*) quelque
any (*pronoun*) du, de la, de l', des, de —, en
anyone quelqu'un (*m*)
anyhow de toute façon
anything quelque chose
anywhere n'importe où
apartment appartement (*m*)
appetite appétit (*m*)
apple pomme (*f*)
appointment rendez-vous (*m*)
(*to*) **appreciate** apprécier
April avril (*m*)
Arab, Arabic Arabe (*m & f*)
architect architecte (*m*)
architecture architecture (*f*)
arm bras (*m*)
army armée (*f*)
(*to*) **arrest** arrêter
(*to*) **arrive** arriver
art art (*m*)
article article (*m*)
artist artiste (*m & f*)

as comme
ashtray cendrier (*m*)
Asia Asie
(*to*) **ask** demander
asleep endormi (*m*), -e (*f*)
asparagus asperge (*f*)
aspirin aspirine (*f*)
assortment assortiment (*m*)
at à
Atlantic Atlantique (*m*)
atomic atomique
attention attention (*f*)
attractive joli (*m*), -e (*f*)
August août (*m*)
aunt tante (*f*)
Australia Australie (*f*)
Australian australien (*m*), -ne (*f*)
Austria Autriche (*f*)
Austrian autrichien (*m*), -ne (*f*)
authority autorité (*f*)
automatic automatique
autumn automne (*m*)
available disponible
avenue avenue (*f*)
average moyenne (*f*)
avoid éviter
away (*not here*) absent (*m*), -e (*f*)

B

baby bébé (*m*)
bachelor célibataire (*m, f*)
back (*of body*) dos (*m*)
(*in*) **back of** derrière (*m*)
bacon bacon (*m*)
bad mauvais (*m*) -e (*f*)
badly mal
bag sac
baggage bagage (*m*)

bakery boulangerie (f)
banana banane (f)
bandage bandage (m)
bank banque (f)
banker banquier (m)
bar bar (m)
barber coiffeur (m)
basement sous-sol (m)
basket panier (m)
bath bain (m)
bathing suit maillot de bain (m)
bathroom salle de bain (f)
battery batterie (f)
battle bataille (f)
(to) **be** être
beach plage (f)
beans haricots (m)
bear (animal) ours (m)
beard barbe (f)
beautiful beau (m), belle (f)
beauty beauté (f)
beauty shop salon de beauté (m)
because parce que
bed lit (m)
bedroom chambre (f)
bedspread dessus de lit (m)
bee abeille (f)
beef boeuf (m)
been été
beer bière (f)
before avant
(to) **begin** commencer
behind derrière
(to) **believe** croire
Belgian belge (m & f)
Belgium Belgique (f)
bell sonnette (f)
(to) **belong** appartenir
below en dessous

belt ceinture (f)
besides d'ailleurs
best (adv.) le mieux
best (adj.) le meilleur (m), la meilleure (f)
bet pari (m)
better meilleur (m), -e (f)
between entre
bicycle bicyclette (f)
big gros (m), -se (f) grand (m), -e (f)
bill note (f)
bird oiseau (m)
birthday anniversaire (m)
black noir (m), -e (f)
blond blond (m), -e (f)
blood sang (m)
(to) **blow** souffler
blue bleu (m), -e (f)
boat bateau (m)
body corps (m)
bomb bombe (f)
book livre (m)
bookstore librairie (f)
booth cabine (f)
born né (m), -e (f)
(to) **borrow** emprunter
boss patron (m)
both tous les deux (m), toutes les deux (f)
bottle bouteille (f)
bottom fond (m)
bought acheté
box boîte (f)
boy garçon (m)
brain cerveau (m)
brake frein (m)
brandy cognac (m)
brassiere soutien-gorge (m)

brave brave
bread pain (*m*)
(*to*) **break** casser
breakfast petit déjeuner (*m*)
breast poitrine (*f*)
(*to*) **breathe** respirer
bride mariée (*f*)
bridegroom marié (*m*)
bridge pont (*m*)
brief bref (*m*), brève (*f*)
briefcase serviette (*f*)
bright brillant (*m*), -e (*f*)
(*to*) **bring** apporter
bring me ... apportez-moi
broiled grillé (*m*), -e (*f*)
broken cassé (*m*), -e (*f*)
broom balai (*m*)
brother frère (*m*)
brother-in-law beau-frère (*m*)
brown brun (*m*), -e (*f*)
(*to*) **build** construire
building bâtiment (*m*)
bull taureau (*m*)
bullet balle (*f*)
bureau bureau (*m*)
(*to*) **burn** brûler
bus autobus (*m*)
bus stop arrêt de l'autobus
business les affaires (*f*)
businessman homme d'affaires (*m*)
busy très occupé
but mais
butcher boucher (*m*), -ère (*f*)
butchershop boucherie (*f*)
butter beurre (*m*)
button bouton (*m*)
(*to*) **buy** acheter

by par
by the way à propos

C

cabbage chou (*m*)
cake gâteau (*m*)
calendar calendrier (*m*)
calf veau (*m*)
(*to*) **call** appeler
camera appareil photographique (*m*)
camera (*movie*) caméra (*f*)
can (*to be able*) pouvoir
can (*container*) boîte
can opener ouvre-boîte (*m*)
candy bonbon (*m*)
cap casquette (*f*)
cape cape (*f*)
captain capitaine (*m*)
car auto (*f*)
carburetor carburateur (*m*)
card carte (*f*)
Careful! Attention!
carrot carotte (*f*)
(*to*) **carry** porter
cashier caissier (*m*), -ière (*f*)
castle château fort, château (*m*)
cat chat (*m*)
catalog catalogue (*m*)
cathedral cathédrale (*f*)
catholic catholique (*m & f*)
(*to*) **cease** cesser
ceiling plafond (*m*)
cellar cave (*f*)
cement ciment (*m*)
cemetery cimetière (*m*)
cent centime (*m*)
center centre (*m*)

central central (*m*), -e (*f*)
century siècle (*m*)
certainly certainement
(*to*) **certify** certifier
chair chaise (*f*)
change (*money*) monnaie (*f*)
(*to*) **change** changer
(*to*) **chat** bavarder
character caractère (*m*)
charming charmant (*m*), -e (*f*)
chauffeur chauffeur (*m*)
cheap bon marché
check chèque
checkroom vestiaire (*m*)
cheese fromage (*m*)
cherries cerises (*f*)
chest (*body*) poitrine (*f*)
chicken poulet (*m*)
child enfant (*m & f*)
chimney cheminée (*f*)
chin menton (*m*)
China Chine (*f*)
Chinese chinois (*m*), -e (*f*)
chocolate chocolat (*m*)
chop côtelette (*f*)
Christmas Noël (*m*)
church église (*f*)
cigar cigare (*m*)
cigarette cigarette (*f*)
city ville (*f*)
class classe (*f*)
(*to*) **clean** nettoyer
(*dry*) **cleaner's** teinturerie (*f*)
clear clair (*m*), -e (*f*)
clerk employé (*m*), -e (*f*)
clever habile (*m & f*)
climate climat (*m*)
(*to*) **climb** grimper
clock pendule (*f*)

(*to*) **close** fermer
closed fermé (*m*), -e (*f*)
closet placard (*m*)
clothes vêtements (*m*)
cloud nuage (*m*)
club club (*m*)
coast côte (*f*)
coat manteau (*m*)
coffee café (*m*)
coin pièce (*f*) de monnaie
cold froid (*m*), -e (*f*)
(*to*) **collect** rassembler,
  collectionner
college université (*f*)
colonel colonel (*m*)
color couleur (*f*)
comb peigne (*m*)
combination combinaison (*f*)
(*to*) **come** venir
comfortable confortable (*m & f*)
commission commission (*f*)
communist communiste (*m & f*)
company compagnie (*f*)
complete (*adj.*) complet (*m*), -ète
  (*f*)
(*to*) **compose** composer
composer compositeur (*m*)
computer ordinateur (*m*)
concert concert (*m*)
condition condition (*f*)
congratulations félicitations (*f*)
contented content (*m*), -e (*f*)
(*to*) **continue** continuer
(*to*) **control** contrôler
convenient commode
conversation conversation (*f*)
(*to*) **convince** convaincre
cook cuisinier (*m*) -ère (*f*)
(*to*) **cook** faire la cuisine, cuire

281

cool frais (*m*), fraîche (*f*)
copy copie (*f*)
cork (*of bottle*) bouchon (*m*)
corkskrew tire-bouchon (*m*)
corner coin (*m*)
corporation société anonyme (*f*)
correct (*adj.*) exact (*m*), -e (*f*)
correspondence correspondance (*f*)
(*to*) **cost** coûter
cotton coton (*m*)
cough toux (*f*)
(*to*) **count** compter
country pays (*m*)
country (not city) campagne (*f*)
cousin cousin (*m*), -e (*f*)
(*to*) **cover** couvrir
cow vache (*f*)
crab crabe (*m*)
crazy fou (*m*), folle (*f*)
cream crème (*f*)
credit crédit (*m*)
crime crime (*m*)
criminal criminel (*m*), -le (*f*)
crisis crise (*f*)
(*to*) **criticize** critiquer
(*to*) **cross** traverser
crossroads carrefour (*m*)
crowd foule (*f*)
(*to*) **cry** pleurer
cup tasse (*f*)
customer client (*m*), -e (*f*)
customs douane (*f*)
(*to*) **cut** couper

D

daily (*adv*) tous les jours
daily (*adj*) quotidien (*m*) -ne (*f*)

(*to*) **dance** danser
dancer danseur (*m*), danseuse (*f*)
dangerous dangereux (*m*), -reuse (*f*)
dark sombre (*m & f*)
date date (*f*)
daughter fille (*f*)
daughter-in-law belle-fille (*f*)
day jour (*m*)
dead mort (*m*), -e (*f*)
dear cher (*m*), chère (*f*)
debt dette (*f*)
December décembre (*m*)
(*to*) **decide** décider
deck (*ship*) pont (*m*)
deep profond (*m*), -e (*f*)
delay retard (*m*)
delighted enchanté (*m*), -e (*f*)
delicious délicieux (*m*), -ieuse (*f*)
(*to*) **deliver** livrer
dentist dentiste (*m*)
(*to*) **depart** partir
department store grand magasin (*m*)
desert désert (*m*)
desk bureau (*m*)
design dessin (*m*)
detail détail (*m*)
(*to*) **destroy** détruire
detour détour (*m*)
devil diable (*m*)
dialogue dialogue (*m*)
diamond diamant (*m*)
dictionary dictionnaire (*m*)
(*to*) **die** mourir
different différent (*m*), -e (*f*)
difficult difficile
(*to*) **dine** dîner
dining room salle à manger (*f*)

dinner dîner (*m*)
direction direction (*f*)
director directeur (*m*)
dirty sale (*m & f*)
disappointed déçu (*m*), -e (*f*)
(*to*) **discover** découvrir
discreet discret (*m*), -ète (*f*)
dishonest malhonnête (*m & f*)
(*to*) **disturb** déranger
(*to*) **discuss** discuter
(*to*) **divide** diviser
divorced divorcé (*m*), -e (*f*)
dizziness vertige (*m*)
(*to*) **do** faire
dock quai (*m*)
doctor docteur (*m*)
dog chien (*m*)
doll poupée (*f*)
dollar dollar (*m*)
door porte (*f*)
dozen douzaine (*f*)
drawer tiroir (*m*)
dream rêve (*m*)
dress robe (*f*)
(*to*) **drink** boire
(*to*) **drive** conduire
driver conducteur (*m*)
driver's license permis de conduire (*m*)
(*to*) **drown** se noyer
drugstore pharmacie (*f*)
drum tambour (*m*)
drunk ivre
dry sec (*m*) sèche (*f*)
dry cleaner teinturier (*m*), -ère (*f*)
duck canard (*m*)
during pendant
dust poussière (*f*)

E

each chaque
ear oreille (*f*)
early de bonne heure
(*to*) **earn** gagner
earth terre (*f*)
easily facilement
east est (*m*)
easy facile
(*to*) **eat** manger
economical économique
egg oeuf (*m*)
eight huit
eighteen dix-huit
eighty quatre-vingts
either one n'importe lequel (*m*), laquelle (*f*)
elbow coude (*m*)
electricity électricité (*f*)
elegant élégant (*m*), -e (*f*)
elephant éléphant (*m*)
elevator ascenseur (*m*)
eleven onze
else autre
embassy ambassade (*f*)
embroidery broderie (*f*)
emerald émeraude (*f*)
emergency urgence (*f*)
employee employé (*m*), -e (*f*)
empty vide (*m & f*)
end fin (*f*)
ending terminaison (*f*)
(*to*) **end** finir
engineer ingénieur (*m*)
England Angleterre
English anglais (*m*), -e (*f*)
enough assez
entertaining amusant (*m*), -e (*f*)

entrance entrée (*f*)
envelope enveloppe (*f*)
error erreur (*f*)
(*to*) **escape** s'échapper
especially spécialement
Europe Europe (*f*)
European européen (*m*), -enne
(*f*)
even même
evening soir (*m*)
ever jamais
every chaque
everybody tout le monde
everything tout
everywhere partout
exactly exactement
(*to*) **examine** examiner
example exemple
excellent excellent (*m*), -e (*f*)
except sauf
exception exception (*f*)
(*to*) **exchange** échanger
Excuse me! Excusez-moi!
exercise exercice (*m*)
exhibition exposition (*f*)
exit sortie (*f*)
(*to*) **expect** attendre
expenses dépenses (*f*)
expensive cher (*m*), chère (*f*)
experience expérience (*f*)
(*to*) **explain** expliquer
explanation explication (*f*)
explorer explorateur (*m*)
(*to*) **explode** exploser
(*to*) **export** exporter
(*to*) **express** exprimer
expression expression (*f*)
exquisite exquis (*m*), -e (*f*)

extra extra
eye oeil (*m*), les yeux (*pl.*)

F

face visage (*m*)
factory usine (*f*)
(*to*) **faint** s'évanouir
(*to*) **fall** tomber
family famille (*f*)
famous fameux (*m*), -euse (*f*)
far loin
fare prix (*m*)
farm ferme (*f*)
farther plus loin
fashion mode (*f*)
fast vite
(*to*) **fasten** attacher
fat gros (*m*), grosse (*f*)
fate destin (*m*)
father père (*m*)
father-in-law beau-père (*m*)
favorite préféré (*m*), -e (*f*)
February février (*m*)
(*to*) **feel** (*se*) sentir
fence barrière (*f*)
fever fièvre (*f*)
(*a*) **few** quelques
field champ (*m*)
fifteen quinze
fifty cinquante
(*to*) **fight** (*se*) battre
(*to*) **fill** remplir
film film (*m*)
final final (*m*), -e (*f*)
finally enfin
(*to*) **find** trouver
finger doigt (*m*)
(*to*) **finish** finir

finished fini (*m*), -e (*f*)
(*to*) **fire** (*a shot*) tirer
fire feu (*m*)
fireman pompier (*m*)
fireplace cheminée (*f*)
first premier (*m*), -ère (*f*)
fish poisson (*m*)
(*to*) **fish** pêcher
fist poing (*m*)
five cinq
(*to*) **fix** (*repair*) réparer
flag drapeau (*m*)
flavor goût (*m*)
flashlight lampe de poche
flight vol (*m*)
floor plancher (*m*)
flour farine (*f*)
florist fleuriste (*m & f*)
flower fleur (*f*)
(*to*) **fly** voler
fly (*insect*) mouche (*f*)
fog brouillard (*m*)
(*to*) **follow** suivre
food nourriture (*f*)
foot pied (*m*)
for pour
(*to*) **forbid** défendre
forbidden défendu (*m*), -e (*f*)
foreigner étranger (*m*), -gère (*f*)
forest forêt (*f*)
forever toujours
(*to*) **forget** oublier
(*to*) **forgive** pardonner
fork fourchette (*f*)
form forme (*f*)
(*to*) **form** former
formal formel (*m*), -elle (*f*)
formula formule (*f*)
fortune fortune (*f*)

fortunately heureusement
forty quarante
fountain fontaine (*f*)
four quatre
fourteen quatorze
fox renard (*m*)
fragile fragile
France France (*f*)
free libre
freedom liberté
French français (*m*), -e (*f*)
fresh frais (*m*), fraîche (*f*)
Friday vendredi
fried frit (*m*), -e (*f*)
friend ami (*m*), -e (*f*)
frog grenouille (*f*)
from de
(*in*) **front** (*of*) en face de
frozen gelé (*m*), -e (*f*)
fruit fruit (*m*)
full complet (*m*), -ète (*f*)
funny drôle (*m & f*)
funeral enterrement (*m*)
fur fourrure (*m*)
furniture meubles (*m*)
future futur (*m*), avenir (*m*)

G

(*to*) **gain** gagner
(*to*) **gamble** jouer
game jeu (*m*)
garage garage (*m*)
garden jardin (*m*)
garlic ail (*m*)
gasoline essence (*f*)
gas station poste d'essence (*m*)
gate porte (*f*)
general général (*m*), -e (*f*)

285

generally généralement
generation génération (*f*)
generous généreux (*m*), -euse (*f*)
gentleman monsieur (*m*)
gentlemen messieurs (*m*)
German allemand (*m*), -e (*f*)
Germany Allemagne
(*to*) **get** (*obtain*) obtenir
(*to*) **get** (*become*) devenir
(*to*) **get off** descendre
(*to*) **get on** monter
(*to*) **get out** sortir
Get out! Sortez!
(*to*) **get up** se lever
gift cadeau (*m*)
girl fille (*f*)
(*to*) **give** donner
glass verre (*m*)
glasses lunettes (*f*)
glove gant (*m*)
glue colle (*f*)
(*to*) **go** aller
(*to*) **go away** s'en aller
(*to*) **go back** retourner
(*to*) **go on** continuer
Go away! Allez-vous-en!
goat chèvre (*f*)
God Dieu (*m*)
gold or (*m*)
golf golf (*m*)
good bon (*m*), bonne (*f*)
goodbye au revoir
goose oie (*f*)
government gouvernement (*m*)
graceful gracieux (*m*), -euse (*f*)
granddaughter petite-fille (*f*)
grandfather grand-père (*m*)
grandmother grand-mère (*f*)
grandson petit-fils (*m*)

grapes raisins (*m*)
grass herbe (*f*)
grateful reconnaissant (*m*) -e (*f*)
gray gris (*m*) -e (*f*)
(*a*) **great many** beaucoup de
Greece Grèce (*f*)
Greek grec (*m*), grecque (*f*)
green vert (*m*), -e (*f*)
group groupe (*m*)
(*to*) **grow** grandir
guest invité (*m*), -e (*f*)
guide guide (*m*)
guilty coupable
guitar guitare (*f*)

H

habit habitude (*f*)
(*a*) **hair** cheveu (*m. singular*)
hair cheveux (*m, pl*)
hairbrush brosse à cheveux (*f*)
haircut coupe de cheveux (*f*)
hairdresser coiffeur (*m*)
half demi (*m*), -e (*f*)
ham jambon (*m*)
hammer marteau (*m*)
hand main (*f*)
handbag sac (*m*)
handmade fait à la main
handsome beau (*m*), belle (*f*)
(*to*) **happen** arriver, se passer
happy heureux (*m*), -reuse (*f*)
hard dur (*m*), -e (*f*)
hat chapeau (*m*) pl: chapeaux
(*to*) **hate** haïr, détester
(*to*) **have** avoir
he il
head tête (*f*)

headache mal de tête (*m*)
(*to*) **heal** guérir
health santé (*f*)
healthy sain (*m*), -e (*f*)
heart coeur (*m*)
heat chaleur (*f*)
heavy lourd (*m*), -e (*f*)
(*to*) **hear** entendre
heel talon (*m*)
helicopter helicoptère (*m*)
hell enfer (*m*)
Hello! Allô!
(*to*) **help** aider
Help! Au secours!
her (*dir. object*) la
(*to*) **her** lui
her (*possessive adj.*) son (*m*), sa
  (*f*) ses (*m & f pl*)
here ici
hero héros (*m*)
hers le sien (*m*), la sienne (*f*), les
  siens (*m*), les siennes (*f*)
herself elle-même
(*to*) **hesitate** hésiter
(*to*) **hide** cacher
high haut (*m*), -e (*f*)
highway route (*f*)
hill colline (*f*)
him (*direct object*) le
(*to*) **him** lui
himself lui-même
(*to*) **hire** louer
his (*possessive adj.*) son (*m*), sa
  (*f*), ses (*m & f pl*)
history histoire (*f*)
(*to*) **hit** frapper
(*to*) **hold** tenir
hole trou (*m*)
honest honnête

honey miel (*m*)
honor honneur (*m*)
(*to*) **hope** espérer
horse cheval, pl. chevaux (*m*)
hospital hôpital (*m*)
hospitality hospitalité (*f*)
host hôte (*m*)
hostess hôtesse (*f*)
hot chaud (*m*), -e (*f*)
hotel hôtel (*m*)
hour heure (*f*)
house maison (*f*)
how comment
however pourtant
hundred cent (*m*)
(*to be*) **hungry** avoir faim
(*to be in a*) **hurry** être pressé (*e*)
(*to*) **hurry** se dépêcher
husband mari (*m*)

I

I je
ice glace (*f*)
ice cream glace (*f*)
idea idée (*f*)
idiot idiot (*m*), -e (*f*)
if si
ignorant ignorant (*m*), -e (*f*)
ill malade
illness maladie (*f*)
illustration illustration (*f*)
imagination imagination (*f*)
(*to*) **imagine** s'imaginer
immediately immédiatement
imitation imitation (*f*)
imperfect imparfait (*m*), -e (*f*)
(*to*) **import** importer
importance importance (*f*)

impossible impossible (*m & f*)
(*to*) **improve** améliorer
in dans
(*to*) **include** inclure
included inclus (*m*), -e (*f*); compris (*m*), -e (*f*)
income revenu (*m*)
(*to*) **increase** augmenter
incredible incroyable (*m & f*)
(*to*) **indicate** indiquer
indigestion indigestion (*f*)
industry industrie (*f*)
industrial industriel (*m*), elle (*f*)
information renseignement (*m*)
inhabitant habitant (*m*), -e (*f*)
(*to*) **inherit** hériter
injection injection (*f*)
insect insecte (*m*)
inside à l'intérieur (*m*), dedans
(*to*) **insist** insister
(*to*) **inspect** inspecter
inspection inspection (*f*)
(*to*) **install** installer
instead of au lieu de
instrument instrument (*m*)
insult insulte (*f*)
(*to*) **insult** insulter
intelligent intelligent (*m*), -e (*f*)
interesting intéressant (*m*), -e (*f*)
international international (*m*), -e (*f*)
interpreter interprète (*m*) (*f*)
into dans
(*to*) **introduce** introduire; présenter
invitation invitation (*f*)
(*to*) **invite** inviter
Ireland Irlande (*f*)
Irish irlandais (*m*), -e (*f*)

is est
island île (*f*)
Israel Israël (*m*)
Israeli israélien (*m*), -ienne (*f*)
it il (*m*), elle (*f*)
its son (*m*), sa (*f*), ses (*m & f pl*)
Italian italien (*m*), -ne (*f*)
Italy Italie (*f*)
ivory ivoire (*m*)

J

jacket veste (*f*)
jail prison (*f*)
January janvier (*m*)
Japan Japon (*m*)
Japanese japonais (*m*), -e (*f*)
jealous jaloux (*m*), -ouse (*f*)
jewelery bijouterie (*f*)
Jewish juif (*m*), juive (*f*)
job travail (*m*), situation (*f*)
joke plaisanterie (*f*)
juice jus (*m*)
July juillet (*m*)
(*to*) **jump** sauter
June juin (*m*)
just (*exactly*) exactement
just now à l'instant même

K

(*to*) **keep** garder
key clé (*f*)
(*to*) **kill** tuer
kilometer kilomètre (*m*)
kind sorte (*f*)
king roi (*m*)
(*to*) **kiss** embrasser
kitchen cuisine (*f*)
knee genou (*m*)

knife couteau (*m*)
(*to*) **know** (*knowledge*) savoir
(*to*) **know** (*a person*) connaître

L

laboratory laboratoire (*m*)
lace dentelle (*f*)
ladies' room toilettes pour dames
  (*f. pl.*)
lady dame (*f*)
lake lac (*m*)
lamb agneau (*m*)
land terre (*f*)
landscape paysage (*m*)
language langue (*f*)
large grand (*m*), -e (*f*)
(*to*) **last** durer
last dernier (*m*), ère (*f*)
late tard
later plus tard
law droit (*m*)
lawyer avocat (*m*)
lazy paresseux (*m*), -euse (*f*)
(*to*) **learn** apprendre
leather cuir (*m*)
(*to*) **leave** partir
left gauche (*f*)
leg jambe (*f*)
lemon citron (*m*)
(*to*) **lend** prêter
less moins
lesson leçon (*f*)
(*to*) **let** (*allow*) permettre
letter lettre (*f*)
lettuce laitue (*f*)
liberty liberté (*f*)
license permis (*m*)
lie mensonge (*m*)

(*to*) **lie down** se coucher
lieutenant lieutenant (*m*)
life vie (*f*)
(*to*) **lift** lever
light lumière (*f*)
light (*color*) clair
like comme
(*to*) **like** aimer
limit limite (*f*)
linen linge (*m*)
lion lion (*m*)
lip lèvre (*f*)
list liste (*f*)
(*to*) **listen** écouter
little (*small*) petit (*m*), -e (*f*)
(*a*) **little** un peu
(*to*) **live** vivre
liver foie (*m*)
living room salon (*m*)
lobster homard (*m*)
long long (*m*), -gue (*f*)
(*to*) **look** (*at*) regarder
(*to*) **lose** perdre
lost perdu (*m*), -e (*f*)
(*a*) **lot** beaucoup
lottery loterie (*f*)
loud fort (*m*), -e (*f*)
(*to*) **love** aimer
low bas (*m*) -se (*f*)
luck chance (*f*)
luggage bagage (*m*)
lunch déjeuner (*m*)
lung poumon (*m*)

M

machine machine (*f*)
madam madame (*f*)
made fait (*m*), -e (*f*)

magazine revue (*f*); magazine (*m*)
magnificent magnifique (*m & f*)
maid bonne (*f*)
mail courrier (*m*)
mailbox boîte aux lettres (*f*)
mailman facteur (*m*)
(*to*) **make** faire
man homme (*m*)
manager directeur (*m*)
manicure manucure (*f*)
(*to*) **manufacture** fabriquer
many beaucoup
map carte (*f*)
marble marbre (*m*)
March mars (*m*)
market marché (*m*)
married marié (*m*), -e (*f*)
mass (*quantity*) masse (*f*)
mass (*church*) messe (*f*)
massage massage (*m*)
matches allumettes (*f pl.*)
may (*as verb*) pouvoir
May mai (*m*)
maybe peut-être
me me, moi (*m & f*)
meal repas (*m*)
(*to*) **mean** vouloir dire; signifier
meat viande (*f*)
mechanic mécanicien (*m*)
medal médaille (*f*)
medicine médicament (*m*)
Mediterranean Méditerranée (*f*)
medium moyen (*m*), -ne (*f*)
(*to*) **meet** rencontrer
meeting réunion (*f*)
member membre (*m*)
(*to*) **mend** réparer
men's room toilettes pour
  hommes (*f. pl.*)

menu carte (*f*); menu (*m*)
message message (*m*)
metal métal (*m*)
meter compteur (*m*)
Mexico Mexique
Mexican mexicain (*m*), -e (*f*)
microphone micro (*m*)
middle milieu (*m*)
midnight minuit (*m*)
mile mille (*m*)
milk lait (*m*)
million million (*m*)
mine le mien (*m*), la mienne (*f*),
  les miens, les miennes
minister (*church*) pasteur (*m*)
minister (*gov't.*) ministre (*m*)
mink vison (*m*)
minus moins
minute minute (*f*)
mirror miroir (*m*)
Miss Mademoiselle (*f*)
(*to*) **miss** manquer
mistake erreur (*f*)
Mr. Monsieur (*m*)
misunderstanding malentendu
  (*m*)
(*to*) **mix** mélanger
mixture mélange (*m*)
Mrs. Madame (*f*)
model modèle (*m*)
modern moderne (*m & f*)
moment moment (*m*)
Monday lundi (*m*)
money argent (*m*)
monkey singe (*m*)
month mois (*m*)
monument monument (*m*)
moon lune (*f*)
more plus

morning matin (*m*)
mosquito moustique (*m*)
most le plus
most of la plupart de
mother mère (*f*)
mother-in-law belle-mère (*f*)
motor moteur (*m*)
motorcycle motocyclette (*f*)
mountain montagne (*f*)
mouth bouche (*f*)
mouse souris (*f*)
(*to*) **move** mouvoir
(*to*) **move** (*residence*) déménager
movie film (*m*)
much beaucoup
mud boue (*f*)
muscle muscle (*m*)
museum musée (*m*)
mushroom champignon (*m*)
music musique (*f*)
musician musicien (*m*), -ne (*f*)
must devoir; il faut
mustache moustache (*f*)
mustard moutarde (*f*)
my mon (*m*), ma (*f*), mes (*m & f, pl*)
myself moi-même
mystery mystère (*m*)

N

name nom (*m*)
napkin serviette (*f*)
narrow étroit (*m*), -e (*f*)
nationality nationalité (*f*)
navy marine (*f*)
near près
necessary nécessaire (*m & f*)
neck cou (*m*)

necklace collier (*m*)
necktie cravate (*f*)
(*to*) **need** avoir besoin de
neighborhood voisinage (*m*), quartier (*m*)
(*to*) **neglect** négliger
neithor ... nor ni ... ni
nephew neveu (*m*)
nervous nerveux (*m*), -euse (*f*)
neutral neutre (*m & f*)
never ne.... jamais
new nouveau (*m*), -velle (*f*)
news nouvelles (*f. pl.*)
newspaper journal (*m*)
New Year Nouvel An
next prochain (*m*), -e (*f*)
nice gentil (*m*), -ille (*f*)
niece nièce (*f*)
night nuit (*f*)
nightclub cabaret (*m*)
nightgown chemise de nuit (*f*)
nine neuf
nineteen dix-neuf
ninety quatre-vingt-dix
no (*adv.*) non
no (*adj.*) pas de
nobody personne
noise bruit (*m*)
none aucun (*m*), -e (*f*)
noon midi (*m*)
normal normal (*m*), -e (*f*)
north nord (*m*)
nose nez (*m*)
not ne .... pas
nothing rien (*m*)
(*to*) **notice** remarquer
noun nom (*m*)
novel roman (*m*)
November novembre (*m*)

now maintenant
nowhere nulle part
number nombre (*m*)
numerous nombreux (*m*), -euses (*f*)
nurse infirmière (*f*)
nuts noix (*f*)

O

(*to*) **obey** obéir
object objet (*m*)
to oblige obliger
occupation occupation (*f*)
occupied occupé (*m*), -e (*f*)
ocean océan (*m*)
o'clock heure (*f*)
October octobre (*m*)
of de
of course bien entendu
(*to*) **offer** offrir
office bureau (*m*)
officer officier (*m*)
often souvent
oil huile (*f*)
old vieux (*m*), vieille (*f*)
olive olive (*f*)
omelet omelette (*f*)
on sur
once une fois
one un (*m*), une (*f*)
onion oignon (*m*)
only seulement
open ouvert (*m*), -e (*f*)
(*to*) **open** ouvrir
opera opéra (*m*)
operation opération (*f*)
opinion opinion (*f*)
opportunity occasion (*f*)

opposite en face
or ou
orange orange (*f*)
orange juice jus d'orange (*m*)
orchestra orchestre (*m*)
order ordre (*m*)
(*to*) **order** commander
in order to afin de
ordinary ordinaire
original original (*m*), -e (*f*)
orphan orphelin (*m*), -e (*f*)
other autre
ought (*conditional of devoir*)
our notre
outside à l'extérieur, dehors
over (*above*) au-dessus (*de*)
over (*finished*) fini (*m*), -e (*f*)
overcoat manteau (*m*)
over there là-bas
(*to*) **owe** devoir
own propre
(*to*) **own** posséder
owner propriétaire (*m* & *f*)
ox boeuf (*m*)
oyster huître (*f*)

P

(*to*) **pack** empaqueter
package paquet (*m*)
page page (*f*)
paid payé (*m*), -e (*f*)
pain douleur (*f*)
painful douleureux (*m*), -euse (*f*)
(*to*) **paint** peindre
painting peinture (*f*)
pair paire (*f*)
pajamas pyjama (*m*)
palace palais (*m*)

pan casserole (*f*)
pants pantalon (*m*)
paper papier (*m*)
parade défilé (*m*)
pardon pardon (*m*)
parents parents (*m pl.*)
Parisian parisien (*m*), -ne (*f*)
(*to*) **park** parquer
park parc (*m*)
part partie (*f*)
partner associé (*m*)
party (*entertainment*) réunion (*f*)
party (*political*) parti (*m*)
(*to*) **pass** dépasser
passenger (*train, bus*) voyageur (*m*) -euse (*f*)
passenger (*boat, plane*) passager (*m*), -ère (*f*)
passport passeport (*m*)
past passé (*m*), -e (*f*)
pastry pâtisserie (*f*)
(*to*) **pay** payer
peace paix (*f*)
peach pêche (*f*)
peas petits pois (*m pl*)
pedestrian piéton (*m*)
pen stylo (*m*)
pencil crayon (*m*)
people gens (*m & f pl.*)
pepper poivre (*m*)
percentage pourcentage (*m*)
perfect parfait (*m*), -e (*f*)
perfume parfum (*m*)
perhaps peut-être
permanent permanent (*m*), -e (*f*)
permitted permis (*m*), -e (*f*)
person personne (*f*)
phone téléphone (*m*)
photo photo (*f*)

piano piano (*m*)
(*to*) **pick up** ramasser
picture tableau (*m*)
piece morceau (*m*)
pier quai (*m*)
pig cochon (*m*)
pill pilule (*f*)
pillow oreiller (*m*)
pin épingle (*f*)
pink rose
pipe (*smoking*) pipe (*f*)
place endroit (*m*)
plain simple (*m & f*)
plan projet (*m*), plan (*m*)
plane avion (*m*)
planet planète (*f*)
plant (*botanical*) plante (*f*)
plant (*factory*) usine (*f*)
plate assiette (*f*)
play (*theater*) pièce (*f*)
(*to*) **play** jouer
pleasant agréable (*m & f*)
please s'il vous plaît
pleasure plaisir (*m*)
plural pluriel (*m*)
pocket poche (*f*)
poet poète (*m*)
poetry poésie (*f*)
(*to*) **point out** indiquer
poison poison (*m*)
poisonous vénéneux (*m*) -euse (*f*)
police police (*f*)
policeman agent de police (*m*)
police station commissariat de police (*m*)
polite poli (*m*), -e (*f*)
poor pauvre (*m & f*)
pope pape (*m*)

popular populaire (*m & f*)
pork porc (*m*)
portrait portrait (*m*)
Portugal Portugal (*m*)
Portuguese portugais (*m*), -e (*f*)
position position (*f*)
possible possible
postcard carte postale (*f*)
post office bureau de poste (*m*)
pot pot (*m*)
potato pomme de terre (*f*)
pound (*weight*) livre (*f*)
practical pratique (*m & f*)
(*to*) **practice** pratiquer
(*to*) **prefer** préférer
pregnant enceinte (*f*)
(*to*) **prepare** préparer
present (*time*) présent (*m*)
present (*gift*) cadeau (*m*)
(*to*) **present** présenter
president président (*m*)
(*to*) **press** (*clothes*) repasser
pretty joli (*m*), -e (*f*)
(*to*) **prevent** empêcher
previous antérieur (*m*), -e (*f*)
price prix (*m*)
priest prêtre (*m*)
prince prince (*m*)
princess princesse (*f*)
principal principal (*m*), -e (*f*)
prison prison (*f*)
private privé (*m*), -e (*f*)
prize prix (*m*)
probably probablement
problem problème (*m*)
(*to*) **produce** produire
production production (*f*)
profession profession (*f*)
professor professeur (*m*)

profit profit (*m*)
program programme (*m*)
(*to*) **promise** promettre
promised promis (*m*), -e (*f*)
pronoun pronom (*m*)
pronunciation prononciation (*f*)
propaganda propagande (*f*)
property propriété (*f*)
(*to*) **protest** protester
Protestant protestant (*m*), -e (*f*)
(*to*) **prove** prouver
psychiatrist psychiatre (*m*)
public public (*m*), -que (*f*)
publicity publicité (*f*)
publisher éditeur (*m*)
(*to*) **pull** tirer
(*to*) **purchase** acheter
pure pur (*m*), -e (*f*)
purple violet (*m*), -te (*f*)
purse sac (*m*)
(*to*) **push** pousser
(*to*) **put** mettre

Q

quality qualité (*f*)
quantity quantité (*f*)
quarter quart (*m*)
queen reine (*f*)
question question (*f*)
quick rapide (*m & f*)
quickly vite
quiet calme
quite tout à fait

R

rabbi rabin (*m*)
rabbit lapin (*m*)

race (*human*) race (*f*)
race (*contest*) course (*f*)
radio radio (*f*)
railroad chemin de fer (*m*)
rain pluie (*f*)
raincoat imperméable (*m*)
rapidly rapidement
rare (*uncommon*) rare (*m & f*)
rarely rarement
rat rat (*m*)
rate taux (*m*)
rather (*somewhat*) plutôt
razor rasoir (*m*)
(*to*) **reach** atteindre
(*to*) **read** lire
ready prêt (*m*), -e (*f*)
real vrai (*m*), -e (*f*)
really vraiment
reason raison (*f*)
receipt reçu (*m*)
(*to*) **receive** recevoir
recently récemment
recipe recette (*f*)
(*to*) **recognize** reconnaître
(*to*) **recommend** recommander
red rouge (*m & f*)
refrigerator réfrigérateur (*m*)
(*to*) **refund** rembourser
(*to*) **refuse** refuser
(*to*) **regret** regretter
regular régulier (*m*), -ère (*f*)
relatives parents (*m*)
religion religion (*f*)
(*to*) **remain** rester
(*to*) **remember** se rappeler
(*to*) **rent** louer
(*to*) **repair** réparer
(*to*) **repeat** répéter
(*to*) **reply** répondre

report rapport (*m*)
(*to*) **represent** représenter
representative représentant (*m*),
  -e (*f*)
republic république (*f*)
responsible responsable
resident résident (*m*), -e (*f*)
(*to*) **rest** se reposer
restaurant restaurant (*m*)
retirement retraite (*f*)
(*to*) **return** revenir
revolution révolution
reward récompense (*f*)
rice riz (*m*)
rich riche (*m & f*)
(*to*) **ride** (*horseback*) monter *à
  cheval*
rifle fusil (*m*)
right (*direction*) droit (*m*), -e (*f*)
right (*correct*) exact (*m*), -e (*f*)
ring bague (*f*)
risk risque (*m*)
river fleuve (*m*)
road route (*f*)
roof toit (*m*)
room chambre (*f*)
rope corde (*f*)
rose rose (*f*)
round rond (*m*), -e (*f*)
route trajet (*m*)
rug tapis (*m*)
(*to*) **run** courir
Russia Russie (*f*)
Russian russe (*m & f*)

S

sad triste (*m & f*)
safe sûr (*m*), -e (*f*); sauf (*m*),
  sauve (*f*)

(*to*) **sail** naviguer
sail voile (*m*)
sailor marin (*m*)
saint saint (*m*), -e (*f*)
salad salade (*f*)
salary salaire (*m*)
sale solde (*f*)
salt sel (*m*)
same même (*m & f*)
Saturday samedi (*m*)
sauce sauce (*f*)
savage sauvage (*m & f*)
(*to*) **say** dire
scarf foulard (*m*)
scene scène (*f*)
scenery paysage (*m*)
school école (*f*)
science science (*f*)
scientist savant (*m*)
scissors ciseaux (*m pl*)
Scotch écossais (*m*), -e (*f*)
Scotland Ecosse (*f*)
sea mer (*f*)
seasickness mal de mer (*m*)
seafood fruits de mer (*m pl*)
(*to*) **search for** chercher
season saison (*f*)
seat place (*f*)
second (*part of minute*) seconde (*f*)
second deuxième (*m & f*)
secret secret (*m*), -e (*f*)
secretary secrétaire (*m*) (*f*)
section section (*f*)
(*to*) **see** voir
(*to*) **seem** sembler
seen vu (*m*), -e (*f*)
seldom rarement
to) **select** choisir

(*to*) **sell** vendre
(*to*) **send** envoyer
(*to*) **send for** envoyer chercher
separate séparé (*m*), -e (*f*)
September septembre (*m*)
serious sérieux (*m*), -se (*f*)
service service (*m*)
seven sept
seventeen dix-sept
seventy soixante-dix
several plusieurs (*m & f*)
sex sexe (*m*)
shape forme (*f*)
shark requin (*m*)
she elle
ship bateau (*m*)
shirt chemise (*f*)
(*to*) **shine** briller
shoe chaussure (*f*)
shop magasin (*m*), boutique (*f*)
short court (*m*), -e (*f*)
shoulder épaule (*f*)
show spectacle (*m*)
(*to*) **show** montrer
shower (*bath*) douche (*f*)
shrimps crevettes (*f pl*)
shut fermé (*m*), -e (*f*)
(*to*) **shut** fermer
sick malade
sign signe (*m*)
(*to*) **sign** signer
signature signature (*f*)
silence silence (*m*)
silk soie (*f*)
silver argent (*m*)
simple simple (*m & f*)
since depuis
sincerely sincèrement
(*to*) **sing** chanter

singer chanteur (*m*), -euse (*f*)
sir monsieur
sister soeur (*f*)
sister-in-law belle-soeur (*f*)
(*to*) **sit down** s'asseoir
situation situation (*f*)
six six
sixteen seize
sixty soixante
size taille (*f*)
(*to*) **skate** patiner
(*to*) **ski** skier
skin peau (*f*)
skirt jupe (*f*)
sky ciel (*m*)
(*to*) **sleep** dormir
sleeve manche (*f*)
slippers pantouffles (*f pl*)
slow lent (*m*), -e (*f*)
small petit (*m*), -e (*f*)
(*to*) **smell** sentir
smoke fumée (*f*)
(*to*) **smoke** fumer
snail escargot (*m*)
snake serpent (*m*)
snow neige (*f*)
so donc
soap savon (*m*)
socks chaussettes (*f pl*)
sofa canapé (*m*)
soft doux (*m*), douce (*f*)
soldier soldat (*m*)
solid solide (*m & f*)
some (*adj*) un peu de
some (*partitive*) du, de la, de l',
des, en
somebody quelqu'un
something quelque chose
sometimes quelquefois

somewhere quelque part
son fils (*m*)
son-in-law gendre (*m*)
song chanson (*f*)
soon bientôt
sorrow chagrin (*m*)
sorry désolé (*m*), -e (*f*)
soul âme (*f*)
sound son (*m*)
soup soupe (*f*)
sour aigre (*m & f*)
south sud (*m*)
South America Amérique du Sud
(*f*)
souvenir souvenir (*m*)
Spain Espagne (*f*)
Spanish espagnol (*m*), -e (*f*)
(*to*) **speak** parler
special spécial (*m*), -e (*f*)
speed vitesse (*f*)
(*to*) **spell** épeler; s'écrire
(*to*) **spend** dépenser
spoon cuiller (*f*), cuillère (*f*)
sport sport (*m*)
spring (*season*) printemps (*m*)
stairs escalier (*m*)
stain tache (*f*)
stamp timbre (*m*)
star étoile (*f*)
(*to*) **start** commencer
state état (*m*)
station (*railroad*) gare (*f*)
statue statue (*f*)
(*to*) **stay** rester
steak steak (*m*), entrecôte (*f*)
(*to*) **steal** voler
steel acier (*m*)
stenographer sténographe (*m &
f*)

still encore
stocks (*shares*) actions (*f pl*)
stockmarket bourse (*f*)
stockings bas (*m pl*)
stomach estomac (*m*)
stone pierre (*f*)
(*to*) **stop** arrêter
store magasin (*m*)
storm orage (*m*)
story histoire (*f*)
straight droit (*m*), -e (*f*)
strange étrange (*m & f*)
stranger étranger (*m*), -ère (*f*)
street rue (*f*)
strike (*labor*) grève (*f*)
string corde (*f*)
strong fort (*m*), -e (*f*)
student étudiant (*m*), -e (*f*)
(*to*) **study** étudier
stupid stupide; bête (*m & f*)
style style (*m*)
subject sujet (*m*)
submarine sous-marin (*m*)
subway métro (*m*)
success succès (*m*)
suddenly soudainement
sugar sucre (*m*)
suit (*for men*) complet (*m*); (*for women*) tailleur (*m*)
suitcase valise (*f*)
summer été (*m*)
sun soleil (*m*)
Sunday dimanche (*m*)
sure sûr (*m*), -e (*f*)
surely sûrement
surprise surprise (*f*)
surroundings alentours (*m pl*)
sweater sweater (*m*), pull (*m*)
sweet doux (*m), douce (f*)

(*to*) **swim** nager
swimming pool piscine (*f*)
swim suit maillot de bain (*m*)
Swiss suisse (*m & f*)
Switzerland Suisse (*f*)
system système (*m*)

T

table table (*f*)
tablecloth nappe (*f*)
tail queue (*f*)
tailor tailleur (*m*)
(*to*) **take** prendre
(*to*) **take away** enlever
(*to*) **take care of** prendre soin de
(*to*) **take a walk** (*or a ride*) faire une promenade
talent talent (*m*)
(*to*) **talk** parler
tall grand (*m*), -e (*f*)
tank reservoir (*m*)
tape ruban (*m*) bande magnétique (*f*)
tape recorder magnétophone (*m*)
(*to*) **taste** goûter
tax impôt (*m*)
taxi taxi (*m*)
tea thé (*m*)
(*to*) **teach** enseigner
teacher professeur (*m*)
team équipe (*f*)
telegram télégramme (*m*)
telephone téléphone (*m*)
television télévision (*f*)
(*to*) **tell** dire
temple temple (*m*)
temperature température (*f*)
temporary temporaire (*m & f*)

ten dix
tenant locataire (*m & f*)
tennis tennis (*m*)
terrace terrasse (*f*)
terrible terrible (*m & f*)
than que
thank you merci
that que
the le, la, les
theater théâtre (*m*)
their leur
them (*dir. obj.*) les
(*to*) **them** eux, leur
themselves eux-mêmes (*m*), elles-
  mêmes (*f*)
then alors
there là
there is . . . , there are . . . il y a
thermometer thermomètre (*m*)
these ces (*m & f*), ceux-ci (*m*),
  celles-ci (*f*)
they ils (*m*), elles (*f*)
thin mince (*m & f*)
thing chose (*f*)
(*to*) **think** penser
third troisième
(*to be*) **thirsty** avoir soif
thirteen treize
thirty trente
this (*adj.*) ce (*m*), cette (*f*)
this (*pro.*) celui-ci (*m*), celle-ci
  (*f*)
those (*adj.*) ces (*m & f*)
those (*pro.*) ceux-là (*m*), celles-là
  (*f*)
thousand mille
thread fil (*m*)
three trois
throat gorge (*f*)

through à travers
(*to*) **throw** jeter
Thursday jeudi (*m*)
ticket billet (*m*)
tie cravate (*f*)
tiger tigre (*m*)
tight serré (*m*), -e (*f*)
time temps (*m*)
tip (*gratuity*) pourboire (*m*)
tire (*automobile*) pneu (*m*)
tired fatigué (*m*), -e (*f*)
to (*direction*) à
to (*in order to*) afin de
toast toast (*m*)
tobacco tabac (*m*)
today aujourd'hui
toe doigt de pied (*m*), orteil (*m*)
together ensemble
toilet toilette (*f*)
tomato tomate (*f*)
tomb tombe (*f*)
tomorrow demain
tongue langue (*f*)
tonight ce soir (*m*)
too (*also*) aussi
too (*excessive*) trop
tool outil (*m*)
tooth dent (*f*)
toothbrush brosse à dents (*f*)
toothpaste dentifrice (*m*)
(*to*) **touch** toucher
tour tour (*m*)
tourist touriste (*m & f*)
toward vers
towel serviette (*f*)
tower tour (*f*)
town ville (*f*)
toy jouet (*m*)
traffic circulation (*f*)

train train (*m*)
translation traduction (*f*)
(*to*) **travel** voyager
traveler voyageur (*m*)
treasure trésor (*m*)
treasurer trésorier (*m*)
tree arbre (*m*)
trip voyage (*m*)
trouble difficulté (*f*)
trousers pantalon (*m*)
truck camion (*m*)
true vrai (*m*), -e (*f*)
(*to*) **try**, (*to*) **try on** essayer
Tuesday mardi (*m*)
tunnel tunnel (*m*)
Turkey Turquie
Turkish turque (*m & f*)
(*to*) **turn** tourner
(*to*) **turn off** (*light*) éteindre
(*to*) **turn on** allumer
twelve douze
twenty vingt
two deux
type type (*m*)
typewriter machine à écrire
typical typique

U

ugly laid (*m*), -e (*f*)
umbrella parapluie (*m*)
uncle oncle (*m*)
uncomfortable incommode (*m & f*)
under sous
underneath en dessous
(*to*) **understand** comprendre
underwear sous-vêtements (*m pl*)

unfortunately malheureusement
uniform uniforme (*m*)
United Nations Nations Unies (*f pl*)
United States États-Unis (*m pl*)
university université (*f*)
unknown inconnu (*m*), -e (*f*)
unless à moins que
until jusqu'à
up, upstairs en haut
urgent urgent (*m*), -e (*f*)
us nous
(*to*) **use** employer
useful utile (*m & f*)
usually d'habitude

V

vacant libre
vacation vacances (*f pl*)
vaccination vaccination (*f*)
valley vallée (*f*)
value valeur (*f*)
variety variété (*f*)
various divers (*m*), -e (*f*)
vegetable légume (*m*)
verb verbe (*m*)
very très
very well très bien
victory victoire (*f*)
view vue (*f*)
village village (*m*)
vinegar vinaigre (*m*)
violet violet (*m*), -te (*f*)
visa visa (*m*)
visit visite (*f*)
visitor visiteur (*m*), -euse (*f*)

(*to*) **visit** visiter
violin violon (*m*)
voice voix (*f*)
voyage voyage (*m*)

W

waist taille (*f*)
(*to*) **wait** attendre
waiter garçon
waitress serveuse (*f*)
(*to*) **walk** marcher
wall mur (*m*)
wallet portefeuille (*m*)
(*to*) **want** vouloir
war guerre (*f*)
warm chaud (*m*), -e (*f*)
(*to*) **wash** laver
washable lavable (*m & f*)
watch montre (*f*)
(*to*) **watch** regarder, observer
water eau (*f*)
watercolor aquarelle (*f*)
way chemin (*m*)
we nous
weak faible (*m & f*)
weapon arme (*f*)
(*to*) **wear** porter
weather temps (*m*)
wedding mariage (*m*)
Wednesday mercredi (*m*)
week semaine (*f*)
weekend week-end (*m*)
(*to*) **weigh** peser
weight poids (*m*)
Welcome! Bienvenue!
(*you are*) **welcome** de rien
well bien

west ouest (*m*)
what (*adj.*) quel, quelle, quels, quelles
what (*pron*) que, qu'est-ce qui, qu'est-ce que, quoi.
wheat blé (*m*)
wheel roue (*f*)
when quand
where où
wherever partout où
whether si
which (*subj.*) qui
which (*obj.*) que
which (*adj.*) quel (*m*), quelle (*f*)
which (*pro.*) lequel (*m*), laquelle (*f*)
while pendant que
white blanc (*m*), blanche (*f*)
who qui
whole entier (*m*), -ière (*f*)
whom que, qui
whose dont
why pourquoi
wide large (*m & f*)
widow veuve (*f*)
widower veuf (*m*)
wife femme (*f*)
wig perruque (*f*)
wild sauvage (*m & f*)
(*to*) **win** gagner
wind vent (*m*)
window fenêtre (*f*)
wine vin (*m*)
winter hiver (*m*)
wise sage (*m & f*)
(*to*) **wish** désirer
with avec

without sans
wolf loup (*m*)
woman femme (*f*)
(*to*) **wonder** se demander
wonderful merveilleux (*m*), -se (*f*)
wood, woods bois (*m*)
wool laine (*f*)
word mot (*m*)
work travail (*m*)
(*to*) **work** travailler
world monde (*m*)
(*to*) **worry** s'inquiéter
worse pire (*m & f*)
(*to*) **wrap** envelopper
wrist poignet (*m*)
(*to*) **write** écrire
writer écrivain (*m*)
wrong faux (*m*), fausse (*f*)
(*to be*) **wrong** avoir tort

X

X-ray rayons X (*m pl.*)

Y

year année (*f*)
yellow jaune
yes oui
yesterday hier
yet encore
you vous
young jeune (*m & f*)
your votre
yours le vôtre (*m*), la vôtre (*f*)
youth jeunesse (*f*)

Z

zero zéro (*m*)
zipper fermeture éclair (*f*)
zone zone (*f*)
zoo zoo (*m*)